# The Making of the Modern Kitchen

# The Making of the Modern Kitchen

## A Cultural History

**June Freeman**

*Oxford • New York*

First published in 2004 by
**Berg**
Editorial offices:
1st Floor, Angel Court, 81 St Clements Street, Oxford, OX4 1AW, UK
175 Fifth Avenue, New York, NY 10010, USA

Berg is an imprint of Oxford International Publishers Ltd.


**Library of Congress Cataloging-in-Publication Data**
A catalogue record for this book is available from the Library of Congress.

**British Library Cataloguing-in-Publication Data**
A catalogue record for this book is available from the British Library.


ISBN   1 85973 694 7 (Cloth)
1 85973 699 8 (Paper)


Typeset by JS Typesetting Ltd, Wellingborough, Northants.
Printed in the United Kingdom by Biddles Ltd, King's Lynn.

**www.bergpublishers.com**

# Contents

# Spotlight on the kitchen: an outline of the scope and approach of the book

The *idea* of the kitchen exerts a powerful hold on the English imagination, evoking images and thoughts of hearth and home, family and domesticity. Indeed, the social and moral role of the kitchen in popular pictorial and literary depictions of domestic life often appears as important as the question of how effective the kitchen is in helping people undertake the various practical household tasks for which it formally exists. English kitchens are commonly perceived as a combination of the 'heart of the home' and 'meal machine'. How these contrasting, though also intertwining, perceptions bear upon and shape kitchen design at the popular level is one of the central concerns of this study.

The widespread perception that the kitchen has a dual role in the house makes it a key site for expanding the scope of analytical thinking about the factors which shape people's design preferences generally. It raises, for example, the question of how people construct relationships between visual appearances and moral attributes and the social significance of this. For a discussion of popular kitchen design to contribute usefully to our general understanding of the emergence of and support for particular design styles, however, requires both empirical and historical data.

The primary methods and perspectives on which the book draws for this data are those of design history and sociology. The use of basic sociological survey methods as a means of developing the study of design history remains virtually untried and a significant part of this book is concerned with exploiting simple, well-established sociological methods of data collection to study the way people approach and make design choices during the purchase of a new kitchen. Some design historians may initially find such an approach alien.

In contrast, the use of oral testimony to advance our understanding of design and the use of material artefacts in our society is a less strange idea to design historians.[1] The last two decades have also seen the incursion of anthropology into areas which abut design history, and design historians are becoming increasingly familiar with the possibilities ethnographical methods offer for exploring the contemporary material world of advanced Western societies, in a bid to advance and deepen our understanding of how people use objects to structure their domestic environment and invest it with meaning.[2] Indeed, the introduction of these methods into the study of design history has significantly begun to affect the way the discipline now conceptualises itself. While acknowledging the huge potential of qualitative, ethnographical data for providing insights into the way we structure our material environment, the primary tools of this study are different.

The fashion for quantitative work in sociology has declined dramatically since its heyday in the 1950s and 1960s. A positive feature of survey work, however, was that it generated an interest in developing research methods which allowed generalisations to be drawn from particular findings.[3] Indubitably the 1950s enthusiasm, which swept across large areas of sociology, for applying methods derived from the natural sciences to the social sciences, together with expectations about what could be learnt about social behaviour from the analysis of quantitative data, was frequently based on simplistic notions about the nature of human motivation and interaction. But the backlash against quantification to which this led can go too far. Despite the inclusion of some judicious provisos, Miller, currently chief champion in this country of the use of anthropological methods for the study of Western domestic material culture, teeters on overreaction, as the following extract from his view of the legacy of quantitative analysis illustrates:

> At present we are only just coming out of a period in which the reliance upon surveys . . . meant that our understanding of the moralities, values and imperatives in consumer action has been limited. These methods . . . seem to have largely stymied investigation in the social sciences – though not entirely.[4]

This study will hope to show that simple, quantitative data drawn from a carefully selected sample remains a helpful and constructive aid to our understanding of the material structuring of domesticity and has a positive contribution to make to the study of design history.

The book will also draw on other disciplinary approaches, though, for the most part, more peripherally. This is not because these other disciplines necessarily have less to offer us in our quest to understand the way we handle the material objects and environments we create for ourselves. But there is a limit to what one can attempt, theoretically and methodologically, in one small book. More work, for example, needs to be done on possible uses of literary sources for studies of the kind attempted here. Claims about the role women have played in domestic decoration historically, for example, are frequently based on articles offering decorating tips and advice found in contemporary magazines aiming at a female readership. Yet it is hard to know what weight to place on such evidence as indicative of general feminine attitudes and values as opposed to its telling us what the writers of the articles thought their audience might be interested in. In default of other available evidence, there is an understandable temptation to depend more heavily on such articles for general information about feminine interests than is logically justified. Backing derived from literary sources, including those where fictional characters are required to appear plausible, though it needs to be handled with care, can thus be both helpful and suggestive. The study will therefore occasionally draw on literary evidence where that seems useful. This, then, constitutes the general method the study will employ to look at how people purchase kitchens today.

Though not planned as a historical study the book recognises that purchasing a new kitchen inevitably takes place within a historically shaped context which acts as an independent variable in buyers' decision-making. The book will not aim to provide a detailed history of kitchens or kitchen design. That is another project. On the other hand, because the development of kitchen design over the course of the last 130 years remains a key factor in determining the way people choose new kitchens at the turn of the twenty-first century, the historical development of the modern domestic kitchen cannot be ignored.

Parts of this history have already been written about in some detail; some are only partly relevant to issues concerning the choice of kitchen design. In immediate historical terms, one of the most striking developments and one which has transformed the average modern domestic kitchen for most people, is the revolutionary change which has taken place in its equipment. The desire for efficient and reliable cooking and cleaning facilities in the kitchen is, of course, long-standing. By the early nineteenth century the kitchens of the wealthy were striking testimonies to human inventiveness in pursuit of the means and equipment for producing ever more complex and elaborate culinary styles. The forms of power available for achieving these styles, however, did not stretch much beyond hand and fire until very late in the century.[5] Whatever cooking and cleaning were done remained heavily labour-intensive. This century, however, has seen a rapid acceleration in harnessing electric and, to a lesser extent, gas power to many of the cooking and cleaning processes formerly done manually.[6] Particularly since the Second World War, commercial companies have bombarded British women with information about labour-saving mechanisation in the household kitchen. Women have generally responded warmly.

Much of this would not have carried the significance it has, however, had not the explosive technological inventiveness of the post-war years, which led to the introduction of a wealth of powered cooking and cleaning aids, helped, as inventions rapidly superseded each other, to lower the relative prices of these new aids. Combined with a growth in the average household income in the country, this brought mechanical kitchen aids within the purchasing reach of the bulk of the population and over the last forty years even modest homes have seen a steady increase in the acquisition of technologically sophisticated cooking and cleaning machinery. Today the average small domestic kitchen boasts a mass of power-driven equipment for performing many of those repetitive daily cooking and cleaning chores that in the not very distant past demanded huge amounts of physical energy and often intimate contact with unpleasant smells or dirt.[7]

While much of this aspect of kitchen history has now been chronicled, other aspects have been less written about. For it is not simply that, if you could magically transpose a working-class woman from a 1946 kitchen into a turn-of-the-century kitchen of a comparable social group, she would be baffled by a good deal of the equipment. She would find the whole concept of how one arranged and worked in one's kitchen strikingly different. Though partly the product of twentieth-century technological development, other factors are at play here too. Many of the changes in kitchen layout and furniture which our 1940s woman would find in a kitchen today derive from ideas developed well before 1946,[8] though, as noted, she would not have been familiar with them because it took the growth of post-war affluence to spark off their widespread dissemination and popular realisation in this country.

Today the layout of many contemporary kitchens reflects both ideas drawn from American turn-of-the-century theories of scientific management and some of the basic canons, aesthetic and technical, of 1920s and 1930s modernist architecture. But while a huge amount of time and space has been devoted to the discussion of modernist architecture, little has been written about modernism and kitchen design, and the debt it owes to American theories of scientific management.[9] The book will therefore provide an outline of the development of these ideas with reference to kitchen design in a separate chapter, before turning to the sample data and the empirical documentation of the effect of these ideas on the way people plan their kitchens today.

Reports on visits to a systematically selected sample of 74 households where new kitchens had recently been installed, and an analysis of the interviews held there with the buyers of these kitchens, will provide the bulk of the study's empirical evidence. The analysis of this data will trace the interplay between buyers' practical considerations on the one hand, and their social and moral preoccupations on the other, as they set about buying and planning a new kitchen. It will also look at how buyers seek to integrate these concerns and express them visually. Against this background the book will then seek to analyse the rationales and aesthetic principles which underlie purchasers' visual choices and preferences in an attempt to delineate the foundations of some popular design tastes today.

One reason for looking at the behaviour of buyers of new kitchens is because of the very considerable outlay of expenditure that setting up a modern domestic kitchen now demands. By the early 1990s British market research showed that the annual turnover in sales of kitchen furniture had reached the billion pound mark,[10] and the real spending on new kitchens was almost certainly significantly higher as current market research data does not include the cost of new machinery bought or the attendant decoration which people do as part of refurbishing a kitchen. Though the level of spending on kitchens displays some fluctuation in the face of recession, market analysts do not see it as a fleeting fashion.[11] When money is tight people spend more cautiously, but the indications are that interest in kitchen refurbishment appears unlikely to fade rapidly. Certainly over the last few years spending on kitchens has steadily increased. This makes the subject interesting in itself.

Interest in the refurbishment of their kitchens across the social strata is, of course, simply one aspect of the huge burgeoning of interest in house decoration and furnishing generally which has accompanied the spectacular growth in house ownership in this country during the twentieth century, most particularly since the last war. If we were to go back just two or three generations most of the forebears of the sample drawn for this book would have spent all their lives in rented accommodation. In 1914, for example, only 10 per cent of the housing stock in England was owner-occupied; by 1938 owner-occupation had risen to 32 per cent; by 1969 it stood at 49 per cent; by 1981 there were more owner-occupied dwellings than the total sum of dwellings in the country in 1938; in 1996, 63 per cent of houses were owner-occupied;[12] and by 2000 calculations put home ownership in Britain at about 70 per cent.

The rate of increase in home ownership has not only been breathtaking in itself, it has also carried in its wake a momentous social change, equal in its impact to the dramatic shift towards the service sector the last decades have witnessed in the occupational structure; the changing position of women; the growth of England as a multicultural nation; and the changes in the country's sexual mores. For the experience of ownership influences people profoundly. A description of the effect of ownership on people is largely still waiting to be described, however.[13] One aim of this study is to make a small start in expanding our understanding of some of the values and feelings ownership leads people to express.

Interest in doing this is heightened because the national increase in house ownership means that owning one's house is now a cross-class phenomenon. Many of today's house owners are the children of people who previously never dreamt of owning their own homes. Among these new home owners many possess significant carpentry, plumbing, electrical, decorating and general building skills. Once they buy a house they can draw on these skills and this has enabled many people to do up their homes, including their kitchens, to a level they could not have afforded had they had to pay for labour. These house owners have played a key role in helping to spawn today's enormous DIY market. This market has further attracted another group of house owners. While in non-manual work they are still on average incomes and have discovered a huge pleasure in learning house-making skills. It is not an aim of the study to provide a history of the growth and influence of the DIY business, though this is clearly a field offering further scope for analysis in design history. That must remain for others to develop. One interest of the study will, however, be the way the possession of practical skills helps people gain access to the latest styles of kitchen design and décor and to use these to express a combination of aesthetic preferences and social concerns as they engage in the process of moulding their material environment. Even those who lack the necessary skills and show little aptitude for learning them can increasingly participate in this activity as the DIY shops improve their installation services.[14]

This takes us back to the issue raised at the opening of the chapter, namely, the kitchen as *idea*. The twentieth-century expansion in house ownership and the development of house decorating and improvment which have accompanied this have made the home available in a historically unprecedented way as a site for the symbolic expression in material form of the role and significance of family and domesticity generally in contemporary society. This raises the question of the degree to which, in acquiring, doing up, maintaining and refurbishing their homes, people today actively avail themselves of the opportunity this offers for exploring their feelings about these issues. The study will consider this as it traces the purchase and installation of new kitchens.

People, of course, express highly personal aesthetic preferences when decorating and furnishing a house. At one level this reflects their sensual responses to the material world around them, experiences they enjoy for their own sake. The study will argue, however, that the purist traditions which emphasise this form of aesthetic experience, and which have been unprecedentedly strong in the twentieth century, profoundly influencing aesthetic values and thinking among art and design historians, do not provide a full or satisfactory account of many people's aesthetic life. In different settings popular aesthetic preferences can include conveying messages about career aspirations, humanitarian concerns, views on parenthood and the family; they can embrace concepts such as respectability, loyalty, decency. The study will therefore look at the extent to which aesthetic experiences continue to be closely enmeshed with and reflective of people's feelings on a broad social front and will consider how, in constructing one particular domestic setting, people simultaneously not only express pure aesthetic partialities but use them to respond to the general social conditions in which they find themselves, and to express their hopes about the kind of domestic life they would ideally like.

This makes popular home decoration a rich field for an exploration of the interface between the past and the future in our society and illustrates the potential of design history for enlarging our understanding of ourselves as *social* creatures. On a number of fronts, then, the book will hope to show that an examination of contemporary kitchen décor and layout offers insights into a number of concerns, practical, moral and aesthetic, which engage house owners today.

Integral to any examination of this has to be an examination of the role of women during the process of purchasing a kitchen. Much feminist thinking has traditionally tended towards seeing the kitchen as both a locus and a symbol of feminine oppression and as a subject area it has not to date appealed strongly to feminists looking to draw attention to the ways and means women have found for realising both independence and individuality. A more popular research area for feminist work on women and consumption, for example, has been the historical development of the department store and the concomitant growth of shopping practices among women. This field has not generally prompted a strong need to problematise the role of woman as consumer. A number of writers in other fields,[15] both substantive and theoretical, have also been happy to take for granted the role of woman as the controller of purchases in the domestic sphere.[16]

The study does not seek to argue that the perception of women playing dominant roles in domestic expenditure is necessarily incorrect.[17] My concern is rather to learn more about the process by which women come to occupy and play out this role. The idea of process has considerable conceptual potential for developing our understanding of women as consumers. One example of its value is provided by De Grazia and Furlough.[18]

The historical case-studies their book brings together seek to unpick the idea of woman as consumer, to show how assumptions about natural gender differences inadequately explain the different patterns of gendered consumption that have been found. De Grazia and Furlough argue that the failure to analyse gender differences as the product of a complex historical interplay of pressures emanating from state action, perceptions of the family and social class, has significantly diminished our understanding of the way we use and give meaning to material objects. The book is persuasive about the benefits of looking at the processes by which gender roles with regard to consumption take shape and are acted out. Like De Grazia and Furlough, this study gives the idea of process a central position.

At a more general theoretical level Slater's critical digest of theories of consumer culture, both historical and across and within different academic traditions, also indirectly lends support to such an approach in that Slater notes that many theories of consumer culture are, in effect, ideologically driven debates, without substantive backing.[19] This points to the need for work which analyses the daily practice of consumption empirically and provides evidence with which to challenge or support different theories of consumption. Analysing the process by which gender roles are currently played out today in terms of the management of domestic budgets during the purchasing of a new kitchen can make a contribution here.

In looking at women as consumers the study will initially review a number of sociological studies, stretching over several decades, which provide an empirically based account of the management of domestic budgeting in British households, and which aimed to establish who, within British households, has overall control of, and responsibility for, household expenditure generally.[20] The study will then trace the scope and degree of control the women in the sample exercised in practical terms during the process of refurbishing a kitchen. This will include reviewing some of the constraints in terms of household budgetary decisions which the sociological data shows that many women face within marriage.[21] It will also look at how spending on new kitchens compared with other forms of household expenditure within the sample. Importantly, it will raise questions about whether we should simply assume that to establish who formally carries responsibility for general budgetary decisions actually provides an accurate understanding of the control of spending within a family. This is where looking at the process by which money is spent can be revealing.

To develop further our understanding of gender roles with regard to domestic design and the role of women as domestic consumers and taste makers the study will examine the degree to which there is evidence of a conscious desire on the part of purchasers when buying a new kitchen to find ways of giving material expression to strongly held moral and social family values. It will also seek to determine who is mainly concerned with and carries responsibility for giving visual expression to such values within contemporary households. This will lead to questions about when we might arguably see the acquisition of a new kitchen as a form of feminine empowerment, even if a woman enjoys only partial budgetary control. To date there is little research about feminine activity and decision-making in this area of the field of furniture buying.[22]

In contrast, the rise of the woman interior designer has attracted considerable attention among design historians. The interior designer's primary concern, however, has usually been the reception and bedroom areas in the houses of wealthy clients. These areas not only belong to different parts of the house socially, they are part of a different social world from the households with which this book is primarily concerned. The research perspective is also significantly different.

In studies of interior design the client occupies a subsidiary role. Here the consumer occupies centre stage and the interviews conducted with them are the study's prime source of interest. This focus of interest derives from an intellectual perspective which remains significantly under-explored among design historians and merits greater analysis than they have vouchsafed it to date. Emerging as it initially did from art practice and art history, design history most commonly starts with the object and/or the designer. Starting with the consumer remains not only relatively uncommon in design history, it stimulates very different questions about design. Different starting-points in the study of design history, furthermore, not only give rise to different approaches to the study of design but have different implications for the kind of design issues and design theory they lead to.

From the point of view of this study, for example, it would be time-wasting to focus on users/consumers if the primary interest in them were as the recipients of designed objects whose meaning and use at the point of purchase they took and accepted as given and fixed. Conducting long interviews in order to analyse essentially passive behaviour would be an uneconomical route to developing a better understanding of the way people express themselves visually. It only makes sense, in fact, to put the user at centre stage and erect a study of this kind if one conceives of consumers as independent, active agents with an interest in and an ability for manipulating the designs they receive so as to make them serve *their* needs as *they* define them.[23] A second and accompanying assumption of such a study is that there are no a priori factors which determine the interest or importance, socially or aesthetically, of any given design style. Most studies of design vigorously reject such an assumption. Many design historians would, indeed, be appalled at the thought of making such an assumption.[24]

While, however, the approach proposed here is relatively new in design history, it has a long history within sociology, where it is linked to a well-rehearsed theoretical debate. During the 1970s and 1980s a central debate in sociology turned on the issue of how far our behaviour is circumscribed and shaped by sets of social constraints outside the individual's control. Different schools of opinion, such as the Marxists, the structural-functionalists and symbolic interactionists, argued over the degree to which human behaviour is socially determined and the degree to which people find ways of manipulating the social situations in which they find themselves so as to further their personal needs and aims. But, though debate was both brisk and partisan, the action–structure debate, as it was known, was not finally resolved by the emergence of a winner. Rather the argument reached stand-off. In addition, by the end of the 1980s major socio-economic changes had begun to erode the traditional industrial base of Western society and this so changed class and work patterns that the terms in which much of this debate had been couched now appeared outmoded. It also led to the emergence of new substantive interests. More people had more money to spend so what and how they spent it was increasingly seen as socially significant. Consumerism began to attract unprecedented attention and by the mid-1990s it had become a major new sociological preoccupation.

In looking for a framework which would give shape to the collection of substantive data for developing descriptions of how people, at all levels of the social system, actively engage with the social constraints and pressures they find themselves facing when they set out to model their homes to reflect their aspirations, the action–structure debate is not irrelevant, however. It continues to provide a useful and simple theoretical framework. The study's theoretical position summarised in a sentence is that consumers are characterised by a self-conscious, willed intentionality which they struggle to realise through the creation and pursuit of instrumentally appropriate patterns of behaviour within the constraints of their social context. The way this plays itself out empirically in shaping a particular part of the English domestic interior is the central interest of this study.

The purpose of outlining a general theoretical stance is to facilitate a systematic assessment of the social meaning of the empirical data collected. The role of the theoretical stance is therefore modest, to provide a way of giving structure and order to an attempt to enhance our understanding of our material environment by means of examining other people's understanding of their environment and their attempts to shape it to their will,[25] in this instance through the analysis of one example of consumer behaviour. Large-scale ontological arguments are left to others.

The foundations on which the approach rested was built on previous work in related fields and derived from arguments, concepts and evidence drawn from a number of key texts. In 1983 Bratlinger's *Bread and Circuses: Theories of Mass Culture as Social Decay*[26] appeared. A study in the history of ideas, it offered an incisive and well-documented account of the repeated eruption, from the Greeks and Romans up to the Frankfurt school, Adorno and beyond, of groups of self-appointed élites who set themselves up as the bearers of cultural standards and took upon themselves a custodial and judicial role with regard to the cultural tastes and preferences of the general population. Bratlinger's book is an account of a continuing intellectual condescension on the part of some of the more privileged sectors of society towards the tastes and pleasures of the less economically and educationally privileged.

The 1980s witnessed other scattered voices raised on behalf of what were still in some cultural circles openly and superciliously called 'the masses'. With *Distinction: A Social Critique of the Judgement of Taste*,[27] published in 1979 in French and in English in 1984, Bourdieu established himself as a powerful dissident voice against this cultural élitism. Working within a Marxist–structuralist framework Bourdieu's main preoccupation was with the process of social reproduction. His analysis of taste was driven by a desire to illuminate the social mechanisms by which old élites retained power across generations. He was not concerned with the process of social change, which he largely denied took place.

As part of his analysis Bourdieu undertook an empirical survey to identify the cultural preferences and tastes of different social strata. In the 1970s this enabled him to identify distinguishable differences of aesthetic preference by social class. Since the publication of *Distinction* twenty-five years ago there have been major modifications to the structure of the economy in both England and France and the class system of that time has changed in significant respects. This has affected the cultural differences that used to distinguish the old social classes. New social groups are also emerging, distinguished by new patterns of cultural interest and preference. Nevertheless, the distinction Bourdieu makes between the economically dominant and the culturally dominant remains valuable in helping to highlight an area of social power play which continues to influence people's social standing and social relationships in our society in important respects. *Distinction* may have limitations but it remains one of the most compelling and persuasive accounts of the social role of culture in the legitimisation of social status and power in the contemporary West during the second half of the twentieth century and into the opening of the twenty-first.[28]

One claim *Distinction* made was that socially less privileged groups not only had different tastes, but also held them in conscious defiance of the social and cultural élite. The book, indeed, provided illustrations of the way the less privileged used their own cultural mores to assert themselves against élite groups.[29] Bourdieu's theoretical framework, however, encouraged him to present this kind of class defiance as a form of cheekiness, what would once have been called cocking a snook. Cultural defiance on the part of the less privileged was theoretically determined for Bourdieu as socially superficial. Whether or not one wants to accept this, *Distinction* adds a new layer of social analysis to the historical narrative Bratlinger provided. Bourdieu's discussion of the relation between judgements of taste and the legitimisation of social status and power for the cultural élite raises fundamental questions about the independence of such judgements and thus about the philosophical status of different sets of aesthetic preferences.

One area where the cultural élitism Bratlinger and Bourdieu describe has found contemporary expression has been in the beliefs of various intellectual coteries about the impact on the general public of twentieth-century marketing techniques, in particular, advertising. These beliefs shaped much of the academic work on advertising until very recently. Sometimes overtly, sometimes by implication, academic studies of advertising repeatedly assumed a hopelessly gullible public who accepted advertisers' claims at face value and were conned into desiring and buying a stream of fashionable gimmickry which had no cultural value and could not deliver the social or personal benefits it promised. The academic perception of public gullibility was so widespread that it was frequently deemed unnecessary to investigate the actual impact of advertising on people. Instead, academic attention focused on the imagery and language of adverts, subjecting them to detailed textual analysis to reveal their manipulative techniques.[30] This position has been increasingly challenged over the last decade but it is, nevertheless, taking a long time to wither away entirely.[31]

Paul Willis's *Common Culture: Symbolic Work at Play in the Everyday Cultures of the Young*,[32] which appeared in 1990, was in sharp contrast to this tradition. Willis approached the study of popular culture and advertising from a new angle. He looked at how 'the masses' responded to the media. This was a notable milestone in the mounting challenge to the intellectual condescension towards the general population which had been so strong in educated circles. Though the young people Willis studied congregated in groups,[33] Willis problematised the commonly made assumption that this meant that any individual member's behaviour would therefore be indistinguishable from that of others in the group and that young, not very highly educated people lacked the ability to discriminate. Drawing on observational and interview evidence Willis argued that these young people displayed a knowing awareness of how the media operated. They looked at what it offered them, selected what they wanted and discarded what did not interest them. You might not like them, you might deplore their tastes, but you could not characterise them as mindless, social automata.

One implication of this approach is that consumers are the final arbiters of the significance of a designed object and, in the attribution of meaning to things, at least the equal of the original creator, if not the dominant actor.[34] With the publication of *Theatres of Memory*[35] in 1994, Samuel added a further slant on this position. As a historian Samuel was concerned with the role a society's historical narratives play in continually changing and shaping our view of society. But he was also concerned that professional historians' preoccupation with archive-based research effected important closures on what counts as knowledge. Believing that history is a social form of knowledge and thus inherently revisionist, Samuel argued that historians can have no sovereign authority over their subject. This made him interested, for example, in popular antiquarianism, including the popular passion for collecting almost any type of memorabilia or antique. Even if such antiquarianism operated with a minimal historiography Samuel saw the knowledge collectors accrue as contributing to the enlargement of our historical and social understanding. For Samuel, therefore, popular collecting was a significant part of contemporary historical endeavour, endowing new groups, activities and artefacts with meaning and thereby making new interpretations of ourselves and the society we inhabit available to us. Samuel's thesis lends supports to the claim here that a study of the visual tastes and interests of the purchasers of new kitchens is of significant social import.

One of the most important new intellectual milestones during the late 1980s, however, was not a book but a movement, post-modernism. Though the term had been around in some disciplines, such as architecture, for well over a decade, post-modernist approaches now emerged across a wide array of academic disciplines and in the field of consumer culture post-modernist debates are now ubiquitous. Although post-modernist debates have not made a significant contribution to the theoretical approach adopted for this study, these debates make the issue of agency a key concept and some response to post-modernism is required. Post-modernism in the field of consumer studies is characterised by a diversity of approaches. As Slater[36] has noted, post-modernist theories of consumption are ambivalent about whether patterns of contemporary consumerism reflect the blossoming of individual agency or the attempts of the socially dislocated to achieve social stability. In the second case, while there appears to be agency, people are, in fact, theorised as profoundly constrained. The status of this position, however, remains to be determined as empirical evidence for it still needs to be gathered. In the meantime the action–structure debate continues to provide a simple, useful conceptual framework for studying the way people manage the material environment of the contemporary home.

Along with writers like Bourdieu, Samuel and Willis, post-modernism has helped to challenge the traditional intellectual framework and accompanying forums which have for a long time controlled and structured the way aesthetic judgements are both made and discussed within our society. As Bourdieu, Samuel and Willis showed, taking consumer agency seriously leads to taking consumer interests and values seriously[37] and challenges the concept of absolute values in aesthetic judgements. It also expands the boundaries of what can potentially count as important aesthetic territory. Despite the challenge that has been mounted against it, the old tradition of cultural élitism is not yet moribund, either in or outside academia, and the concept of a general population as a foolish and easily malleable body continues to thrive in various educated coteries. These developments are therefore refreshing.

It is not an aim of this study to deny that many people can be and are foolish on occasion, or to assert the superiority of the hitherto cultural underclass. But the study does argue for confronting the fact that the phrase 'the general population' covers huge numbers of people who cannot be simply lumped together; for recognising that the time has come to stop making taken-for-granted assumptions about what constitutes worthwhile aesthetic activity; for extending the range of artefacts that can qualify for serious cultural discussion; and, without assuming the outcome of the debate, for subjecting the role of absolute values in aesthetic judgements to reappraisal and for considering possible new sets of criteria for evaluating different modes of cultural activity.[38]

This study seeks to make a start on some of these fronts. A major assumption behind the study, for example, is that an enquiry into how a sample of purchasers set about choosing and installing new kitchens in their homes addresses a significant cultural area of contemporary life. There seems no reason otherwise for taking the time to do the study.

Though, in ascribing agency to people, the study problematises any easy assumption of public malleability and gullibility, it also limits itself to an account of one particular, specialised form of purchase. It does not attempt any general pronouncement on the intellectual independence of the population as a whole in the face of the mass of marketing blarney now surrounding the sale of almost all forms of commercial products, both cheap and expensive. It also disclaims any suggestion that, by looking at how people set about selecting a new kitchen, we can learn how people select other goods, either small ephemeral items like a can of fizzy drink or large expensive items like a new car. What it does claim is that whether people show signs of being driven by clever marketing strategies which bamboozle and cajole them into buying what the market wants to sell or whether they display a proactive and independent approach in formulating and expressing their aesthetic tastes is not a matter of opinion. It is an empirical question and, as such, resolvable only through a process of empirical examination. This is coupled with the belief that a study of the purchase of new kitchens will help us develop a more nuanced understanding of the intellectual and aesthetic underpinning of a key area of contemporary domestic and social life.

Such an approach requires and makes no evaluation of the artistic merit of any given example of design or décor. But, by bringing the goals of the user to the fore and concerning itself with the degree to which people aim to communicate these goals through their handling of given designs, it presents design historians with some new questions. To recognise the consumer's right to determine the goals they want design to serve raises questions about what we wish to define as 'good' design.

This might give rise in some circles to a concern that a consumer-driven approach could lead to a denigration of design as a professional activity. The history of design has now achieved the status of a recognised academic field, but the subject would not exist without the concept of the professional designer consciously working within the context of twentieth-century visual art.[39] This both sustains and shapes it. The analysis of kitchen design as developed in this study does not operate from this perspective and might seem to subordinate questions of design to issues about the nature and meaning of contemporary cultural mores, popular or élite. That, some design historians might argue, effectively diminishes both the idea of design and the concept of the designer, when what is needed is an informed public understanding of the designer as a figure of artistic and social significance, whose activities and products have the power to make a positive contribution to the quality of our lives.

To conceive of these contrasting approaches to the study of design as competitive with each other would, however, be to misunderstand them. It is true that the approach adopted here denies the authority of the designer in judgements of meaning and taste, and refuses any claim they might make to the right to legislate about taste. But this is far from negating the role of the designer. The designer remains a vanguard figure in the process by which people create new visual languages to express the values and aspirations of a given period, and thereby expands the means available to us for communicating with each other visually.[40] The fact that people may take, leave or modify these visual languages does not invalidate the claim that, through their work, designers enlarge and enrich our visual vocabularies. This is no mean thing. In a democracy it is as much as any group should expect.

In addition, though it starts with the consumer, the book is also concerned with developments in design. A central interest will be what non-designers like or find useful in professional design work sufficiently to take and adapt for their own purposes. This presupposes that the study of design exists as an independent discipline. Design developments are not left to one side here, as might be considered proper in an anthropological study. Instead the book will seek to straddle two very different disciplines, the art-historical and the sociological, each with its own distinctive analytical styles.

This has implications for the kind of data which will be appropriate to the arguments of the book. The potential value of simple quantitative data for exploring the way people select new kitchens has been noted. Quantitative data has a limited contribution to make, however, to the discussion of aesthetic questions. The study will therefore draw on qualitative data as well.

The cross-disciplinary interests of the book also create problems for the layout and presentation of its argument. Empirical studies in sociology, which would include the kind of fieldwork done for this study, have a well-established and distinctive format for reportage. Previous work in the field is reviewed; the choice of sample and other pertinent methodological issues are described; a theoretical position is outlined; and one or more theoretical issues relating to this position are selected for further debate and clarification in the light of the empirical data collected. At this point the empirical findings are presented. It is an approach closer to that of the natural sciences than history. For those not attuned to it, it can seem ponderous. In historical writing, in contrast, a narrative mode continues to dominate. At its best it offers a clear, absorbing story. Historians, of course, face important theoretical and methodological issues. Frequently, however, their discussion of such issues is reserved for specific debates on historiography. Some historians, indeed, remain unconvinced about the benefits of theorising.[41]

The study was planned to attract a mixed audience, embracing readers from both the humanities and the social sciences. This meant it had to meet different sets of reader expectations. But the primary audience for the book was to be design historians. The book had to gain their attention first. So, though the heart of the book is a report on an empirical project, employing methods drawn directly from mainstream sociology, the book does not follow a conventional sociological format in a number of respects. Yet neither does it adopt the kind of narrative mode which still dominates the writing of design history. Theoretical and methodological issues receive more attention than they would customarily get in a mainstream work of design history but, from the point of view of a sociologist, theoretical issues may seem too cursorily handled. Setting up a format for the book which would be acceptable to design historians led to a more discursive presentation than one would get in either a straight sociological or a straight design history study.

The difficulties interdisciplinary work faces goes beyond finding ways of marrying different styles of presentation and forms of data, however. Interdisciplinary work is currently fashionable and its benefits, much lauded. Yet such work commonly demands intellectual adjustments from both practitioners and readers which can be disorientating and threatening. It often, for example, problematises important taken-for-granted assumptions in the disciplines involved. As a result people often settle for a more manageable multidisciplinary approach, that is to say where one discipline brings its perspective to bear on an issue which is also of interest to another discipline. This offers a way of avoiding the need to penetrate the boundaries between disciplines. Without a real exploration of another discipline's traditional territory, practitioners involved in a multi-disciplinary exercise are also free to retreat from each other as soon as they start to feel insecure.[42]

This study, however, aims at an interpenetration of different ways of thinking. This means asking design historians to try to think like sociologists and sociologists to try to engage with the world like a design historian. In other words it means asking people to move from the role of a spectator of to the role of a participant in another intellectual universe. This raised two problems. First, there were virtually no tried or tested formats for doing or presenting such work. Finding a structure for the book which seemed appropriate to people from different disciplines was difficult but to have waited until a structure was devised which satisfied everyone would have led to an indefinite delay in publishing. It seemed better to publish and hope that constructive criticism of the format would help writers engaged in the interdisciplinary endeavour in future.

Secondly, interdisciplinarity for writers means submitting to a range of concepts and methods in which they continually find themselves in the disorienting position of being novices again. The difficulties inherent in this position are not helped by the fact that powerful social forces, the analysis of which is beyond the remit of this book, continue to make disciplinary specialisation the dominant organisational principle shaping and regulating activity among the tribes of Academia today, prescribing for their individual members both the boundaries of their intellectual activity and the structure of their intellectual personas.[43] An inter-disciplinary approach can therefore be uncomfortable and difficult for writers,[44] leaving them feeling academically marginal. Ultimately, of course, significant advances in intellectual understanding are rarely built on the basis of one kind of intellectual approach alone. They occur rather by a process of osmosis between different modes of intellectual thinking. The persistent privileging of one kind of approach, a strong emphasis on a subject-centred approach, for example, as has certainly occurred in many intellectual fields, can act as a serious barrier to making progress. It is not, however, an aim of this study to mount an attack on subject specialisation *per se*. The study certainly assumes that for narrowly focused, detailed specialist studies to achieve intellectual significance they normally need to be located within more widely conceived contexts. But specialist studies continue to occupy an important place in intellectual life while studies which primarily operate in terms of broad, general claims unsup-ported by detailed back-up studies can fail to rise beyond grand but essentially speculative intellectualising.

What this book offers the general quest to improve our ways of knowing is a small subject, buying a kitchen, combined with a wide-ranging approach. There is finally only one way, however, of judging the usefulness of the kind of interdisciplinary approach proposed here, namely, by putting it into practice and then reviewing its results.

Early in this chapter the argument was put that human behaviour does not occur in a vacuum, but in a particular social setting and against a specific historical backdrop, and both the setting and backdrop, within and against which people act, are invariably, to some degree, independent variables influencing and shaping that action. The first step in our interdisciplinary endeavour must therefore be to outline the historical context within which the sample set about the process of acquiring a new kitchen.

The next chapter therefore moves the study into gear by way of a short review of how the concept of the fitted kitchen developed historically. The following chapter describes the rationale behind the way the sample was drawn. Subsequent chapters take up and discuss different aspects of the data collected.

## Notes

1. I was using oral testimony myself extensively in the 1980s, as a way of gaining insight into the aesthetic and social significance of the design of handcrafted objects, initially in exhibitions and exhibition catalogues and later in articles such as Freeman, June (1989) 'The Discovery of the Commonplace or Establishment of an Elect: Intellectuals in the Contemporary Craft World', *Journal of Design History*, vol. 2, numbers 2 and 3, and Freeman, June (1990) 'The Crafts as Poor Relations', *Oral History*, vol. 18, number 9.
2. Miller, Daniel (ed.) (1998) *Material Cultures: Why Some Things Matter*, University of Chicago Press, and Miller, Daniel (ed.) (2001) *Home Possessions: Material Culture Behind Closed Doors*, Berg, provide two examples.
3. Some of the recent anthropologically inspired studies of contemporary domestic culture can display a somewhat cavalier attitude towards methodology, leaving the rationale informing the selection of respondents unclear. While not a blanket assertion, one or two of the essays in Miller (1998), for example, are weak on this front. It can make them vulnerable to the charge of being akin to journalism.
4. Miller, D. (ed.) (1995) *Acknowledging Consumption: A Review of New Studies*, p. 52, Routledge.
5. Hardyment, Christina (1988) *From Mangle to Microwave: The Mechanisation of Household Goods*, Polity Press in association with Basil Blackwell.

6. This is not the same as saying that poverty has been abolished, of course. But the point is illustrated by the kinds of kitchens shown in sitcoms, films and soaps set in relatively modest contemporary English social conditions.

7. Cowen, Ruth Schwartz (1989) *More Work for Mother*, Free Association Books, has argued that the time saved as a result of the development of household machinery has led to led to ever higher standards of cleanliness rather than the release of time for other things. The argument here does not gainsay this: the point being made is a different one.

8. Bullock, N. (1988) 'First the Kitchen – then the Façade', *Journal of Design History*, vol. 1, numbers 3 and 4.

9. Ibid.

10. See Mintel, Marketing Intelligence, 1989 and 1992.

11. Ibid., 1992.

12. McCulloch, Andrew (1983) 'Owner Occupation and Class Struggle: the Mortgage Strikes of 1938–40', Ph.D. thesis, University of Essex; and *Social Trends* (1996) Office of National Statistics.

13. Saunders, Peter (1990) *A Nation of Homeowners*, Unwin Hyman, has looked at one aspect of this though his perspective is different from that adopted here.

14. The DIY market has certainly attracted the attention of design historians, though there is not yet a major study of this market.

15. Parr, Joy (1999) *Domestic Goods: The Material, the Moral and the Economic in the Post-war Years*, University of Toronto Press, for example, basically proceeds on this assumption in tracing the emergence, through an examination of household objects, of a distinguishable Canadian style of domestic consumption in the years following the Second World War.

16. Slater, D. (1996) *Consumer Culture and Modernity*, Polity, makes this assumption a major plank in his criticism of the limitations of liberalism's theory of consumer culture.

17. At one level, therefore, I have no quarrel with Parr and Slater and certainly not with Slater's sharp appraisal of liberalism's belittling of feminine consumption.

18. De Grazia, V. and Furlough, E. (eds) (1996) *The Sex of Things: Gender and Consumption in Historical Perspective*, University of California Press.

19. Slater (1996), p. 209.

20. See Oakley, Ann (1985) *The Sociology of Housework*, Basil Blackwell; Pahl, Jan (1989) *Money and Marriage*, Macmillan; Laurie, Heather

(1996) 'Household Financial Resource Distribution and Women's Labour Market Participation', Ph.D. thesis, University of Essex;

21. See Laurie (1996) and Pahl (1989).

22. Miller, D. 'Appropriating the State on the Council Estate', in Putnam, T. and Newton, C. (eds) (1990) *Household Choices*, Futures Publications, remains about the only study which has looked at kitchens, and the study is not concerned with women's roles in particular: the perspective is different.

23. In contrast, connoisseurs and other collectors are essentially passive in terms of their physical relationship to the objects they buy, revering them or making them a focal point for contemplation. They may, of course, be very active subsequently in using the objects they buy as a means of enhancing their social status. But this is to use objects in a very different way.

24. This is not to claim that it is impossible to make meaningful value judgements about different kinds of design. On the contrary. It only rules out the idea that there are absolute standards of judgement available to the well-trained design or art historian.

25. What Giddens, A. (1984) *The Constitution of Society: Outline of the Theory of Structuration*, Polity Press, has called 'the double hermeneutic'.

26. Bratlinger, P. (1983) *Bread and Circuses: Theories of Mass Culture as Social Decay*, Cornell University Press.

27. Bourdieu, P. (1984) *Distinction: A Social Critique of the Judgement of Taste*, Routledge and Kegan Paul. *Distinction* was first published in French in 1979.

28. Warde, Alan (1997) *Consumption, Food and Taste: Culinary Antinomies and Commodity Culture*, Sage, argues that despite recent social changes we should not drop the concept of social class too quickly in analysing contemporary social mores. The evidence of this study supported retaining the concept of a cultural élite as a distinct and significant class group. For the purposes of this study, however, other traditional class distinctions did not seem to operate, as the data shows.

29. Bourdieu (1984), p. 184. Bourdieu describes, for instance, how in working-class circles at the time he was writing it could be a conscious slight to insist on someone accepting a plate with certain kinds of food and working-class groups might employ this exclusionary gesture against a member of the middle class, who, one suspects, probably did not know how to read it.

30. Williamson, Judith (1980) *Consuming Passions: The Dynamics of Popular Culture*, Marion Boyars, is a classic text in this tradition of discussing advertising.
31. Jackson, P. and Thrift, N. 'Geographies of Consumption', in Miller (1995), p. 218, make the same point about the way commentators have ignored the consumer in discussions of adverts, preferring to base their understanding of advertising on their personal interpretations of the signs and symbols found in them. Examples, coming from different perspectives, of the growing challenge to this position, would be: Leiss, W., Kline, S., and Jhally, S. (1990) *Social Communication in Advertising*, 2nd edition, Routledge; Willis, Paul (1990) *Common Culture: Symbolic Work at Play in the Everyday Cultures of the Young*, Open University; and Cook, Guy (1992) *The Discourse of Advertising*, Routledge. An example of its persistence would be Isenstadt, Sandy (1998) 'Visions of Plenty: Refrigerators in America around 1950', *Journal of Design History*, vol. 11, no. 4, p. 311. The two brothers in the American sitcom *Frasier* offer an example of the persistence of aesthetic snobbery but also the developing challenge now being mounted against such snobbery. The actors' rendering of Niles and Frasier Crane and their cultural pretensions turns the brothers into objects of gentle but constant ridicule.
32. Willis (1990).
33. This, of course, does not distinguish them from other people. The cultural élite notoriously congregates in groups. For some reason it is not generally assumed that members thereby lose their individuality, unlike the members of some other groups.
34. This remains true whether or not the consumer accepts or seeks to modify the designer-given significance or meaning of an object or design. There is also an analogy to be drawn here with Roland Barthes's (1977) 'The Death of the Author', in *Image Music Text,* Essays selected and translated by Stephen Heath Fontana Paperbacks. At this juncture it is worth noting Slater's (1996) comment, p.157, however, that even when different branches of Western philosophy have dealt with the issue of the autonomous actor in discussions of consumption there has been a very strong tendency to 'structure' women out of the discussion. The autonomous actor is all too frequently conceived of as male.
35. Samuel, R. (1994) *Theatres of Memory*, Verso.
36. Slater (1996), pp. 203–9, provides a succinct account of these, noting how some post-modernists see current patterns of consumption as the ultimate in anomie, others as the ultimate in freedom. Yet other coteries continue to embrace old patrician élitist attitudes.

37. Miller, Daniel (1987) *Material Culture and Mass Communication*, Basil Blackwell, and McRobbie, Angela (1999) *In the Culture Society: Art, Fashion and Popular Music*, Routledge, both claim that certain cultural forms still tend to be privileged, nevertheless.

38. Docker, J. (1994) *Postmodernism and Popular Culture: A Cultural History*, Cambridge University Press, is a post-modernist approach which draws heavily on Bakhtin for this purpose.

39. This consciousness of being players within an ongoing history of design remains a major part of the self-perception of those designers whether they work to commission for wealthy private or corporate clients or are employed by the public or commercial sectors.

40. See Forte, Adrian (1986) *Objects of Desire*, Thames and Hudson, on the designer and ideas.

41. Glennie, P. 'Consumption within Historical Studies', in Miller (1995), p. 164, comments on how distrustful many historians are of theorising. De Grazia and Furlough (1996) are an exception here.

42. Dobash, Emerson and Dobash, Russell (1998) *Rethinking Violence Against Women*, Sage, provide a tart account of the kind of shameless discourtesies in which academics will indulge when 'cross-border' discussion is attempted. The book, a collection of essays on the contentious subject of domestic violence, bypasses this problem by adopting a multidisciplinary approach. An example of a similar approach being adopted for the discussion of design history was *Ideal Homes? Towards a Sociology of Domestic Architecture and Interior Design*, a conference held at the School of Human Studies, University of Teesside (1994).

43. Even a cursory analysis of the way people advance in terms of career, salary and status in our universities also makes apparent to any discerning and ambitious young academic the advantages of sticking to subject-centred research activity.

44. Particularly in view of the kind of intellectual socialisation trainee academics are customarily subjected to and which Basil Bernstein neatly described in his essay 'On the Classification and Framing of Educational Knowledge', in M.F.D. Young (ed.) (1961) *Knowledge and Control*, and which still rings true today. Samuel (1994) also talked of how professional historians learn to fetishise archive-based research. This helps to create a pressure for them to conceive of their work 'within an existing form of enquiry and respecting its limits', p. X.

# Kitchen design as an expression of twentieth-century proselytising

Daily household chores and general home care absorb so much of our time today that it is easy to forget what a recent feature of many people's lives they are. Until well into the nineteenth and even twentieth century, there were still considerable segments of the populace, particularly in agricultural areas, for whom not merely general household management but such apparently basic things as cooking and cleaning occupied very little time indeed.[1] Some of the older members of the sample, indeed, could still tell stories about the kitchens of their childhood, which seemed to belong to a world light-years away from their present trim and spotless domains. One man, recalling the mice in his now demolished childhood home, broke into laughter as he remembered a mouse jumping out of a loaf from which he was cutting a slice of bread at the kitchen table one day. Another man remembered with amusement the stone sink with a bucket underneath for the slops, which, together with the contents of the privy up the garden, he used to help his mother carry and spread over the vegetables they grew. And it was not just older respondents who remembered kitchens with little adjoining pantries and sculleries, so important in the days of the fridgeless kitchen. A middle-aged woman, in recalling the pleasure of shouting as she ran along the long stone-flagged hallway leading to her grandmother's kitchen, was jolted into remembering the separate stone-flagged scullery where the family stood the milk and meat on the floor in an attempt to keep them cool and fresh in the hot weather. Even young people could remember kitchens which now seemed very impoverished. A young woman in her early thirties, for example, remembered her grandmother folding old newspapers to line the open shelves on which she kept her crockery, and, standing in her fully fitted, amply cupboarded, spotlessly clean kitchen, shuddered fastidiously at the recollection. With the huge rise in the general level of wealth, education, nutrition and health that the twentieth century has seen, such old-style kitchens have disappeared, even among the poor.

The English kitchen today is simultaneously a product of greater wealth and a cause of better health in the country. Its genesis can be traced back to the second half of the nineteenth century. Certain strains of thinking began to emerge in the United States at that time on the newly coined subject of household management, which were later taken up and developed alongside new thinking about design in Germany, Holland and Vienna. By the late 1920s in Vienna and Germany the new thinking and design were beginning to find expression in actual housing. Then the Second World War broke out.

The United States recovered from the war more rapidly than Europe. In addition, as well as being traditionally a more flexible and open society culturally than Britain, the United States also experienced a considerable economic boom during the 1950s. The new surge of wealth this brought to many Americans allowed for the successful introduction into private homes of commercially produced fitted kitchens displaying new design ideas on an increasingly large scale. By the 1960s, however, Europe had also largely recovered from the war and fitted kitchens started to appear on the English market and were being installed in English houses. Since then, fitted kitchens have become increasingly common. Today they are a virtually taken-for-granted feature of English homes.

These changes did not take place overnight. Nor does the fitted kitchen, in the forms in which it is predominantly realised in English homes today, reflect, in any simple way, the growth of an unqualified acceptance of the outlook and ideas of a design avant-garde by the general public. The nature and degree of popular acceptance for the new design ideas about kitchens constitute a complicated and rambling story, as will become increasingly apparent in subsequent chapters. Certainly an account of the appearance of today's fitted kitchens includes an account of the growing public annexation of various professional design ideas[2] and ideological perspectives with regard to the domestic kitchen, but it will become clear that the story of the fitted kitchen in England is also a story of selection on the public's part.

An account of the development of the fitted kitchen will need to cover a number of issues. It will want to consider how professional designers have won the general public over to new ideas about the design of the domestic kitchen, but it will also want to include a discussion of what the public has persisted in rejecting in terms of design ideas and the material form designers have given these ideas. As a significant strand in under-standing the form the fitted kitchen has taken in English homes, it will, at the same time, want to consider how the public has sought to amalgamate various professional design ideas with their own ideas and design preferences. The aim here will not only be to show how the buying public has modified certain professional design ideas profoundly in a number of respects but will also be part of an attempt to highlight the aims and goals purchasers of kitchen furniture seek to realise today through the layout and décor of their new kitchens.

In this chapter, however, the immediate task is to provide an account of the rise of the modern kitchen historically in terms of the ideas which lie behind its genesis and the design features which developed in association with these ideas and continue to help shape its appearance. In offering this historical account the provisos of the previous paragraph will need to be borne in mind. For the structure and style of this account is necessarily heavily marked by the nature of the evidence on this subject which has come down to us, and historiographical biases in the past significantly determine the information available to us today for retrieving the story of the development of the fitted kitchen. For example, almost none of the material we have today to work with covers popular responses to new ideas about kitchens. History has not, until the last few decades, generally been conceptualised as being shaped in an interesting or significant way by popular values about design, so few people thought either of collecting information on this front or of storing it. Historical changes in kitchen design have been overwhelmingly conceived of as being driven by professional architects. The bulk of the information on which this historical account is based is perforce from people and groups who came from more privileged, financially comfortable, often highly educated social strata, even more narrowly, indeed, from self-appointed campaigners for new ideas and specialist trained groups within these strata. These providers of our present information tended to be characterised by a more than average self-confidence and a strong sense of self-esteem, which made them more likely than average to engage in public debate and to write for the public. Their words and thoughts thus dominate the archival information available. In later chapters the opinions of the general public will find expression but an account of the origins of the fitted kitchen can contain very little about popular responses to the new ideas. Nevertheless, the archival information we have remains essential to an understanding of how today's buyers of domestic kitchens make their purchasing choices.

The starting-point of the thinking which led to today's fitted kitchen is often seen as being Catherine Beecher's *The American Woman's Home, on Principles of Domestic Science*, published in 1869.[3] 'The chief cause of women's disabilities and sufferings', Catherine Beecher asserts in the Introduction, is 'that women are not trained as men are for their peculiar duties'. She aims to rectify this and to this end seeks 'to elevate the honour and remuneration of domestic employment' according to 'the principles and teachings of Jesus Christ' as these constitute 'the true basis of women's rights and duties'. Her religious beliefs lead Beecher to locate happiness 'in an efficient family sustained and adorned by family *work*' (my emphasis). On the one hand this leads her to denounce 'the falsity of the idea that to be a lady and be waited on is desirable', but it also supports her belief that 'Woman's mission is self-denial.' Her discussion of good kitchen organisation takes place within and is structured by this moral framework.

Some feminists have seen Catherine Beecher as an early proponent of women's rights. But despite an occasional mention of rights Beecher is driven overwhelmingly by a concern with duties which do not obviously entail any rights and certainly none we would immediately recognise today as feminine rights.[4] Beecher's concern with 'efficiency' has nevertheless been significant for the development of kitchen design.

Early in the book Beecher advises arranging a kitchen so as to help women avoid excessive walking while cooking.[5] The idea that there is a positive virtue in striving to employ an economy of means and having 'efficiency' as a goal remains, however, largely undeveloped in terms of her subsequent practical recommendations. She advises, for example, hugely cumbersome arrangements for washing up demanding three types of dishcloth for different categories of utensil and an equal number of tea towels, all of which are to be systematically arranged and have their own special pegs.[6] Even bearing in mind the vastly dirtier and more difficult conditions of nineteenth-century cooking Beecher makes little serious attempt, as she outlines her rules and systems of kitchen practice, to weigh the possible gains from cleanliness for women against the disadvantages in terms of increased outlays of effort and concomitant exhaustion. Rather the idea of a woman's duty, deeply infused with a fervent puritanism, dominates. Nor, regarding, as she does, playing cards and dancing as 'sinful', is she much motivated anyway to find ways of releasing time for women to engage in light-hearted pursuits.[7] At one point, for example, Beecher writes, 'the only legitimate object of amusement is to prepare the mind and body for the proper discharge of duty'.

Ultimately Beecher's conceptualisation of efficiency centres on the achievement of order rather than economy of effort. Her concern with order, indeed, verges on the obsessional, swamping all other considerations. Her attitude to the kitchen clock provides an illustration of this. Having a clock in the kitchen has long been a common practice. Sometimes when there was only one clock in the house it was found in the kitchen.[8] There are possibly many good reasons for having a clock in the kitchen, but it is characteristic that Beecher recommends it because it enables the housewife to make sure that everything is done with 'regularity'.[9] Regularity and efficiency may be interconnected in a number of ways but they are not the same thing. On occasion efficiency demands the abandonment of regularity.

Beecher's concept of efficiency emerges from a pinched and blinkered puritanism, which to most modern eyes produces a parody of the concept. To make a fair assessment, however, of the extent to which Beecher's recommendations can be seen as precursors to subsequent suggestions about the improvement of kitchen management, we need to try to separate the narrow religiosity from the actual practical suggestions she makes about kitchen organisation. This act of separation helps one to move beyond Beecher's obsession with order and see the beginnings of a more conceptual interest in system. And, in so far as a concern with system is a prerequisite for analysing work processes, one then begins to see in Beecher's writing the germs of certain later ideas. For it is not a huge move from a concern with system to the idea that, with proper planning, the performance of kitchen routines could be conducted more economically in terms of the time and energy required and thereby be made less onerous for the housewife. And this opens up a radical new way of thinking about kitchen routines.

The frame of mind required for developing such thinking is different from Beecher's, however. While the impetus behind Beecher's thinking was religion, it was a belief in the power of science to improve the human condition that constituted the decisive stimulus in changing the way people thought about kitchen routines. The leading figure in setting this new style of thinking in motion was Christine Frederick.[10] And the fact that her faith in science was not necessarily less obsessional than Beecher's concern with order and was often very romantic is not a decisive argument against her ideas and certainly has not prevented them from spreading and having an impact still apparent today on contemporary kitchen design.

Mrs Frederick, like Charlotte Beecher, was an American. A one-time teacher, she turned journalist and wrote a series of articles for the *Ladies Home Journal* in 1912 entitled 'The New Housekeeping'.[11] By 1919 she had produced a book, *Household Engineering: Scientific Management in the Home*,[12] on the same theme. The publication of this book proved seminal. Her use of the magic words 'scientific management', combined with the book form, helped to lure a much wider audience than a *Ladies' Home Journal* article would have done, an audience which included architects. When presented in book form, Christine Frederick's ideas precipitated a train of professional design thinking which became an important factor in the development of the fitted kitchen as we know it today. It seems likely that another factor which contributed to Mrs Frederick's extensive influence is that, while embracing the language of modernity, and thereby attracting the attention of professional designers, her writing style was finely attuned to ordinary women with an ordinary education. This made her ideas readily accessible to large numbers of her female contemporaries.

To trace all the factors, economic, political, cultural and technical, which, in interaction with each other at this period, combined to make people review the way they approached and conceptualised various domestic routines is beyond the scope of this short historical chapter. This is not primarily a historical study: it is a piece of contemporary empirical analysis. Though set within a historical frame, only a limited amount of primary historical research could be undertaken. Thus, for example, ideas about privacy and cleanliness, which, alongside more instrumental considerations, resonated with moral strictures, will only be touched on in passing, though it seems likely that their impact on the way people use and conceive of domestic kitchens today continues to be significant. This must remain a theme for someone else to take up, however. And, as noted above, there are other problems. Historiography has largely privileged narratives which dwelt on the shaping influences of eminent individuals. There is a general paucity of data about consumer attitudes to the development of kitchen design.

Mrs Frederick's book opens very much as a *Ladies Home Journal* article might. In a chatty, informal style Mrs Frederick bemoans the difficulty of trying to do 'justice to all the household tasks, and yet find enough time for the children' and the problem of becoming 'more and more tired out' so that when her husband came home she had no interest in 'listening to his story of the day's work'.[13] She then proceeds to recount how one day her husband came home with talk about the new scientific management and how it immediately flashed upon her that here was the answer to her problems. She then describes how she threw herself into learning about the new movement and its theories and set about visiting factories employing 'scientific management' to see how this new system worked.

As she began to appreciate 'the marvellous improvement this efficiency idea had brought' to so many commonplace jobs, the more strongly she felt that it 'could save time and effort and money in my business – the home'. In the same way that it was now apparent that bricklayers commonly stooped unnecessarily over their bricks it was clear that women stooped unnecessarily over sinks. 'Couldn't we perhaps standardise dishwashing by raising the height of the sink . . .?' Women needed to work out the least demanding way of performing each household chore so as to conserve their time. 'Did we not waste time and needless walking in poorly arranged kitchens – taking twenty steps to get the egg-beater when it could have been hung over my table, just as efficiency insisted the workmen's tools must be grouped?'[14] She set about counting every step she took to complete her various domestic chores and by carefully tracing her movements and reorganising her kitchen she discovered that she could significantly reduce the number of steps and thus, she deduced, the amount of energy she had to expend on this work. 'Every day I tried to find new ways, new methods and new short cuts in my home problems.'[15]

Her enthusiasm is enormous. No chore, she insists, is 'too small or too unimportant' to be subjected to analysis. She clearly revels in the challenge of finding new ways of accomplishing her different household tasks with a minimum number of steps and movements, and thus, it is assumed,[16] of time and effort. And she provides detailed accounts of a host of experiments and calculations she has undertaken. One example will suffice to illustrate her approach, her 'careful experiments made with dishwashing over a period of two months and analysis of each of the six steps in the dishwashing process'. This set of experiments enabled her to reduce the time it takes to wash fifty dishes from '43 minutes to 23 or nearly one-half the time'.[17] Such experiments led her to believe that the adoption of her methods would prevent housewives being ground down by domestic drudgery and its dreadful accompanying tiredness, thereby freeing them to be more responsive wives and mothers.

To demonstrate that Christine Frederick's recommendations won more free time and/or a greater respite from weariness for American housewives generally would clearly be important.[18] But it is far from clear that, for herself, Mrs Frederick won any additional free time. As she herself acknowledges, the gains she predominantly derived were 'poise and determination', 'faith in myself and in my work' and status by association with what many intellectuals at the time saw as the key motors of social progress, science and industry: 'I felt I was working hand in hand with the efficiency engineers in business, and what they were accomplishing in industry, I too was accomplishing in the home.'[19]

She became an evangelist for her ideas and a prominent public figure. Thousands of women wrote to her and she had a message for those who aimed to develop and implement her thinking: 'You are going to be one of a great band of women investigators, working towards the splendid aim of putting housework on a standardised, professional basis.'[20] What Christine Frederick did was to offer women a means to self-improvement within the safe framework of conventional gender roles. It was the same message, albeit without the stridency, that Charlotte Beecher had preached. Whatever reservations one might have about this line of argument they are not a good reason for dismissing Mrs Frederick's ideas. Her ideas not only encouraged a safer use of the kitchen but also made efficiency and the notion of time-saving in kitchen work a socially acceptable goal for women. Her influence is still apparent in the layout of today's kitchens and, in terms of encouraging efforts to ease the burdensome work of domestic chores, remains benevolent. Though never part of a serious challenge to the unequal position of women generally in society, it undoubtedly helped to foster a way of thinking about kitchen work which had the potential for making women's lives freer. This meant that as occupations, particularly middle-class ones, were opened up, women's ability at a practical level to take advantage of their new opportunities was increased even though they might still have other barriers to cross.

As far as the appearance of the kitchen was concerned, however, Mrs Frederick lacked any aesthetic vision which could partner and reflect the time- and effort-saving arrangements she recommended. Aesthetically her own kitchen reflects nothing of the ideas which structure its organisation and layout. Photographs of it depict it as visually inchoate, a design hotchpotch (plate 2.1). The impetus for developing a new aesthetic for the kitchen came from elsewhere.

**Plate 2.1** Photograph of Mrs Frederick's kitchen about which Mrs Frederick wrote: 'Note unusually deep porcelain sink at left and china shelves at left of drainer and dish "scrapping" table at right.'

The pursuit and development of ideas about scientific management and kitchen organisation continued, however. In the United States, another key figure was Lillian Gilbreth, a psychologist and widow of Frank Gilbreth, a leading researcher in motion studies in industry. Lillian Gilbreth wrote in a vein similar to Mrs Frederick's. When the Brooklyn Gas Company asked her to undertake a study on the kitchen as workplace, in 1930, her report[21] describes how, by dint of rearranging the equipment in the kitchen, she discovered she could substantially reduce the number of operations required for various kitchen tasks. When she turned her attention to the kitchen appliances available to women, however, she found that almost no thought had been given to how they could best be designed to help with the efficient pursuit of domestic chores. If change were to be effected on this front the manufacturers had to take the initiative. Housewives were limited in what they could do. Once such machines came onto the market, of course, women could stimulate further production significantly by buying them. This is taken up in a later chapter.

As already indicated, however, it is to Europe, rather than the United States, that we have to look for the emergence of the idea that the design of kitchen furniture could be consciously developed so as to harmonise with the overall layout of the kitchen, and that this would not only help to smooth work processes in the kitchen further, but would also reflect the new efficiency visually. This idea emerged predominantly in Germany, Austria and Holland as part of a militant architectural avant-garde which aimed to achieve a sweeping rejection of the widespread architectural aesthetic of the nineteenth century, which had enthusiastically combined revivalism, eclecticism and new technological developments and revelled in the wealth of decorative possibilities these offered. The new architectural asceticism, under the rubric of 'functionalism', which now arose in opposition to the lavish ebullience of so much nineteenth-century architectural taste, effected a significant and lasting influence on kitchen design.

The Europeans' single most significant contribution to the development of the contemporary kitchen has been the provision of an aesthetic of efficiency which American kitchens, even when following the new organisational principles, still blatantly lacked. Specifically, European functionalism provided a concrete design style which visually complemented the 'scientific' approach to kitchen layout which was now being widely debated at a popular level in the United States.

In addition, some of the most influential sections of the European architectural avant-garde at this time also actively embraced a socialist outlook including a strong concern with social welfare. This was to be important because it led a number of avant-garde European architects to welcome the chance to design modest or working-class housing, and some became involved in housing projects as part of slum-clearance programmes. This work, which was publicly funded and thus imposed on people, gave architects the opportunity to structure the design of kitchens for a significant number of people in terms of their new architectural as well as social creed. Over time and with changing social circumstances some of the ideas they imposed were rejected or abandoned but others were accepted.

Nicholas Bullock has written a thorough and well-informed account of the interplay of ideas between proponents of architectural functionalism and debates about the role of women within the socialist movement in terms of its outcome for kitchen design in Germany in the 1920s. Programmes for the liberation of women which the women's arm of the German socialist movement put forward in the nineteenth century included releasing them from kitchen drudgery so that they could work outside the home.[22] Bullock notes, however, that the aim of making women equal to men and giving them the same right to work brought the women's socialist movement into conflict with the trade unions, which feared the appearance of a mass of cheap female workers on the labour market. The result was the emergence in the early years of the twentieth century of a revisionist ideology which shifted the emphasis away from getting women out of the home to easing the work of women within it. By the 1920s this line of thinking had gained considerable ground and in Europe, as in the United States, a vision emerges of women being freed, not for work, but to be better wives and mothers. Diverting attention from the idea of women having jobs did not, however, damp down interest in the *process* of housekeeping. It remained avant-garde to engage with this problem and it would therefore seem an a priori reason for supposing that this has contributed to making the easing of household drudgery a socially acceptable design aim.

Much of the debate about this, however, was now also a smoke-screen against other fears. Just as in Britain and the United States, where, throughout this period, hundreds of thousands of working-class women were trudging into mills and factories day after day for long hours, many working-class Austrian women had always had to work outside the home. Though in general outline this was well known, it does not appear to have penetrated architectural awareness. Ideological rather than empirical considerations seem to have predominated and driven the imagination of the planners. And as far as the trade unions were concerned the dislike of women working, Bullock suggests, was often based on the covert anxiety that women would begin to demand better pay and better jobs, thereby threatening male preserves, if they were given any positive encouragement to believe they had a right to decent jobs. It was better to encourage them to see work as something a woman was forced to undertake to make ends meet when people were poor. So what the unions said and what they thought did not always match. The result was all too frequently a tacit male ganging up against women.[23]

Alongside this, however, the clearly desperate social need combined with a political desire to effect slum clearance with minimum financial outlay had generated a close interest in standardisation within German industry.[24] So, as ideas about so-called scientific management began to be explored in the United States, the Germans responded with an immediate and lively curiosity. Ford, Taylor and Gilbreth were quickly translated and eagerly read. Such an atmosphere also aroused interest in Christine Frederick's work, and it, too, was soon translated and equally rapidly read and absorbed both into socialist thinking about women and avant-garde architectural thinking. As a combination of the ideas of household engineering with an interest in the production of standardised building units constitutes the basis of the fitted kitchen, these developments were seminal. They made the idea of the fitted kitchen, and with that a new kitchen aesthetic, possible.

Another widely attributed influence on the way new kitchens were now being planned has been the disappearance of servants. Though Charlotte Beecher had believed that it was a moral virtue for women to participate practically in the daily running of their homes her writing still assumes the ready availability of servants. True, they display, by Miss Beecher's standards, dreadful inadequacies and require the most stringent training, but they nevertheless remain a taken-for-granted background presence in her book. By the time Mrs Frederick is writing, however, the perceived 'problem' of the servantless household had started to engage the middle-class public.

On the one hand, it seems clear that as alternative and often more lucrative work than domestic service became available to working-class women they moved out of an occupation which was poorly paid and frequently demeaning. At the same time, Adrian Forty offers a convincing rebuttal of the idea that domestic machines were invented in response to the decline of the servant class. Forty comments that 'The myth that the work once done by servants has been taken over by gadgets and machines has been repeated so often it has acquired the authenticity of historical truth.' And he argues that 'This idea has had a compulsive attraction both to housewives and to manufacturers of domestic appliances.' What he should perhaps have also added is that academia has also fallen heavily for the idea.[25] In challenging these beliefs Forty calculates the decline in the number of servants on the basis of an examination of the Census Reports for Great Britain, 1891 to 1931. Census data, he argues, offers evidence that though the First World War saw women moving out of domestic service they returned afterwards so that by 1921 there were almost as many domestic servants as there had been prior to the war. The disappearance of domestic servants during the course of the twentieth century was a gradual process which took place over half a century, from 1890 to 1940. More has been attributed to the decline in domestic service than is justified. A very significant decline did, of course, ultimately take place and in doing so gave an additional boost to ideologies of household efficiency in which economy of effort was the prime concern. The fact that the chapter entitled 'The Servantless Household' in *Household Engineering* does not appear until chapter 9 in Mrs Frederick's book coupled with Forty's calculations, however, suggests that it was not a prime concern of Christine Frederick. Indeed, she gives the impression of being driven by ideas much grander than ones generated by simple pragmatism.

One element, indeed, in Mrs Frederick's thinking, which was probably more important for the future of kitchen design than the decline of the availability of servants, was that Mrs Frederick as a middle-class woman was accustomed to homes where different household activities were clearly demarcated spatially. Furthermore, the clear differentiation of domestic space was intimately bound up for the American middle classes with concepts of propriety and decency.[26] There is no indication that Mrs Frederick questioned the assumption that the kitchen was only a room for cooking. As a result the idea that the kitchen should be used for cooking only became, for many European intellectuals, part of the concept of modernity and the scientific approach to household management generally.

In Germany the concept of a scientific form of household management received a further boost in popularity with the publication of Erna Meyer's *Der neue Haushalt* in 1926.[27] Bullock points out that Meyer's arguments were not original. But her message was undoubtedly in harmony with prevailing thinking on social reform at the time and she clearly offered people what they were ready to hear for the book became a huge popular success, rapidly achieving enormous sales. Giedion suggests that the idea, already noted in Mrs Frederick's book and now widely touted in the United States, that housekeeping was a profession is one key to Meyer's success, and this idea provides a useful complement to the account Bullock gives of the socialist revisionist writing on women's social position current in Germany at the time. Whatever the reasons, Meyer's book made a strong impression on a significant public. And in popularising the idea of the *Kochkuche* or cooking kitchen Meyer played a significant role in innovative thinking about kitchen design for a period.

Meyer's popular success, for example, helped to counter another strong tradition about the nature of the kitchen. The German working class had long used their kitchens for living as well as for food preparation. Indeed, where heating was expensive and people were poor, families often slept in the kitchen, a practice which sent shudders down the spines of middle-class European reformers, for whom, as for middle-class Americans, the custom of functionally separated household space was deeply tied up with concepts of decency.

Other developments also came to the support of the new reformers and designers. Once gas for cooking appeared, people no longer had to rely on a single source of heat for hot water, cooking and general warmth. A clearer spatial separation of domestic activity, as well as satisfying middle-class fastidiousness, became more practical. And, though there were those who remained reluctant to see the disappearance of the kitchen as the centre of family life, its strong connection with rural practice was, in itself, sufficient to worry many Continental socialists, for whom, under the spell of Marxist thinking, 'rural' read 'backward'.

Where new building was planned there also appeared to be financial economies in building small, galley kitchens. Not only did such kitchens appear to save on movement and so were seen as being in tune with the ideas of scientific management, but it was impossible to use them for sleeping. A variety of factors thus conspired to make the favoured form of kitchen among reformers and public-minded architects the small kitchen used only for cooking. Such a format was, in addition, general enough to allow for a variety of layouts. Variants were also possible such as the English kitchen–diner, which appeared in the new houses built in the immediate post-Second World War years.

There is little evidence that working-class opinion was seriously solicited about any of this.[28] But several notable kitchen plans produced in Europe constitute concrete expression of the growth of this strain of thinking. The Georg Muche and Adolf Meyer kitchen in the Haus am Horn, built for the first Bauhaus exhibition in 1923 as part of a display of design suitable for mass production, and the J.J.P. Ouds kitchen for the Weissenhof Settlement, Stuttgart, in 1927 are two examples. By later standards they look to many eyes grim, harsh places (plates 2.2 and 2.3) with an aesthetic more appropriate to an institutional than a domestic setting. At the same time, their visual impact is strikingly different from that of Mrs Frederick's kitchen. These kitchens are not simply carefully

**Plate 2.2** Kitchen of Haus am Horn, Bauhaus, 1923. Though raw in appearance to today's eyes, this illustrates the introduction of continuous working surfaces in the kitchen as an integral part of the design of the house.

organised, they announce visually that they are carefully organised. Their continuous working surfaces and their built-in or, at least, unified cupboard arrangements are a visual commitment to orderliness and efficiency: they give concrete expression to the idea of scientific management.

By 1928 an amalgamation of government agencies in Germany, known as the Rfg,[29] had been set up to look into all aspects of housing production and design and they produced six design alternatives for small cooking kitchens. If judged by the extent of its implementation, the most important of all the cooking-kitchen designs of this period, however, was the 'Frankfurt kitchen'. Its designer, Margarete Schutte-Lihotsky, was a determined young woman who, in the face of vigorous attempts to dissuade her, persisted first in training as an architect and subsequently in practising as one.[30]

Born in Vienna, at a time when the city boasted a strong socialist movement and extensive urban poverty, Grete Schutte-Lihotsky was

**Plate 2.3** J.J.P. Oud, kitchen in Weissenhof experimental settlement, Stuttgart, 1927, again showing the introduction of continuous work surfaces in the kitchen. It too, seventy-five years on, now seems brutal and unattractive in design.

already conscious of and concerned about the squalor the city harboured by the time she embarked on her architectural training, also in Vienna, and was brought into close contact with the latest architectural avant-garde. In 1919, the year she qualified, she visited the Netherlands where she saw Oud's work. By 1921 she was employed as an architect on a housing estate managed by Adolf Loos and in 1926 she moved to Frankfurt. Here she found expression for both her social and professional concerns in working with Ernst May on a number of major housing projects. It was at this point that she designed her celebrated kitchen.

The design of what became known as the Frankfurt kitchen clearly reflected the debate on scientific management and household engineering. Grete Lihotsky had not only read Christine Frederick, she was a disciple. Despite the fact that she saw the living kitchen as encouraging communality and she liked that, she bowed to the intellectual theories of the day and arguments about the economics of mass housing projects and opted in her design for a purely cooking kitchen. A time and motion study was conducted to determine its optimum size. The answer arrived at was 1.9 m × 3.44 m, though subsequently some people regarded this as unsatisfactory as it only allowed one person to be in the kitchen at once. But dimensions could be changed even if the square footage was fixed and eventually Schutte-Lihotsky developed a variety of kitchen plans in a number of different shapes to fit in with different flat layouts, though the galley shape has continued to be regarded as the classic one.

Lihotsky's galley kitchen had a generous window and a wide sliding door gave access to the living-room. Fittings were designed carefully and Lihotsky paid close attention to the height of the cupboards to ensure they could be reached, planned a suspended lamp which could be moved along a runner on the ceiling so as to get light to every part of the room, and a height-adjustable stool to make it easier for people to sit while working. There was also a ventilator hood above the cooker and a fold-down ironing-board. Concerned to make the room look attractive Lihotsky also planned a colour scheme for her kitchen: ultramarine-blue cupboards and drawers, grey-ochre splash tiles, a black floor, worktops and cooker and metal fittings in white and aluminium (plate 2.4). Although black and

**Plate 2.4** Grete Schutte-Lihotsky's 'Frankfurt' kitchen. Compared with plates 2.2 and 2.3 this kitchen displays a markedly greater elegance. A comparison between this and Christine Frederick's kitchen is instructive.

white photographs might be regarded as an inadequate basis for making aesthetic judgements they nevertheless suggest that the Frankfurt kitchen had an elegance and design cohesion not discernible in photographs of the Haus am Horn or Ouds kitchens. Between 1926 and 1930 different versions of Grete Lihotsky's kitchen were installed in ten thousand housing-project flats. There is no record, however, of anyone asking the occupants of the new housing how they felt about their kitchens or whether they thought some variants of the use of space were preferable to others. The large number of these kitchens built encourages the idea that they were a significant architectural development historically. And doubtless people were generally delighted to move out of the slums of Vienna into more wholesome housing. But both the new flats and their kitchens represented design handed down; they did not reflect user opinion.

In 1989 when she was ninety-two Grete Lihotsky provided an interesting postscript on the Frankfurt kitchen when she commented that she had planned the kitchen for women who worked, rather than with cooking in mind, adding that she had never concerned herself with cooking in her life.[31] The defiance she had shown as a young architectural student is still engagingly there in the old lady. But it also reflects a form of middle-class thinking and it cannot compensate for the fact that a major problem with the new cooking kitchens was that they were simply beyond the means of the people for whom they were designed. Bullock calculates that it would have taken an average working-class family of the 1920s at least five years to buy the basic equipment such kitchens assumed for their effective functioning. Inherent in the very concept of the Schutte-Lihotsky kitchen is a casual thoughtlessness and design self-indulgence. That is, of course, a judgement made from within the framework of modern thinking. At the time, Grete Schutte-Lihotsky's attitudes reflected caring concern.

Both Lihotsky's and the new cooking kitchens generally were, however, ultimately Utopian conceptions and did not resolve the contemporary social problems they set out to address. Nevertheless, they laid down a way of thinking about kitchen design, by reference to kitchen work, which was so powerful that there was no return for subsequent professional designers. Whatever the limitations of this movement, all subsequent professional kitchen design is predicated on a belief in its enduring contribution to the conceptualisation and organisation of modern domestic kitchens. And with the growing affluence of the last fifty years the domestic kitchens of English people on average incomes have increasingly utilised the ideas of these early pioneers, whatever new design preoccupations they have also displayed.

New ideas about kitchen design were initially realised on any significant scale in public housing, where they were imposed on people. The financial constraints which characterise all public housing also ensured that the ideas of the early prototypes were significantly modified in their implementation. The introduction of changes in the layout and design of domestic kitchens for the middle classes, whether German, American or English, was slower. For at this social level designers could not impose their ideas; the public had to be convinced of the virtues of the fitted kitchen. However convinced themselves of the value and desirability of their new ideas, designers had to win this public over if they were to see their ideas realised on any scale. This took time. Equally important, the new kitchens were expensive. The public not only had to be convinced of their desirability, they had to be prepared to pay out the considerable amount of money needed to acquire them. One result of this was that the move from an old-style kitchen among the middle classes to what became known as a fitted kitchen often passed through what might be termed the Era of the Commodious Cupboard.

In *Mechanisation Takes Command* Giedion has an illustration of a single large, multi-doored and drawered, free-standing cupboard from the American *Kitchen Maid* catalogue of 1923 (plate 2.5). Its various

**Plate 2.5** An example of the Commodious Cupboard from the catalogue of *Kitchen Maid*, 1923.

**Plate 2.6** Another Commodious Cupboard, the white lacquered '*Ideal* model kitchen' manufactured by Poggenpohl in 1923. *Courtesy, Poggenpohl Ltd.*

compartments are organised to allow for the storage of brushes and brooms, pots and pans, crockery and cutlery and bagged and bottled foodstuffs.[32] In Germany in the same year Poggenpohl introduce their '*Ideal* model kitchen'.[33] This is not what we would call a kitchen but a free-standing cupboard with a white lacquered finish combining a variety of compartments for use in the same way as the American *Kitchen Maid* cabinet (plate 2.6). And in 1925 in England George Nunn and Len Cooklin set up Hygena Cabinets Ltd in Liverpool also to produce individually crafted, free-standing kitchen cupboards suitably divided to accommodate an array of food and a variety of household tools and utensils. Over the next fifteen years these cupboards were continually elaborated, even to the incorporation of pull-down worktops and fold-down ironing-boards. But they did not lose their free-standing, independent format. In 1938 Hygena went into liquidation but was shortly re-established under Arthur Webb, who once again made the all-purpose kitchen cabinet the mainstay of the business.

The thinking about kitchen organisation which these commercial cupboards reflect lacked the breadth of vision of the architect-designed kitchens. Following the 1920s experiments in kitchen design, architectural ideas were developed on modularisation, standardisation and co-ordination, which embraced appliances as well as furniture and conceived of the kitchen space as a single co-ordinated design unit, and architect-designed kitchens started to display increasing visual sophistication. Meanwhile, at the popular level, many of the houses and flats on the new council estates which began to spring up in the twenties and thirties, while planned with cooking kitchens in terms of the allocation of space, continued to remain innocent of most of the equipment the European prototype cooking kitchens boasted. War, however, was now about to break out and this put an end to design developments and new building for some years in both Germany and England.

In Europe the first years following the conclusion of the war were spent recovering from it. Young designers and architects with the energy of youth, however, were soon railing against conservatism and producing idealised drawings of the kinds of kitchens we could have if we were less stuffy and, though they were not always frank about this, much richer. Poggenpohl and Hygena meanwhile continued to manufacture commodious cupboards. But by the mid-1950s Germany was on the way to recovery and in Britain full employment and the establishment of the welfare state were producing a new sense of national well-being.

The United States had not been affected by the war to the same degree as Europe and they also recovered materially from the war very much more quickly than Europe. Even during the war the Americans were pushing ahead with the design of kitchen furniture and in 1943 the Libbey-Owens-Ford Company commissioned H. Creston Dohner to design a model kitchen for them. Dohner gave his kitchen an uncompromising modern appearance. Entitled the *Day After Tomorrow's Kitchen*, it combined being an advertisement for an electric cooking-range, an architectural experiment in the reorganisation of interior domestic space, an exercise in streamlining and a fantasy. Displayed in department stores throughout the United States it was estimated that over one and a half million people saw it. The widespread post-war longing for a brave new world to follow five years of destruction helped to encourage a new interest in and sympathy for forward-looking design and thinking, while the unprecedented wealth many Americans now began to enjoy gave more people than ever before the wherewithal for translating this desire into material form. Everywhere the Dohner kitchen was set up it aroused enormous interest. Forward-looking kitchen design had begun to attract significant popular support.

The manufacturers' marketing strategies for the new fitted kitchens went straight back to Charlotte Beecher and Christine Frederick.[34] Their sparkly clean appearance, the ease with which this cleanliness could be maintained and their many convenient and labour-saving arrangements were all much paraded. Advertisements showed prettily pinafored ladies in high-heeled shoes painlessly accomplishing their kitchen tasks under conditions which relegated the worn-out housewife-drudge to history. Not infrequently, women were shown doing things for or with their children in the kitchen or being hostesses. Once again the suggestion was that a modern fitted kitchen with all mod-cons would enable women to be better mothers and wives. There was never any suggestion that such kitchens might lift the burden of domestic work to the extent that women could contemplate seeking fulfilling employment, including a monetary return, outside the home.

But, whatever the level of American women's content or discontent about their social position generally, it was certainly the case that by the mid-1940s many American women were thoroughly attuned to the ideas about the desirability of kitchen efficiency on which the fitted kitchen was premised and, where finances allowed, there was a widespread interest in owning such a kitchen. A good decade before they began to appear in significant numbers in Britain fitted kitchens had become a well-established feature of American homes.

By the 1960s, however, an economic boom was under way in Britain. Living standards, including housing standards, began to improve rapidly and in unprecedented ways. Domestic facilities which had appeared to be the prerogative of a minority of the better off now came within the reach of a much larger spectrum of society. There were the usual conservatives who decried any kind of change, but, with more money at their disposal, the bulk of the population, and certainly the young, eagerly embraced technologies which promised easier and more efficient housekeeping. The sale of refrigerators rose rapidly, and food stopped going bad in summer and generally stayed fresh longer. The sale of domestic washing-machines also rose, to the extent that commercial laundries started to go out of business. And increasingly people replaced their open fires with central heating systems. At long last English houses began to be warm in winter.

No room in the English home was more affected by the new affluence than the kitchen. As in the United States the post-war mood was for putting the past behind and embarking on a new start. This mood underlay the widespread popular excitement the Festival of Britain generated in 1951, with its strong emphasis on the future and the futuristic. Popular taste from clothing to interior design in the late 1950s and 1960s favoured the new and modern. The forms of some of the latest scientific discoveries pro-vided an artistic stimulus and the kinds of colours favoured, raw, acid, primary, spoke more of chemistry than nature. With regard to kitchens young designers and architects again took up pre-war avant-garde concerns and styles, and eagerly began to develop them.

The new designers not only needed public support, they also needed manufacturing and retail support. Commerce continued to be cautious. The vague phrase commonly used to justify this was 'the time is not ripe', though the idea now being touted had been around since the 1920s. The manufacturers, of course, usually had considerably more to lose than the eager young designers. An unsuccessful product could bring a business to the edge of ruin or even topple it into liquidation. Business understandably was reluctant to fill the market with goods the public would not buy.

In the early 1950s in Germany, however, Poggenpohl, under the leadership of Walter Ludewig, began to think there might be a market for an alternative kind of kitchen furniture. They began to produce standard-ised kitchen units in series as their response to their sense of a burgeoning interest in the new and the modern. This new kitchen furniture consisted of base units covered with a continuous worktop and matching wall units, though there was as yet no fitted cooker. In addition, these units were designed with what would later be termed ergonomic considerations in mind. By the 1960s Poggenpohl had replaced conventional door handles on their kitchen units with strip handles integrated into the cupboard fronts, which were now rendered in glossy laminate finishes, giving them a smooth, sleek, modern look. Soon they were also producing cupboard fronts in five different colours, which could all be combined with silver or black strip handles in a choice of seven finishes. At the end of the decade Poggenpohl introduced a wooden kitchen and the choice of finishes, colours and unit combinations began to acquire that air of endlessness which is so strong a feature of kitchen furniture today.

Like the Germans, English manufacturers were also cautious, con-cerned that they could find themselves facing commercial ruin. A leading figure in introducing new ideas about kitchen design in this country was George Féjer, an emigré Hungarian who had trained as an architect in Zurich. Féjer has left us various pieces of illuminating information about his relationship with commerce and the public as an avant-garde designer.

George Féjer arrived in England in 1939 just as manufacturing and product development were being turned to the needs of war and design considerations were being forced into a secondary role. Féjer's first project, therefore, was developing a glass substitute as part of the government's attempt to contain air-raid damage. At the same time, however, he began to write a series of articles outlining the wonderful possibilities for design once the war was over. And when, in 1943, the Selection Engineering Company appointed him as a development consultant Féjer designed a range of kitchen furniture replete with co-ordinated kitchen appliances. Looking back at this period Féjer recalled how:

> In the darkest days of World War Two working for post war homes was a hypnotic dream. I got involved in kitchen design because here was an area where all the arts and techniques of living, design and manufacture seemed to meet, and where unsolved problems were a [*sic*] legion, and where so many new products were evidently waiting to be born . . . Who could resist such a challenge? . . . I could not believe my luck![35]

At the same time the real world continued to exert a sobering influence on a young man's design enthusiasms. As Féjer wryly comments:

> There was just one snag. In those days there was no way of making my kind of furniture because we just could not get the timber licence needed for this sort of standardised flow production.[36]

So Féjer's ideas became, as he put it, 'an underground movement for another ten years'.

By the mid-1950s, however, Féjer had met Arthur Webb of Hygena and his colleague, George Nunn. Looking back at this period, as an older and less impatient man, Féjer reflected on how he learnt from Arthur Webb:

> a lesson I never forgot since, i.e. never to attempt to design a client out of his business. In 1953 there was no way to try to make or sell split level cookers and metric 'system furniture', but we could improve kitchen cabinets, made and sold by the thousands to cheer up the horrible kitchens, tenants and houseowners alike, had in those days.

Féjer's words provide clear evidence of the way manufacturers and their young designers had to try to communicate their own enthusiasm to the public as part of asking them to make an unprecedentedly large outlay on the purchase of new kitchen furniture. Getting people to do this involved a process of slow incremental steps, as Féjer describes.

> By the mid-fifties quite a lot of old sinks were replaced so we designed those a shade better, and our sinks had 'bases' and we designed other 'base' units to go with them . . . So gradually we meandered back to the 1946 concept of the 'built out', unit system kitchen.[37]

Slowly, then, Hygena moved into the fitted-kitchen market. It first produced an *F Range* which exploited some of Féjer's 1940s ideas and manufactured pieces which people could 'build' into their kitchens but, significantly, without scrapping the kitchen furniture they already had. The commercial success of the *F Range* encouraged Webb to the degree that he felt able to allow Féjer to develop a fully co-ordinated modularised range of kitchen units. Years later Féjer acknowledged the positive part Webb's sharp business acumen played in realising the success of his own forward-looking design:

> I was very young and very foolish . . . and flew in the face of providence by trying to introduce a completely new concept to be absorbed by a market which was not there. That is of course a failing of many designers, that although they can see new trends they don't know how best to make money. This is indeed a completely different kind of sixth sense and is where the designer needs the Arthur Webbs of this world with a flair for success in knowing when to go slow and when to accelerate . . .[38]

As Féjer's designs continued to sell, Arthur Webb began to feel the market was ready for the introduction of fully fitted kitchens, and started to make the considerable financial investment in the machinery and tools the production of new designs like Féjer's required. By the early 1960s Féjer was designing floor-to-ceiling, wall-to-wall, modularised, inter-changeable units. There were also housings for lighting systems and for appliances like cookers, and refrigerators were 'built-in'. More and more design refinements appeared – a swivel corner cupboard, a pull-out exten-sion surface. Féjer also attempted to foresee every potential problem and design it away. Among the many design niceties he came up with were plastic injection-moulded door handles which concealed a 180 degree opening hinge and simultaneously sealed the upper door edge, always susceptible to water absorption, which could be hugely damaging. By the 1970s Hygena had established itself as a leader in England of modern kitchen design using smooth, clean lines. It was Hygena's design team which devised the first kitchen furniture 'flat pack'.

Following Arthur Webb's retirement, however, marketing became more cautious and other changes in production policy led the company to lose its market edge. German imported kitchens increasingly began to attract buyers with a taste for the modern and in 1982 Hygena had to cease trading. MFI, one of the new trading sheds, subsequently bought the brand name.

The other major kitchen furniture brand name at this time was Wrighton. The firm was established in 1882 but only moved into the production of kitchen furniture in 1952. In 1958 Nigel Walters produced his *Californian* kitchen range for the company. Its design seemed very modern to con-temporary purchasers with its clean lines, high-gloss finish in bold, strong colours, formica worktops in contrasting shades and aluminium handles attached to the tops of the cupboard doors. In time, however, Wrighton also began to feel the impact of German competition.

And it was not only that the Germans were producing competitive modern design styles. Equally, if not more, importantly, their production and distribution methods were ahead of British ones. So they were able to penetrate the British market while the British made little inroad into the German one. The Wrighton brand name was eventually bought, like Hygena, by another of the sheds, Texas, itself subsequently bought out by Sainsbury Homebase. By this stage, however, the business difficulties British kitchen furniture manufacturers were facing were not to do with winning people over to the idea of the fully fitted kitchen.

Alongside these developments work on the efficient use of kitchen space continued. In 1960 Joan Walley, Head of the Household Science Department at Queen Elizabeth College, University of London, produced *The Kitchen*.[39] The book runs once again through the, by now, tired ideas about time and motion work, the most efficient arrangement of kitchen furniture and the issue of the optimum heights for different items of kitchen equipment. The discussion is almost entirely derivative and nearly all the references are to American work.

The COSMITH kitchen plan, the product of collaboration between the Council of Scientific Management in the Home and the Building Research Station and exhibited in the Ideal Home Exhibition in 1955, is one of the few English contributions to thinking about kitchen planning described in the book. Curiously, however, although this model kitchen includes a refrigerator located beneath a worktop, the plan still incorporates a sizeable walk-in larder.[40] Academic staleness in England was now running in parallel with our loss of innovative edge in kitchen design and marketing.

From the point of view of the English consumer, of course, this was of little interest or concern. There is no reason, after all, why the public should be expected to know or be concerned about the fact that English thinking had lost its innovative edge in terms of exploring questions about the spatial planning of kitchens or the ergonomics of kitchen furniture. Similarly, few English purchasers of fitted kitchens were aware or worried much, at the point of purchase, that certain English companies producing designs whose emphasis on clean straight lines made people see them as modern were going out of business because they had failed to keep abreast of the Germans in their production and distribution methods. What mattered to purchasers was what they liked, what was available in the shops and, within these givens, what they could afford. For this is what would determine the purchasers' prime and immediate concern, namely, the appearance and arrangement of their own kitchens.

On this front it was clear that by the 1970s English consumers had become highly receptive to certain aspects of the new designer-planned kitchens. Thus, as people's disposable incomes grew, the fitted kitchen became increasingly common in the English home. The public was now widely convinced of the benefits of furnishing their kitchens with standardised, modularised units and had begun to spend considerable sums to acquire them. Today's public is fully attuned to purchasing kitchen units built to standardised measurements and to kitchen machinery for cooling, freezing and washing, similarly constructed along standardised lines. Indeed, the public not only accept this form of standardisation, they demand it. Sales also suggest they welcome the increasingly refined modularisation systems which now characterise the construction of kitchen furniture and machinery and facilitate ever tighter, more space-efficient forms of kitchen layout.

The history of the development of the fitted kitchen is one of considerable triumph for the professional designer. Professional designers wanting to justify their existence could surely point to the public's wholesale adoption of the principles of the fitted kitchen. It might have taken decades but it was a huge achievement. Unlike public or corporate building, which does not require public approval for its construction, the spread of the fitted domestic kitchen could only happen because the general buying public were won over. There are few examples of international architectural modernism being embraced by the public in the way the concept of the fitted kitchen has been. Subsequent chapters, furthermore, will present evidence of continuing public enthusiasm for the basic design principles which underlie such kitchens. Designers can surely congratulate themselves on the impact the trained design imagination and vision has had in helping to ease kitchen routines and give coherence to the appearance of domestic kitchens.

But, though the public accepted the general architectural principle on which the fitted kitchen was based, a major claim of this study is that they have been conspicuously less willing to accept the styles which designers and architects have tended to favour for 'clothing' the new modularised kitchen units. Many have markedly failed to share architect and designer enthusiasm for styles informed by an aesthetic based on a visual celebration of the structure of the new technology. Instead they have tended to favour design styles bearing very different messages. Just what these messages are and how people, left to their own devices, have actively sought to convey these messages through the visual management of their environment are the subject of a later chapter, however. In preparation for a discussion of this the immediate next step for this study is to look at patterns in the acquisition of kitchen furniture and machinery today across the country as a whole.

## Notes

1.  See, for example, Burnett, J. (1979) *Plenty and Want: A Social History of Diet in England from 1815 to the Present Day*, Scholar; and Woodforde, J. (1969) *The Truth about Cottages*, Routledge and Kegan Paul. Woodforde has a telling passage from J.L. Green, a sanitary inspector who produced a book in 1900 entitled *English Country Cottages*. Green recommended that a kitchen should have a grate which did not fall apart in a couple of years and

    > an arrangement on which the plates, cups, etc., may be washed. This arrangement may be of metal, stone or brick cemented over . . . It should be connected from one corner with, if possible, a drainage system; as, otherwise, if the waste water after washing-up is run off into a pan . . . instead of being emptied with regularity, will certainly stand at times to ferment and become a nuisance (Woodford, 1969, p.58).

    Green also recommended that fireplaces were constructed so that people did not have to keep the house door permanently open to get rid of the smoke and that every room had a window that would open. He also noted that many cottage kitchen-cum-living-rooms were too small for the family to sit and eat together and many had no arrangements for washing clothes. Woodforde also has descriptions of actual cottage living at the turn of the century which make horrifying reading.
2.  See, however, Adrian Forty (1989) on the complex relation between design forms and ideas, p. 242.
3.  Beecher, Catherine E. and Stowe, Harriet Beecher (1869) *The American Woman's Home, on Principles of Domestic Science, Being a Guide to the Formation and Maintenance of Economical, Healthful, Beautiful and Christian Homes*, University Microfilms Inc., Ann Arbor, Michigan. This publication followed an earlier one in 1841, written by Charlotte Beecher alone and entitled *Treatise on Domestic Economy*. Although *The American Woman's Home* of 1869 was, formally, co-authored, the text here follows the precedent set by Giedion, S. in *Mechanisation Takes Command* (1948), Oxford University Press, pp. 514–18, and attributes the text of the 1869 publication just to Charlotte Beecher.

4. Such a position is, I think, rather like seeing Harriet Beecher Stowe's publication of *Uncle Tom's Cabin* as the beginning of the civil rights movement.
5. Beecher and Stowe (1869), p. 34.
6. Ibid., pp. 372–3.
7. Beecher theoretically believes that people should take some relaxation and indulge in laughter and claims to be opposed to asceticism. But she imposes enormous strictures on what one is allowed to derive pleasure from. The idea that playing ring-a-ring-a-roses with one's children is a wonderful mode of adult enjoyment would fail to convince many highly conventional people today.
8. Harrison, Molly (1972) *The Kitchen in History*, Osprey.
9. Beecher and Stowe (1869), p. 371.
10. Though she was not the only proponent of a 'scientific' approach to kitchen management, she became the best known, see Forty (1989), p. 216.
11. Frederick, Christine (1912) 'The New Housekeeping', *Ladies Home Journal,* vol. 26.
12. Frederick, Christine (1919) *Household Engineering: Scientific Management in the Home,* American School of Home Economics.
13. Ibid., p. 7.
14. Ibid., p. 12 and p. 14.
15. Ibid., p. 15.
16. This assumption should be treated with caution. The efficient execution of a chore probably depends on the interaction of a number of factors. One can, for example, readily imagine that under certain circumstances the worker could become totally bored and that this would lead to inefficiency. Certain inefficiencies in theoretical terms might, therefore, in practical terms, actually enhance efficiency.
17. Frederick (1919), p. 79.
18. Christine Hardyment goes further than this. She sees the movement as a craze which simply wasted the housewife's time 'on the elusive task of self-organisation', pp. 38–9. While suspecting that Christine Frederick's claim that her approach significantly eased the housewife's lot were probably exaggerated, I would nevertheless hesitate myself to be quite so sweeping. And certainly, in terms of the development of modern kitchen layouts, I think there is strong evidence to suggest that Christine Frederick's impact was a lasting one.
19. Frederick (1919), p. 15.
20. Ibid., p. 17.
21. Gilbreth, L. (1930) 'Efficiency Methods Applied to Kitchen Design', *Architectural Record*, March, pp. 291–2.

22. It has always to be remembered, of course, that huge numbers of working-class women worked anyway outside the home and always had done. The fight for the right to work was essentially a middle-class women's fight to enter professional jobs.

23. The story of the way women have historically been pulled into the labour market during periods of labour shortage and then pushed out again when jobs were needed for men is a long one. One cannot go into it at length here. And the tactics working-class men have used in conniving with this is a story in itself. The important point is that European interest in kitchen design proceeded without any serious analysis of the social relations between men and women in industrial society but on the basis of middle-class complacency and self-serving union arguments. This is not to say that the result, on a whole range of criteria, was not ultimately better kitchens than in the past.

24. Bullock (1988), p. 179.

25. Forty (1989), p. 209 and p. 213. See also Davidson, Caroline (1982) *A Woman's Work is Never Done*, Chatto and Windus, p. 174.

26. Bullock (1988), p. 181.

27. Meyer, Erna (1926) *Der neue Haushalt, ein Wegweiser zur wissenschaftlichen Hausfuehrung,* Franklische Verlagshandlung.

28. It is often noted that Grete Schutte Lihotsky visited the slums of Vienna as a student to find out what kind of living accommodation people there wanted. However sensitive and imaginative this was, it does not appear to have constituted more than one or two visits and certainly does not seem to have been a careful, systematic enquiry, and I have yet to come across evidence of more extended and serious enquiries by any other avant-garde architects. Generally speaking, the reformers appear to have thought they knew what was good for the working classes. One should not, of course, dismiss the idea that they might, in part, arguably have been right. On the other hand, a serious attempt to elicit popular preference in this area would surely have raised some important issues.

29. Its full title was the Reichsforschungsgesellschaft für Wirtschaftlichkeit im Bau- und Wohnungswesen e. V.

30. See Oedekoven-Gerisher and Frank, P. (1989) *Frauen im Design*, Haus der Wirtschaft, Exhibition catalogue, Design Centre, Stuttgart, vols 1 & 2, for details of her career.

31. Ibid., p. 168.

32. Giedion, S. (1970) *Mechanisation Takes Command*, Oxford University Press, p. 520.

33. Poggenpohl Möbelwerke GmbH & Co. (1992) *100 Years of Poggenpohl: Tradition Orientated Towards the Future*, Poggenpohl, p. 9.

This is a celebratory catalogue produced by the company to mark its first hundred years of trading.

34. With American soldiers returning to civilian life anxious to find jobs after the unemployment of the 1930s the Beecher–Frederick view of women's role hit just the right note. It projected an apparent respect for women without challenging the conventional view of gender roles.

35. Féjer, George (1984) *Design Process: Inside Story of Familiar Products*, pp. 71–2, Exhibition catalogue, Manchester Polytechnic.

36. Ibid.

37. In acknowledging the power of the market to make or break imaginative design ventures Féjer is also concerned not to kill initiative. In his just slightly foreign English he writes:

> To young designers of today I would say don't stop the flow of ideas in designing against the tide of convention and general stick-in-the-muddery, you can easily do so as part of the University or Polytechnic study projects – before knuckling down to realities of short term tasks. (Ibid., p. 75)

38. Ibid., p. 78.

39. Walley, Joan E. (1960) *The Kitchen*, Constable.

40. Ibid., p. 193.

–3–

# From the general to the particular and how it was done

The sale of kitchen furniture is big business, and seems set to remain so. In the early 1990s the turnover in kitchen furniture sales was running from somewhat under to somewhat over the billion pound mark annually. By 2000 annual spending on kitchen furniture had risen to over one and half billion pounds.[1] This sum does not include the sale of kitchen appliances such as cookers, microwaves, washing-machines or tumble-driers, or the cost of new floor coverings or wall tiles widely used in kitchens. Nor are the costs of installation included in any systematic way. If one started with the customer rather than the retailer and calculated the cost of a new kitchen to the buyer, the annual turnover in spend on kitchens would be significantly higher than market research figures currently suggest.

Market research is not concerned with such calculations, however. Its purpose is simple, to help manufacturers and retailers make sales. The concerns of this project are different. Nevertheless, work in the sociology of culture can usefully draw on the work of the major market research firms. For if businesses selling kitchen furniture are to be successful they have to be able to offer people the kinds of things they want to buy. The Spring 2000 National Shoppers Survey makes this point:

> Your answers to the *New* survey are important. You've heard that old saying: 'The customer is always right.' Well, it's true. If shoppers don't like a product, the manufacturers lose money. And the manufacturers get it wrong more than you think. Eight out of ten new products actually fail in the shops . . . they survive for a few months and then disappear forever.
>
> So it's important for big firms to know what customers like yourself actually prefer. Your answers in the *New* Summer National Shoppers Survey will influence these famous companies in providing products and services that customers really want.
>
> Just by ticking the boxes in the Survey, you'll help to make shopping more enjoyable for yourself and others.[2]

Whatever the limitations of market research it remains a valuable source of information about the purchasing of new kitchens today and a brief review of the market research over the last few years into the sale of kitchen furniture provides helpful background information about people's interests and concerns as they embark on the process of designing new kitchens for themselves.

The sale of kitchen furniture fluctuates with the ebb and flow of economic growth and recession. When people feel economically insecure, are worried about their jobs or anxious about negative equity, they spend more cautiously. Nor, during a recession, do people buy new houses readily, and market research shows that the purchase of a new house correlates positively with buying a new kitchen. But, whether the house market is booming or sluggish, market research done over the last decade strongly suggests that the kitchen furniture market will continue to enjoy expansion.

In 1996 Mintel's on-going survey of market trends encouraged them to report a 'pent-up demand' for refurbished kitchens and in 2000 Keynote was still finding that the replacement market for kitchens was strong.[3] In 1990 Keynote also suggested another way of looking at the desire for new kitchen furniture. They estimated that the number of people employed in the manufacture, selling and installation of new kitchens stood at between thirty and fifty thousand. It is hardly a precise figure but even the bottom estimate is not negligible. And, to put it in some kind of context, by the end of the 1990s the number of coalminers in the country had, in contrast, fallen to ten thousand.[4]

Market research also shows that the majority of kitchens installed today are fitted kitchens, that is to say they are characterised by matching units and appliances built to standardised measurements compatible with the dimensions of the units. This helps people both to position their gas and electrical appliances in the most suitable place in terms of their function and to exploit the space available to best advantage. Fitted kitchens also have long worktops which run continuously over a number of base units, and their walls carry rows of matching cupboard units also planned to maximise the use of the space available. The preference for such kitchens among the population generally is now so deeply entrenched that even purchasers who wish to avoid an obviously fitted look are unlikely to buy free-standing, non-matching work units or kitchen machines with non-standardised measurements.

However, by 1996 Mintel noted that people were also buying supplementary free-standing items of furniture for their kitchens, such as pine tables and dressers or butcher's blocks to assist with food preparation. This will be taken up in analysing the sample data, along with the Keynote's 1990 claim that people were now regarding the setting up or refurbishment of a kitchen as part of the process of embellishing their homes, as much as a matter of meeting practical requirements. In 1992 Mintel also found that 29 per cent of respondents, that is, just under a third, thought the kitchen was the most important room in the house.[5] By the time their next big review of the kitchen furniture market came round in 1996, Mintel expressed the opinion that a family's lifestyle is a significant factor in determining the type of kitchen a household wants and that the kitchen plays an important role in a household's general life.

This does not mean that interest in the practical requirements of a kitchen has declined. On the contrary, certain appliances designed to ease kitchen work are now so widespread in English homes they are virtually regarded as necessities. In 1996 Mintel reported that refrigeration was almost universal in British households, or, in market jargon, ownership had reached nearly maximum penetration. Automatic washing-machines were also widely regarded as essential, with 80 per cent of households possessing them. With the increase in the number of women working, the demand for quickly prepared meals has also grown, making both prepared foods and quick cooking facilities popular. Microwave cookers may also be on the way to attaining the status of necessity, with 66 per cent of households owning them in 1996 and 74 per cent owning them in 1999. Tumble-driers, in contrast, remain less common. Only 33 per cent of households had them in 1996. And dishwashers continue to be relatively uncommon, being found in only 18 per cent of households in 1996 and 23 per cent in 1999.[6]

In the early 1990s some Mintel reports had begun to explore the incidence and spread of 'snacking' and 'grazing' eating habits. The 1996 report on kitchen furniture, however, makes no further reference to this. One must assume there had been no significant developments on this front. Instead, the 1996 report reviews the persistence of shared family food preparation and family meals, reporting that 42 per cent of their respondents thought it was important to have one family meal together each day and that 56 per cent ate their main meals at a table. In contrast, far fewer, 11 per cent, said they were too busy to eat proper meals, presumably snacking and grazing instead.

In 1996, therefore, Mintel concluded that, for a substantial proportion of the population, attitudes to food are closely related to people's desired lifestyles, and this gives the kitchen, as the site of food preparation, a central role in domestic life. These findings support the claim made in chapter 1 that many people today see their kitchen as playing a symbolic and shaping role in the material realisation of their views about what constitutes a desirable family living style. This, then, summarises the information available at the outset of the research on current trends among and interests displayed by purchasers, with regard to the use and furnishing of kitchens today.

Market research firms work to a narrow brief. Their aim is simple, to find ways of boosting the sale of kitchen furniture and/or equipment. They draw on huge samples and emphasise quantitative analysis, though they also incorporate focus-group work with small numbers of respondents. Here, in contrast, the study would aim not only to identify the main factors which influenced the way people set about buying a new kitchen, but would try to learn more about how these different factors shaped people's design preferences. It would also seek to look at the interaction between these factors as people sought to select and arrange their new kitchen furniture so that their kitchen would communicate some of their social ideas and values visually. To undertake this exercise a sample of purchasers had to be found who would agree to be interviewed in detail, particularly as such a study would also require the collection of qualitative data closer in type to the kind one would get from focus-group discussions. The sampling procedures for the project were set up with these data needs in mind.

Empirical studies can never be better than their methodologies. Drawing the sample was therefore a critical part of the exercise. And, despite the fact that it might seem tedious, it is important for readers to understand, at least in outline, the principles by which the sample used here was drawn. A sample drawn on the basis of a systematic application of a carefully argued set of relevant criteria would increase the likelihood that the findings and conclusions based on the data collected would be relevant to a larger universe. A way had to be found, therefore, to make the sample properly reflect the spread of current buyers of kitchen furniture. Haphazard sampling, so common in the media, for example, can never provide more than anecdotal information. This is inherently incapable of providing the basis for social generalisation.[7]

This is one reason why sociologists sometimes appear to non-sociologists to be obsessed with problems of methodology. At the same time, generating the means and acquiring the necessary permissions for drawing a properly representative sample are not only costly and time-consuming but frequently present huge practical problems. Very few sociologists avoid some methodological compromise. Sampling is thus both critical and usually imperfect. This is apparent in the brief sketch, now offered, of how the sample for this project was drawn.

In their 1992 report on kitchen furniture sales Mintel had figures for the share of market sales achieved by different types of retailer. Nothing more recent was available.[8] These figures are shown in table 3.1, in

**Table 3.1** *Percentage of kitchen furniture market sales commanded by different types of retail outlet*

| Type of retail outlet | Col 1. Market share in 1992 % | Col. 2 Adjusted market share % | Col. 3 Recalculated market share % |
|---|---|---|---|
| MFI | 31 | | |
| Other DIY/sheds | 25 | 56* | 66 |
| Kitchen specialists/studios | 19 | 21 | 24 |
| Builders' merchants | 8 | 8 | 9 |
| Direct sales | 5 | | |
| Other retail | 2 | | |
| Contract | 9 | | |
| Total | 99 | 85 | 99 |

* This figure now represents the market share commanded by MFI and the other sheds combined.

column one. Contract sales were not relevant to this study, which sought to examine personal buying; 'Other' retail was probably bespoke, and adding this to 'Kitchen specialists/studios' could be defended; direct sales was very small and has since fallen, so was dropped as a category; MFI could reasonably be grouped with other DIY companies under the general heading of 'sheds'. Column two then shows the share of the market achieved by these adjusted categories of different kinds of kitchen furniture retailers. One could argue that this 85 per cent of kitchen furniture sales represented a 100 per cent of relevant sales for the purposes of this study. At this point, therefore, the percentage of kitchen furniture sales which each of these new categories commanded was recalculated. This is presented in column three.

This left one problem. I was interested in people's actions and opinions when purchasing a new kitchen and these percentages were based on the value of kitchen sales. In the absence of any other appropriate data I could think of no alternative but to convert these percentages into percentages of kitchens purchased. This clearly involved a doubtful assumption. But after discussion with some market researchers this is what I did on the grounds that it was the best I could do under the circumstances.[9]

The next question was to decide on the size of the sample and the geographical area it would cover. Practicalities decreed that the geographical range had to be limited. However, if the sample was drawn according to the kind of retailer purchasers used and reflected the same proportion of purchasers as the national pattern of market share by type of retailer, the argument could, with caution, be put that findings based on this sample were more than just anecdotal. As pilot interviewing indicated that each interview was likely to take about two hours, excluding travelling time, practicalities further decreed that the final sample could not exceed more than 70–75 cases.[10]

A shed, a studio and a builder's merchant from the same town agreed to participate in helping me draw a sample. This made interviewing practical as most of the sample came within a thirty-mile radius of my base. Table 3.2 shows the distribution of purchasers in the final sample by type of retailer, against the national distribution of purchasers by type of retailer. The distribution is identical.

**Table 3.2** *Distribution of sample purchasers by type of retail outlet*

| Type of retail outlet | % of kitchen sales nationally commanded by different type of retail outlet | % of purchasers in sample by type of outlet used | Number of purchasers in sample by type of outlet used |
| --- | --- | --- | --- |
| Sheds | 66 | 66 | 49 |
| Studios | 24 | 24 | 18 |
| Builders' merchants | 9 | 9 | 7 |
| Total | 100 | 100 | 74 |

Given the hope that the sample of 74 purchasers of new kitchens shown in table 3.2 would provide interview information which, used carefully, would allow one to generalise about the concerns and interests which engage people purchasing new kitchens in this country, it is worth reviewing some of the general social characteristics of the sample, before turning to an examination of the interview data.

There was no way of making social class a variable during the drawing of the sample. Nor was it, from the beginning, expected that the sample would include people living on very low incomes, the premise being that a new kitchen would be a luxury they could not afford. Indeed, because of the cost of new kitchens it was expected that the distribution of social class would be skewed. This was borne out: social classes A and B were over-represented in terms of national patterns while social class D was under-represented (table 3.3). Nevertheless, for the reason given above, the distribution of social class in the sample was regarded as acceptable for the purposes of the study.[11]

**Table 3.3** *Social class distribution of sample compared with the national distribution*

| Class distribution | Number | % of sample | % nationally |
|---|---|---|---|
| Social class A | 4 | 6 | 3 |
| Social class B | 21 | 28 | 16 |
| Social class C1 (non-manual) | 17 | 23 | 30 |
| Social class C2 (manual) | 24 | 32 | 29 |
| Social class D | 7 | 10 | 22 |
| No information | 1 | – | – |
| Total | 74 | 100 | 100 |

The changing nature of our economy and its creeping impact on our class system was noted in chapter one. By recording social class it would be possible to make at least some examination of the continuing importance of social class as an explanatory variable in terms of people's design tastes and to consider Warde's claim that we are in danger of dismissing class differences in English culture too lightly. The study's primary concern, however, was with popular tastes and the cultural élite's beliefs about the origins of those tastes.

In terms of distribution by age, the purposes for which national data is collected lead to its publication in such a different way that no national comparisons with the sample proved possible. The sample, however, showed a fair cross-section of ages.[12]

With regard to gender the sample was very heavily skewed. As this was again expected, it was not disconcerting. The skewing itself came about in the following way. Once the sample of 74 buyers of new kitchens had been drawn, the format of the interview had to be the choice of the interviewees. They were doing me a favour and to ensure their co-operation I felt I needed to accept their terms. Thus, in the case of couples who, I had been informed, had bought kitchens together, *they* decided whether they would both be interviewed or one of them would suffice. From the beginning an important concern of the project was to look at the role of women in popular kitchen design and their influence on the symbolic role kitchens play in English domestic life. In this way, respondents' choice of interview format became part of the study's findings.

The concept of chief respondent was introduced. A chief respondent was defined as a person who took the initiative during the interview in answering questions and to whom the other member of the couple openly deferred on questions of design and décor. Where only one person took part in the interview the issue of chief respondent did not arise, but it was an important distinguisher when couples were interviewed together because it was the chief respondents' answers which were used for the purposes of overall counts.[13] Secondary respondents' answers were not used for this purpose, though they were also not ignored and they proved particularly useful when they took the form of the secondary respondent engaging in interactive discussion with the chief respondent. On such occasions secondary respondents often helped to enhance the meaning or significance of the chief respondents' answers, though they also enriched the qualitative data independently.

As table 3.4, shows, 58 per cent of the sample were interviewed on their own. Of these, thirty-two, or 43 per cent of the whole sample, were women. This included two widows and a divorcee, but the rest of these women were in partnerships. When phoned to request an interview, however, it was not uncommon either for a woman to self-select or for her partner or husband to select her as the appropriate interviewee. Many women were quite comfortable during the initial telephone conversation about saying that they could see no reason for involving a male partner or husband in our discussion, while when men picked the phone up they frequently assumed my call had nothing to do with them and passed me over to their wives or got me to call again. I accepted respondents' judgements on this. A further 34 per cent of the sample consisted of couples who chose to be interviewed together. Twenty-one of the chief respondents in these couples, or 28 per cent of the sample as a whole, were women. Finally, 9 per cent of the sample, or seven couples, chose to be interviewed together but not consistently. These interviews were characterised by one member of the couple joining in halfway through or, alternatively, sporadically leaving and returning to the interview. Women dominated in six of these interviews. Women, indeed, overwhelmingly dominated as chief respondents, accounting for 79 per cent of chief respondents of the sample as a whole. This supported a pre-project expectation that kitchens are women's territory. Some of the implications of this socially and aesthetically will be taken up later.

**Table 3.4** *Form of interview by gender of chief respondent*

| Form of interview | % male | Number | % female | Number | Total % | Number |
|---|---|---|---|---|---|---|
| One person alone | 14 | 10 | 43 | 32 | 57 | 42 |
| Couple together | 5 | 4 | 28 | 21* | 34 | 25 |
| Couple sporadically | 1 | 1 | 8 | 6 | 9 | 7 |
| Total | 20 | 15 | 79 | 59 | 100 | 74 |

* In one case here two women, a mother and daughter, were interviewed with one man.

These then are the general characteristics of the sample. Its limitations are apparent even to the non-sociologist and a sharp mind would detect problems with it which have not been touched on here. I am grateful therefore to Tilly and Tilly for their neat summing up of the problems of empirical methods:

> . . . that there are errors in our numbers we are sure. That they are open to disproof we take to be a virtue. That our procedures could be improved we have no doubt; we hope that someone else will soon take up the task. In the meantime, we want to make it clear that we did not adopt our particular methods and our particular sources because they were quick, easy and cheap. They were none of these. We adopted them because they were the best we could manage.[14]

On this note, which combines humility and challenge in equal parts, this chapter closes. The next chapter will start to examine the findings this sample yielded.

## Notes

1. Keynote Market Survey (1990), (2000); Mintel (1992), (1996), (1998). It should perhaps be noted that Mintel (1998) calculated that some of this increase in spending was not, however, an increase in terms of the amount of people's personal disposable income which was spent on this market sector. This does not alter the claim that the sale of kitchen furniture is big business today.
2. National Shoppers Survey (2000) Summer. The National Shoppers Survey (2002) made a similar point.
3. This was partly calculated on the basis of using the SPSS time series.
4. As reported by the BBC, 17 April 2000.
5. Mintel, British Lifestyles (1997), Keynote (2000).
6. The categories were not mutually exclusive.
7. This is why the description of the sampling process, though, on the one hand, significantly truncated by sociological standards, has, on the other, not been relegated, as it often is in a sociological study, to an appendix. It will also be recalled that in chapter 1 the claim was made that some anthropological studies fail to give enough information about how respondents have been selected. This study therefore had a strong obligation to be clear about its sampling process.

8. And when Mintel reported again in 1998, after the sample had been drawn, they had changed their classification of distribution outlets so no comparisons with earlier reports, as they themselves appreciated, were possible.

9. It included extensive discussion with a major DIY kitchen retailer's market research department, who could think of no way round the problem. The data required to check the degree of error this assumption would produce was unavailable and there was no way in which an individual researcher could collect it.

10. It was also clear that to increase the final size of the sample significantly over this would generate huge administrative difficulties, be very expensive of time and seriously delay the production of any results. In addition, to attain this number of usable interviewees more purchasers would inevitably have to be followed up and some would turn out to be unsuitable, e.g. they had bought a kitchen for an elderly mother or for a house they rented out rather than for themselves.

11. The final social class distribution of the sample compared with the national distribution pattern using the Market Research classification system is given below. The Market Research Society (1991) *Occupational Groupings: A Job Dictionary*, 3rd edn, Market Research Society, was used to allocate respondents to social class, as opposed to the Registrar General's classification of occupations was used. The great changes in the social structure of Britain over the last few decades has led to a full-scale review of the latter. But, given that the study was concerned with the process of purchasing, the Market Research classification seemed adequate.

12. *Respondents' age by decile*

| Age | Number | % |
| --- | --- | --- |
| 20–29 | 5 | 7 |
| 30–39 | 21 | 29 |
| 40–49 | 20 | 27 |
| 50–59 | 12 | 16 |
| 60+ | 15 | 20 |
| Missing | 1 | 1 |
| Total | 74 | 100 |

13. Valentine, Gill (1999) 'Doing Household Research: Interviewing Couples Together and Apart', *Area*, vol. 31, pp. 67–74, contributes to the debate about how far interviewing couples in the way described here provides a refined and accurate account of how decisions are

reached in households. Both Valentine and Jan Pahl (1989), whose work is discussed later, were able to elicit more refined accounts of couple relationships by interviewing couples both together and separately and Valentine argues cogently for the Pahl approach. My difficulty with this interviewing method was less conceptual than practical. The demands of the Data Protection Act meant that getting a suitable sample was laborious and time-consuming. The 74 households in the final sample were widely scattered geographically so visiting was not easy. The interview was lengthy. To get 74 couples who fulfilled my criteria as purchasers to also agree to doing a series of interviews seemed an enormous problem. Though one of Valentine's studies involved 70 couples, the other used just 12 families. Given that this study was moving into uncharted territory, the value of a good-sized sample arguably outweighed the advantages of interviewing in the style of Pahl and Valentine. Ultimately you do what you can and accept that it will fall short of perfection.

14. Tilly, L. and Tilly, R. (1975) *The Rebellious Century*, Harvard University Press, p. 16.

# −4−

# First findings from the sample

Between them the sample buyers had made a financial outlay of £381,350, though it should be borne in mind, as noted earlier, that this sum does not include the cost of new building work, such as making two rooms into one or adding a room onto their house, which a number of respondents had done. It represents simply the cost of kitchen equipment and kitchen decoration. On this the mean, or arithmetical average, spend per household was £5,225; the median financial outlay, or the sum which divided the sample so that there were as many above this spending line as below it, was £3,200; the mode, or most frequent amount, spent was £2,000. Three-quarters of the sample spent £7,499 or less. Overall spending per kitchen ranged from £800 to £30,000. The amount of money spent on a new kitchen therefore varied widely but whatever was spent it virtually always represented a significant outgoing from most respondents' annual incomes.[1] Under these circumstances it seems reasonable to suppose that people would not undertake the refurbishment of a kitchen lightly, that, given the sums of money they were laying out, most people would be planning their purchasing carefully. A by-product of this ought to be that, in looking at refurbished kitchens, it would be possible to explore the relative importance people gave to practical as opposed to aesthetic concerns when thinking about kitchens. This will be pursued later.

To contextualise the sums spent on new kitchens further and simultaneously to begin to acquire an indication of respondents' perceptions of the importance of the kitchen area within the household, as far as it is possible to do that by making financial comparisons, respondents were asked to estimate what they would expect to spend on refurbishing their kitchens in comparison with what they would expect to spend on refurbishing other rooms and on a small number of other major items of household expenditure.

People consistently expected the kitchen would cost more to do up than other household rooms: 72 per cent of people in the case of the sitting-room, 84 per cent in the case of a bedroom, 89 per cent in the case of the bathroom. With regard to the dining-room 26 per cent of people had kitchen-diners so the question did not apply to them, but 85 per cent of the remainder thought refurbishing the kitchen would prove more expensive.[2] This pattern did not vary significantly by social class. We should not immediately assume on the basis of this, however, that because so many people thought they would spend more on refurbishing a kitchen than on refurbishing various other domestic spaces this reflected an unqualified belief that kitchens had a more important role in the house.

The standard of machinery that respondents were installing in their new kitchens has to be one reason kitchens have become so comparatively expensive in terms of domestic furnishing. On top of buying and fitting new kitchen units, the majority of buyers, 88 per cent, were simultan-eously replacing substantial items of kitchen machinery, such as cookers, washing-machines, fridge-freezers, as part of their kitchen refurbishment. Some were replacing every machine. This may have been related to the fact that modern kitchen design which involved the installation of new kitchen units generally necessitated stripping the room bare first. One effect of such radical action seemed to be that people felt it was sensible to update their kitchen machines at the same time. Very few people seemed to feel that refurbishing a sitting-room required a comparable initial room gutting. Sitting-rooms also tended to contain fewer costly machines. So we need to bear these considerations in mind. Nevertheless, the majority of those interviewed expected to, and were prepared to, make a greater financial outlay on their kitchens than any other room. The kitchen was an important room in the house.

Continuing the endeavour to evaluate the relative importance of kitchens, respondents were asked to make two further comparisons between what they would expect to spend on refurbishing a kitchen and on other items of household expenditure, namely, their main annual holiday and the family car. The bulk of respondents, 87 per cent, calculated that their new kitchen was more expensive than their main annual holiday. The commonest exception to this was when people had recently made long antipodean trips, to Australia, for example, to visit children or other family.

The final cost comparison respondents were asked to make was between a new kitchen and replacing the family car. Here the pattern of expectation among respondents was different. Stereotypes about male and female interests commonly link men with cars and women with kitchens. If we accept that this stereotyping accurately reflects certain widespread differ-ences between male and female interests, a sense of justice would suggest that families should spend similar amounts on their family cars and family kitchens. In fact, as table 4.1 shows, only 16 per cent of respondents

**Table 4.1** *Respondents' estimate of cost of a new kitchen in comparison with their expected expenditure on a new family car*

| Cost of kitchen compared with family car | Number | % |
|---|---|---|
| Kitchen cost more | 23 | 31 |
| Kitchen cost the same | 12 | 16 |
| *(Total of above* | *35* | *47)* |
| Kitchen cost less | 39 | 53 |
| Total | 74 | 100 |

thought they did this, while 31 per cent thought kitchens cost more and 53 per cent thought their family car cost more. The question is thus whether, despite the fact that people were spending substantial sums on new kitchens, these figures illustrate, yet again, how women lose out to men in our society. However, the figures are not entirely straightforward. Although only 16 per cent of respondents thought the family car and the new kitchen cost about the same, 47 per cent thought the kitchen cost as much as or more than the car as opposed to 53 per cent who thought the car cost more. At this stage it is hard to know what to make of this and the issue will be returned to later.

From the beginning a major issue was the emphasis people put on practical considerations when they embarked on installing a new kitchen. The efficient pursuit and management of practical household tasks were undoubtedly a priority if judged in terms of people's possession of machinery designed to expedite domestic chores. Using Mintel (1996) it is possible to compare national and sample figures on this front.[3] As has been noted, Mintel reported that refrigeration facilities were now virtually universal in British kitchens, and within the sample 99 per cent had refrigeration and 100 per cent had freezing facilities. Virtually all, 99 per cent, of the sample also had a washing-machine, in comparison with Mintel's figure of 80 per cent of households, and 65 per cent, as against Mintel's 33 per cent, had a tumble-drier.[4] The difference between the sample and Mintel's 1996 figure for the whole population was even greater with regard to dishwashers. Within the sample, 55 per cent, as opposed to Mintel's 18 per cent, had dishwashers. Microwaves were also commoner among the sample. By 1996 Mintel was reporting that 66 per cent of households had them: the figure for the sample was 85 per cent. Some of these differences must be explained by the skewed distribution of social class, with the poorer social classes being under-represented in the sample, and by the fact that young, less settled people, who tend to live in rented accommodation, did not appear, as they were not buying kitchens.

Within the sample there was also some variation by social class in the possession of certain items of kitchen machinery, though the pattern was not clear-cut. Putting social classes A and B together, 60 per cent had dishwashers. Of those who fell into social class C1, 64 per cent had a dishwasher, while the comparable figure for social classes C2 and D put together was 45 per cent. Separate ovens and hobs, which give greater flexibility in positioning furniture as well as ruling out the need for people to bend down when taking heavy things out of the oven, were widespread, with 61 per cent of the sample owning them. They also tend to be more expensive than the conventional cooker and ownership again varied by social class, with 72 per cent of social classes A and B having separate appliances, in comparison with 47 per cent of social class C1 and 61 per cent of social classes C2 and D combined. The variation between the social classes with regard to the ownership of this machinery is sufficiently erratic, however, to suggest that factors over and above socio-economic ones are also at play when people decide whether to opt for separate ovens and hobs or for an appliance in which they are combined, possibly issues of habit and personal preference.

The general message behind these figures is that people today are fully receptive to the idea of using mechanised kitchen aids designed to ease the handling of routine domestic chores.[5] The scepticism about kitchen machinery which was still marked thirty years ago has gone. This scepticism may, of course, have been partly a by-product of the expense of such machinery.[6] Today's kitchen machines are both relatively cheaper and more efficient. But more women are also working for longer periods of their life and concomitantly are consciously looking for ways of expediting housework. But, whatever the factors at play, machines are in.

Certainly they are in among people installing new kitchens. Having a new kitchen correlates with possessing noticeably more kitchen machinery than the population on average. In this sense buyers of new kitchens see the kitchen as, in the words of more than one respondent, the engine-room of the house. The proliferation of kitchen mechanisation found in the homes of the sample is important evidence of the emphasis people place, when refurbishing their kitchen, on it being an efficient workplace.

From the beginning of the study, however, an important concern was the way people conceived of the kitchen's social role within the house and the extent to which they sought to express this in material terms. Some preliminary evidence about the way people planned their kitchens in terms of perceived family and general social needs was therefore collected as part of establishing the foundation for a more detailed exploration of this question subsequently.

The age range within the sample was considerable so there were people who were just beginning to raise families, people who had decided not to have children and empty-nesters, whose children had long since left home. Family requirements had consciously influenced the planning of some kitchens with 14 per cent of respondents reporting that children's needs or habits had influenced their design and décor and a further 4 per cent of buyers mentioning teenage needs. One mother had selected a colour for the new kitchen units because it would not show the bump marks made by her children when riding their tricycles. Another mother had chosen a floor covering because it would soften her toddler's falls.

For 70 per cent of respondents, however, family needs, expressed as a product of the stage in which people currently found themselves in the family life cycle, were not perceived as significant in determining the design of these new kitchens. And even when family needs were a factor influencing design they often turned out to be amusingly idiosyncratic, but unclassifiable. One young mother of three, for example, had given priority to installing a wine rack in her new kitchen because she badly wanted somewhere to keep her children's lemonade bottles. Another older woman had carefully planned a space under her worktop to accommodate a dog basket in which her labrador could curl up out of her way. She had thereby sacrificed storage space, only to find the space turned out to be cold and the dog continued to flop out in the middle of the floor so that it was continually under her feet, an inconvenience she thought she had found a way around (plate 4.1).

**Plate 4.1** Kitchen showing a carefully planned but never used cubby-hole for the dog.

However, although the impact of family needs on the design of new kitchens did not turn out to be significant, we cannot assume that this shows that people's feelings about family life and desirable family conduct generally did not colour the way they thought about design when planning their new kitchens.

As part of exploring the way people conceptualised their kitchens as distinctive domestic spaces, preliminary information was also sought about the time people spent in their kitchens and the way they used them. The kitchen was a heavily used part of the house during people's waking hours. Only one room, the sitting-room, alternatively known as the lounge, was used more. Only 7 per cent of people used any other room more than these two during their waking hours.

How people used these two rooms, however, was strongly patterned by gender. Women overwhelmingly reported spending more time in the kitchen than their menfolk and the men, in the couples who chose to be interviewed together, confirmed this. Even among chief respondents this different pattern between men and women still held. A total of 47 per cent of male chief respondents, in contrast to 12 per cent of women chief respondents, thought they spent less than an hour a day in the kitchen, and a further 20 per cent of men, as opposed to 44 per cent of women, estimated that they spent between three and six hours there daily. In addition, 86 per cent of male chief respondents estimated they spent between three and six hours a day in their sitting-room in contrast to 71 per cent of women chief respondents who thought they spent about this amount of time there. There was, however, a group of women, over a fifth, who estimated they spent over six hours a day in the sitting-room. Women therefore spent more time in the kitchen than their male counterparts but, although there was a tendency for men to match this by spending more time than women in the sitting-room, there was one group of women who constituted an exception to this. A possible explanation for this is that those women who were not employed outside the home both spent longer in the kitchen than men respondents and also longer in the sitting-room because they were in the house for substantially more hours every day.

The kitchen and sitting-room are thus the most heavily used areas in English homes today. This suggests the value of a closer examination both of how people used and how they would have ideally liked to have used their kitchens. In looking at this the aim is not only to record habitual patterns of behaviour in domestic life but, equally importantly, to start to consider the role of the kitchen in respondents' general conception of domestic life.

For centuries eating has been a major social activity. People can and often do eat alone. But the consumption of food frequently meets more than a biological need. It is an important means of generating a sense of social solidarity among people. Eating together helps people to structure and infuse with meaning the activity of both formal and informal human groups, thereby establishing or consolidating the importance and significance of such groups socially. An examination of the use of the kitchen for eating is therefore an important first step in the process of identifying the role of the kitchen in people's conceptualisation of domesticity and family today. Subsequent chapters will develop this theme but the initial step is to establish the extent to which people aimed to eat and actually ate together.

In doing this, however, it has to be borne in mind that for a significant number of people the social uses to which they put their kitchens was architecturally determined in marked respects. Only a small number of people had built on or radically remodelled the room which housed the kitchen. The high cost of such work deterred most. However, a greater number of people had made relatively modest changes to their kitchens which did not require major structural alterations, changes such as removing a door or a non-bearing partition wall or altering a window-frame. And a considerable number of people had tinkered with their kitchens, by, for example, changing the position of major electricity, gas or water outlets, shifting the fuse box or adding or moving electrical sockets. Only one couple had simply taken out the old units and machines and returned new ones to the same place. Virtually everyone was engaged in looking for ways of managing the space available to them. Though conscious that there were major constraints on what they could physically alter, given their financial means, people were far from quiescent. On the contrary, they actively embarked on making the space they had available serve their ends as best it could.

Thus, while architecture was an important determining factor with regard to how extensively a kitchen was used for eating, people's desire to eat in the kitchen had, despite considerable architectural constraints, stimulated the production of an array of ingenious devices for accommodating kitchen eating despite considerable obstacles. This, in itself, indicated the strength of people's desire to eat in the kitchen. It was also an indication of the liveliness of popular creativity.

In looking at the use of the kitchen for eating, however, two architectural factors had to be taken into account. A significant number of kitchens, fourteen in total, were so small that finding space for even one person to eat in them was impossible. Once upon a time an architect had decided that the kitchen was to be just for cooking and this had been made material fact in such a way that there were no practical means of combating it. Secondly, some houses had been initially designed and built with a kitchen-diner complex, limiting people's choice about where they ate in another way. No-one in this group, however, said they would prefer not to be able to eat in the kitchen, though one or two said they would have liked a second dining area for more formal occasions and in one instance this had led a couple to erect a divider so as to partially separate the cooking from the eating area.

The use of the kitchen for eating has to be considered against this background. Table 4.2 shows that 50 per cent, or half the sample, had kitchens or kitchen-diners with a table and chairs which they used for eating. A further 13 per cent who could not manage a table and chairs had devised other means of arranging to eat in the kitchen, such as having a breakfast bar and stools, while 19 per cent of the sample, whose kitchen structures defied the introduction of any arrangement for eating, said they would have liked to be able to eat in the kitchen. Overall, therefore, a substantial majority, 82 per cent, wanted a kitchen they could eat in. This left 18 per cent for whom eating in the kitchen was not a matter of concern.

**Table 4.2** *Respondents' desire for eating facilities in the kitchen*

| Desire for eating facilities in the kitchen | No | % |
|---|---|---|
| Yes and had them | 37 | 50 |
| Stools and breakfast bar only possible | 7 | 9 |
| Other device organised | 3 | 4 |
| Desired but no room | 14 | 19 |
| Did not desire | 13 | 18 |
| Total | 74 | 100 |

These then were the kitchen eating facilities available to people or which they had constructed. Solitary eating need not concern us here, for the key question is the extent to which people used their kitchens for social eating. Family eating on a regular basis took place in 53 per cent of the sample kitchens, and, if we include occasional family eating, in 58 per cent of cases. The evidence shows that, where the facilities were available for family eating in the kitchen, people actively took advantage of them.

Beyond close family eating there is also the question of how far people used their kitchens for entertaining other family members, friends and acquaintances, informally and formally. The use of the kitchen in some form for this purpose was widespread. Only 11 per cent reported no form of socialising in their kitchen. Even among the twenty-seven respondents who did not have a table and chairs in their kitchen (fourteen of whom were in this position only because they were unable to accommodate them), eleven reported that visitors frequently followed them into the kitchen. And half of those who said they were not interested in having eating facilities in the kitchen still reported that friends and guests followed them into the kitchen to socialise.

Guests did not apparently feel it was intrusive or discourteous to walk without invitation into someone's kitchen in order to open up or pursue a conversation. Even when it was physically awkward for both visitor and host to be in the kitchen together, visitors still felt no requirement to wait for an invitation before entering. Not even the pokiest kitchen deterred them from squeezing in. The kitchen appears to be an open-access, public space in English homes regardless of its size or its facilities for socialising.

Among those whose kitchens were furnished with tables and chairs everyone reported using the kitchen for some form of entertainment. For those with kitchen-diners there was obviously not much choice about this. But among those who had some choice 21 per cent offered cups of tea and glasses of wine to visitors in the kitchen; 33 per cent offered cups of tea and glasses of wine and also provided light or informal meals in the kitchen; a further 33 per cent not only used their kitchens for these casual forms of entertaining but were also prepared to offer formal meals there as well, when the occasion suited. It seems fair to say that the kitchen is widely accepted today as a major site for social discourse within the domestic setting.

This is not to say that people spent more of their waking hours in the kitchen than in other rooms. As has already been noted many people spent more time in their sitting-rooms/lounges than they did in their kitchens. Rather, people appeared to conceive of different kinds of relaxation and to allocate different forms of socialising and entertainment to different parts of the house. Thus, though the kitchen might be a model of cleanliness, respondents repeatedly indicated in discussion that it was quite acceptable for people in dirty clothes to flop down in the kitchen. Kitchens were places where tired, grimy people could relax and recuperate after a day's work without feeling they had to get themselves cleaned up first. It was even acceptable to eat a meal in the kitchen before cleaning yourself up. Once refreshed by rest and food, people would then often go off to shower and change. When they reappeared in clean leisure wear, they did not return to the kitchen, however.

Not all the people in the sample of course, did work which involved getting dirty. But a similar set of social principles and expectations seemed to hold for white-collar workers, namely, that people needed time to revive when they first got home from work, and this often involved hanging round the kitchen in your business clothes and frequently included having a meal there. Then people would change from suits into casual wear, such as slacks and a sweater. Once people had changed they moved on to the sitting-room/lounge.

The sitting-room/lounge was where one most commonly found the television and there, in more luxurious surroundings, people's evenings often finished watching television. Lounges were characteristically furnished with soft carpets, huge sofas and capacious armchairs, uphol-stered in plush fabrics, very different textures from those found in most kitchens. The incidence and use of radios and televisions in these rooms was in keeping with these behaviour patterns. Forty-five, or 61 per cent, of the sample kitchens had a radio, but only nineteen, or 26 per cent, of them contained a television, and in seven of these people watched the kitchen television for less than an hour a day.

Today listening to the radio is not the social activity it once was. It is frequently an activity people do on their own, while driving a car or doing household chores.[7] In addition, even though they may have other important functions as well, kitchens are workplaces and watching television while doing something manual is often intrinsically impossible. In addition, watching television these days, though it can certainly be done on one's own, is also a social activity which people do together. If they are really tired, they may just sit companionably, leaving the tiredness to drain away and, apart from the odd wisecrack, say very little. Frequently, however, people like to intersperse their watching with appreciative or critical comments among themselves about the programmes. Neither kitchen layouts nor their furnishings, however expensive, are physically as well suited to this kind of activity as sitting-rooms/lounges.

For the most part people did not, of course, articulate domestic rules in this way. They remained unspoken or elliptically referred to in terms of describing family practices. But this is not to say they did not exist. And they could be quite refined. So one woman, describing the way they used their kitchen and sitting-room, noted how her husband, who did long hours of dirty work, was sometimes too tired to change. Sitting in her spotless kitchen she described how he would then stay in his work clothes and spend the evening sprawled at the kitchen table where they would chat until he went to clean up before going straight to bed. It was clear that she felt there was no impropriety in staying in your dirty clothes for long periods in an otherwise spotless kitchen, a room, furthermore, where hygiene was important.

The role of the sitting-room or lounge is reflected in its name. Intrinsic to both names is the idea of a leisure or, at least, non-work space. In contrast, whatever other role the kitchen has in a house it is invariably a workplace too. Kitchens are for preparing food. This is usually immediately obvious on entering a kitchen from the machinery alone.

But it goes further than this. Today's kitchens not only proclaim their role as workplaces by dint of their contents, or even by the way they are planned and arranged. The surfaces and texturing of kitchen furniture as well as the kinds of textiles found in kitchens also proclaim the kitchen's role. Modern kitchens have their own distinctive visual aesthetic. It is also an aesthetic deeply rooted in non-aesthetic judgements about how kitchen work is best done, one frequently heavy with moral overtones. The intermeshing within kitchen design today of aesthetic values with moral and social values was steadily consolidated as the century progressed and is distinctively twentieth-century, though now carried on into the twenty-first century. And, though of recent origin, this socio-moral aesthetic is now so pervasive that purchasers of new kitchens often take it for granted. That is to say, they read it fluently, they accept it and they like it visually even when they do not articulate it verbally in detail.

A major aim of this study is to learn to interpret the visual messages contemporary purchasers incorporate into the design of a new kitchen so as to achieve a more nuanced understanding of this aesthetic. An important precursor for learning to do this, however, must be to trace the way purchasers go about the process of buying. Knowing how the sample approached the business of buying constitutes a necessary backdrop to a closer analysis of the design features of the sample kitchens: it becomes the next task.

## Notes

1. In 1997, when the main body of the interviewing was done, pre-tax average incomes per annum fell as follows:

   Manual men – approx. £16,340 for a working week of 45 hours.
   Non-manual men – approx. £25,000 for a working week of 39 hours.
   Manual women – approx. £10,460 for a working week of 40 hours.
   Non-manual women – approx. £16,525 for a working week of 40 hours.

   Source: *New Earnings Survey, Office of National Satitistics.*

2. Mintel Keynote (2000) found that in 1999 the population overall was spending more on living-room furniture than on any other kind of furniture. But as kitchen machinery is not included in these figures these calculations may not correspond to people's own perceptions about what they spent on their kitchens. This omission would explain why my sample, in apparent contradiction to Keynote's findings, thought they spent more on their kitchens than on any other room in the house.

3. Mintel (1996) was selected for making these comparisons because most of the interviewing was done in 1997. Any later figures therefore seemed inappropriate.

4. Though the majority of these machines were sited in the kitchen, a significant number, for reasons of convenience or space, were kept elsewhere. This, however, does not affect the argument that machines which offer to ease the drudgery of housework are now widely accepted.

5. This, of course, does not challenge Ruth Schwartz Cowen's (1989) thesis about the expansion of housework. It is a separate argument about the receptivity and acceptance of kitchen mechanisation.

6. See Adrian Forte (1986) on the enormous expense of the early cleaning machines, p. 214.

7. Or increasingly radio is used to occupy the patient while the dentist works on their teeth.

# –5–

# Shopping begins

The persistent belief in some intellectual circles that marketing techniques in the twentieth century have made substantial sections of the population the victims of fashionable gimmickry and life-style demands was noted in chapter 1. The point was made that whether or not this was true was an empirical question but that the debates in which this argument often features are commonly ideologically rather than empirically driven, and people can be very cavalier about the empirical evidence for their arguments. This chapter takes up the question of the impact of advertising and salesmanship on purchasers of new kitchens.

Chapter 2 outlined the gradual development of the fitted kitchen from design idea to commercially viable design form. During this time the advertising of the new fitted kitchens in England was similar to the American approach. They were lauded as offering a state-of-the-art technology and the enhanced comfort and efficiency that, it was claimed, accompanied this. That the public was won over to this opinion and to the general concept of the fitted kitchen is borne out by the fact that when the economic boom of the 1960s occurred people started to invest in these new kitchens with some enthusiasm. And during the prosperous 1980s the purchase of fitted kitchens accelerated to the degree that by the early 1990s the market research firm, Mintel, estimated that 66 per cent of English homes now had fitted kitchens.[1]

The choice of style had also taken off from the 1960s when Poggenpohl had made cupboard doors available in five different colours. Production techniques had developed so that manufacturers now thought nothing of offering cupboard finishes in fifty different variants. Together with the numerous worktop finishes and colours and the wide range of handles on offer the different kitchen styles available to customers had become enormous. Though theoretically one might expect that the more one had to spend the greater the choice, even at the middle and bottom end of the market the choice available was, by now, huge. Manufacturers catered for almost every kind of taste. Buyers could select kitchens in cool, restrained hues or bright, saturated colour; doors could be flush or panelled, with laminated or wooden fronts and shiny or matt finishes. The final installation could be left severely unadorned or decorated with architraves, pilasters and fretwork. It was therefore open to people to create a clinically modern or cosily traditional effect, an urban or a countrified feel, or any hybrid of these they fancied.

Purchasers today have enormous scope for stamping their own taste on their kitchens, and marking them with their personal visual preferences. Nevertheless, there is still a belief in some quarters that the marketing of consumer goods is now so wily and its practitioners so deeply accomplished in customer manipulation that they are hugely successful at stopping most consumers from acting as autonomous social agents. Today's customer, the argument goes, has lost the ability to act with independent initiative or imagination. Purchasers are basically conned into buying what the manufacturers and retailers want them to buy. The apparent variety in styles available to buyers is often defined by those making this argument as essentially superficial. In defence of this they point to the fact that these styles are essentially clothing standardised carcasses.

Accounts and analyses of the ploys of advertising are also often brought in to buttress this argument. These analyses used commonly to take the form of textual analyses, verbal, visual or both, offering an interpretation of the intentions of the copywriter or artist as the basis from which to deduce consumer responses. Logically, of course, such deductions are quite indefensible.[2] Actual consumer responses, however, were virtually never investigated in such analyses. While such analyses are now much less popular, they have not disappeared.[3] More commonly, however, the argument has changed its emphasis. So, for example, recent years have witnessed an interest in the way marketing tactics have been increasingly directed towards encouraging people to adopt particular lifestyles.

One popular theory has been that, ensnared by advertising and sales talk, consumers now aim to construct themselves and their surroundings according to the preferences of the other members of the social group to which they belong, or aspire to belong. They thus seek to set up similar kinds of domestic décor, pursue the same leisure activities, dress similarly and patronise the same kind of restaurants as people whom they hope to impress or emulate. The problem with the concept of lifestyle preferences is not that it contains no truth at all. The problem is that it is so frequently incorporated into a much wider view of social life which seems to assume, first, that prior to the huge spread of advertising people did not adopt 'lifestyles' and, secondly, that the social pressures which draw people into adopting particular lifestyles reflect a population essentially reduced to social dupes, except, by implication, the presenters of the argument, who, for some reason, remain immune to the pressures to which everyone else succumbs. In an attempt to provide a sounder means of assessing how far people are influenced by others' opinions and how far they make choices we can describe as independent, the approach adopted here starts with the purchaser, not the advert or a theory of lifestyles, and it concentrates initially on collecting information from purchasers about what they saw as their concerns and motivations when they began the process of planning a new kitchen and deciding on one layout and design rather than possible others.

In putting together a description of the initial stages in the process whereby people install a new kitchen, this chapter starts with the very earliest stages of the interaction between purchasers and the market in kitchen furniture, presenting the reasons people gave for their initial decision to buy a new kitchen, and then turning to look at the preliminary steps they took to gather information about what the market had to offer them, how they handled advice from salespeople and shops and how they finally arrived at a decision about what they would buy. Covering this will include looking at how people responded to the blandishments of advertising. By the end of the chapter the aim is to have produced a broad overview, up to the point of purchase, of the way people operate as purchasers in this field.

The picture of shopping behaviour this initial data analysis produces should begin to establish the extent to which these purchasers act in a spontaneous, ad hoc manner, and the degree to which their decisions are carefully weighed and planned. This will constitute the first stage in making an informed assessment of how far the behaviour of the sample can properly be described as rational and purposeful and how far purchasers appeared to be the playthings of external forces bearing down upon them.

At the beginning of the interview people were asked why they decided to buy a new kitchen. Sixty-one per cent said their previous kitchens were old and in a state of disrepair. The other 39 per cent of responses constituted a hotchpotch collection of answers, none of which occurred with sufficient frequency to warrant separate categorisation. So one answer stood out, given by over half the respondents. It seems an obvious answer; it also sounds a reasonable one. A number of respondents described in some detail the dilapidated condition of their old kitchen. One woman described with feeling, for example, how 'lovely' it was in her new kitchen to have drawers that opened and closed smoothly after the sticky, jerky movement of her old drawers, which it had been a constant battle for her to close. Her husband similarly recalled how he used to break his nails opening and closing the old drawers.

The sample overwhelmingly rejected the idea that they might have just got bored with the old style and decided to go for something new and trendy. They were insistent that though they might not have liked the style of the old kitchen furniture this was not the main reason for their going out and buying new furniture At this stage, and by itself, this is not proof that such a consideration was not a factor in determining their behaviour. But if it was people were not saying so. And if we decide to disbelieve a respondent's answer we ought to have sound reasons for doing so.

People also reported mulling over the decision to buy a new kitchen for a considerable time before embarking on the actual process, with 43 per cent saying they had spent about a year or more thinking about it and a further 38 per cent saying they had thought about it for several months. Impulsive decisions to buy were rare. Only 7 per cent had both made the decision to buy and embarked on the process of purchasing in under a month. Thus any influence marketing hype had on the respondents was not taking the form of making people rush out to buy on the spur of the moment. In addition, one cannot assume that because the decision to buy was made quickly the subsequent process of purchasing was similarly rapid.

Once people had decided to buy, exploratory forays into the market could be extensive. A handful of people visited as many as twelve or more showrooms. One hardy soul thought they must have visited twenty. Most, however, 53 per cent, visited between three and six showrooms (table 5.1). The number of showrooms visited does not, of course, tell us anything about the quality of effort people put into their review of the market.

**Table 5.1** *Number of showrooms buyers visited*

| No. of showrooms visited | No. of buyers | % of buyers |
|---|---|---|
| 1–2 | 16 | 22 |
| 3–6 | 39 | 53 |
| 7–10 | 13 | 17 |
| 12–20 | 6 | 8 |
| Total | 74 | 100 |

While only a few people, 15 per cent, sent away for brochures just over half, 53 per cent, brought between one and five brochures home to look at, and a further 27 per cent, or over a quarter, collected between six and ten brochures to browse through. Gleaning what the market overall had to offer by going through catalogues, listing the pieces of kitchen furniture available and looking at pictures illustrating the different ways in which they could be combined and arranged, was thus extensive. In addition, 85 per cent of the sample subsequently had plans and/or drawings made, or, in the case of competent DIY people, did ones themselves, detailing possible or proposed new kitchens they could have. This leaves just 15 per cent who did not bother with drawings or plans. In addition, over two-thirds of the sample also collected prices from showrooms as part of their initial general review of the market. Then, as part of deciding on just what they would buy, 74 per cent got one or more costings done for them and 41 per cent got costings from more than one retailer.

These figures, particularly when put together, suggest widespread forethought and care among purchasers of new kitchens both in consider-ing the general layout and arrangement of the furniture and in attempting to ensure they got value for money. They do not offer any clear support for a contention that the general public are swept along by commercial blarney.

The cost of the new kitchen was a matter of continuing concern for pur-chasers. Price was mentioned by 62 per cent as a reason for selecting the retailer they used as opposed to 35 per cent who said that one reason for their choice of retailer was that they stocked a particular design of furniture. Roughly a further quarter of buyers said that, had they been able to allocate themselves bigger budgets, they would have selected a different style of furniture from the one they did choose. One cannot, however, deduce from this that they would have chosen a radically different style of furniture, for very similar styles of kitchen furniture are produced today in cheaper and more expensive versions. Indeed, one or two of the sample explained that, for budgetary reasons, they had settled that parts of their kitchen would be in some form of simulated wooden finish though ideally they would have liked real wood.

On the other hand, a keen concern about price should not be read as evidence that price was of greater concern than design among the sample. Money indubitably was a major determining factor in what people purchased, but, as we trace the run-up to buying further, it will become clear how important design was to purchasers. At the same time, people did not appear to be tempted in any obvious way by marketing hype. For they did not spend carelessly. Whatever they might have fancied buying was balanced against careful financial calculations.

Mock-ups of kitchens using actual furniture are now standard in kitchen furniture salesrooms. Retailers set up a variety of layouts to imitate different kitchen conditions ranging from the little galley kitchen to luxuriously spacious kitchens capable of various domestic usages. They also set them up using a wide array of styles, from those embracing the latest design interests and more dated modernist styles through Shaker pastiche and 'country' pine to oak, both dark and limed, and more or less ornately embellished. Buyers used these extensively in the run-up to deciding what to buy. There was only one buyer who said they had not bothered with them while almost a third thought they had looked at more than forty-five such mock-ups and many others had looked at considerable numbers (table 5.2).

**Table 5.2** *Number of mock-ups buyers examined*

| Mock-ups examined | No. | % |
|---|---|---|
| None | 1 | 1 |
| About 5 | 9 | 12 |
| 6–15 | 21 | 28 |
| 16–45 | 19 | 26 |
| More than 45 | 23 | 31 |
| No ans. | 1 | 1 |
| Total | 74 | 100 |

Most people, 89 per cent, had not simply looked at these displays but said they had examined them in detail. And they regarded them as helpful. As many as 81 per cent said they enabled you to see what the units really looked like and the same number that they helped you find out what their quality and workmanship was like. Men, in particular, liked mock-ups. Some exploited to the maximum the opportunity they provided for assessing the quality of the furniture, and men who showed no interest in any other aspect of buying a kitchen could become hugely energised when it came to examining mock-ups. Several wives described how their husbands managed to squeeze themselves completely inside some of the units. Others recalled how all they could see of their husband was his bottom. These men also opened cupboards to examine hinges, took drawers out, turned them upside down, tapped them and held them up to the light. These detailed examinations reduced some women to a state of acute embarrassment. The men who undertook them, however, felt no compunction about effectively dismantling parts of the showroom.

Fewer, though still half, 51 per cent, found mock-ups were a positive help in enabling you to see what it was hard to visualise in your imagination, and another half, 54 per cent, felt they gave you ideas about possible arrangements for your own kitchen, even though a number of people commented that, despite the retailers' best attempts, mock-ups invariably had an unnatural feel.

Mock-ups are customarily set up replete with splash tiling, floor tiles, curtains, cushions and even crockery. Among the sample 46 per cent found these accessories stimulated ideas about what they might try in their own kitchen. The usefulness of these mock-ups as a visual aid or their effectiveness as a sales technique, depending on how you choose to characterise it, is clearly shown by the fact that 77 per cent of purchasers had actually seen a mock-up which used the furniture design they finally selected. Again, however, one should be cautious about classifying this as evidence of consumers succumbing to manipulative sales methods. It is equally plausibly an example of a usefully informative sales technique, allowing people to examine workmanship as described above, for example, albeit with the aim of making sales, and the evidence presented here is plausibly open to being interpreted as evidence of the public's intelligent use of it. Additional evidence of proactive behaviour among purchasers, however, would considerably strengthen any claim that purchasers were neither readily nor easily manipulated. And there was evidence of people from all walks of life engaging in such behaviour.

People did not just choose a style. They had to accommodate their layout preferences to the exigencies of their own kitchen. A third of the sample felt the architecture of their kitchen and/or the positioning of services as significantly inhibiting what they would have liked to do. A number of these, though not all, lived in more modest housing. Several, for example, had galley kitchens of the Schutte-Lihotsky genre, in which, try as they might, they could not arrange to eat informal meals or snacks. One painter-decorator and his wife still living in a rented council house described in detail their futile efforts to overcome this. A bus-driver's wife with a very small kitchen was similarly defeated as she could not afford to do the building work which would have made eating in the kitchen possible. Others with small kitchens who had found ways of offsetting this problem were still often conscious that they had not got what they would really have liked. This was true of both a divorced salesman in a modest bungalow and a retired director of a printing company and his wife in a more spacious detached 1960s house (plate 5.1).

Others, however, had houses in which it was both possible and within their financial ability to undertake building work to get a kitchen which more closely met their ideal. As noted earlier, this did not usually extend to radical construction work but typically involved removing partition, as opposed to bearing walls or relocating doors and/or windows. Occasionally, however, extensive building was undertaken, though, not surprisingly,

**Plate 5.1** An illustration of how keen some people were to incorporate eating facilities into their kitchens. At the back on the left-hand side one can just see how these owners have squeezed in a tiny table with a radio, toaster and fruit bowl, together with a stool and a chair. When the owners were eating it would be hard to use the kitchen door.

this only occurred among social classes A and B. The most dramatic example was that of a couple who designed their ideal kitchen, had all the measurements logged and then handed these to the builder with the instruction that he was to construct a room on the back of their house which would accommodate this design. When they discovered some of the builder's measurements were out by about four inches, they refused to alter their design and insisted he move his walls instead. The builder complied. Literally turning a dream into reality did therefore happen. But for most people cost prohibited this. Any design ideals they might cherish were tempered from the beginning by what they perceived as being realistic.

The other structural constraint on the redesigning of a kitchen was the location of water, gas and electricity outlets. Again, as noted, some people relocated fuse boxes, moved electric-cooker and other electric sockets and changed the position of the kitchen sink. More, however, felt they had to leave cookers and sinks where they were. The problems of moving them were too great. For a third of the sample, designing a new kitchen was a major exercise in manipulation, a kind of assault course you had to go through to get what you wanted in the face of considerable odds. Even for those who did not have such acute problems with the layout of their kitchens, getting what they wanted was still often a problem-solving process and it was clear that this aspect of kitchen installation had engaged a good deal of people's time. Many were full of how they had tackled the limitations imposed by the physical proportions of their kitchens and they could and often did talk about them at length. Some people certainly sought advice from the retailers about such layout problems. Few, however, appeared to have handed over the resolution of their difficulties to retailers.

The most striking characteristic of people's responses on this front was their strong feeling of personal involvement, and their answers conveyed the energy and zest with which they set about tackling the constraints they faced. Resolving these constraints often displayed a considerable ingenuity, involving a play of both practical and visual imagination. And, when recounting the discovery of a resolution or neat compromise by dint of moving a fuse box up or down, putting a false back or front on a cupboard, turning a machine at right angles or changing the position of a window, people often expressed a strong sense of satisfaction.

In summary, purchasers generally appeared to sort out their layout problems for themselves. Some, as we see below, drew on sales-staff experience for advice. Yet they saw the final resolution of their difficulties as their own. Buyers had complaints about retailers but these typically concerned the delivery of wrong, incomplete or damaged goods, or a failure to deliver on time. When things went wrong, as with the buyer cited earlier who planned a hole under her counter for the dog which it never used because it was too cold, people took the blame on themselves. They did not blame the retailers or installers.

Before an assessment of the degree to which today's purchasers are the victims of market hype and blarney is offered, more probing is required, however. For a considered assessment of the degree to which salespeople shaped purchasers' decisions we need an analysis of customer interaction with sales staff. People were therefore questioned about the way sales staff approached them and they approached sales staff. Just over a quarter, 27 per cent, said they actively avoided sales staff while deciding what to buy. Once they had made their selection this group also said they put in their order and paid for it without discussion. A further 16 per cent said they made their choices without discussions with sales staff but checked various things with staff at the point of purchase. Over half, 57 per cent, however, said they had consulted sales staff as part of the process of deciding what to buy. Further questions were put to these last two groups. These yielded a picture of customer interaction with sales staff in terms of the frequency with which different kinds of advice were offered to and taken by customers.

The area in which purchasers reported sales advice was least frequently proffered was over the choice of design or style of kitchen furniture they might select. Here 10 per cent said they had received such advice and 3 per cent said they had taken it. Sales advice about the placement of the main service outlets for gas, electricity and water in the kitchen was similarly infrequent, again 10 per cent. On this front, however, a similar number took it, 10 per cent. More advice about the placement of lighting was given, with 18 per cent of customers receiving it and 15 per cent taking it. Advice about quality was more common, being received by 24 per cent though taken by only 15 per cent. Almost a third of purchasers, 31 per cent, were given advice about the selection of particular units and over a quarter of customers, 27 per cent, took it. Advice was most commonly offered, however, about the way odd spaces could be used up and not go to waste and about how cornices and other comparable trims could be added to the selected design, being offered to 41 per cent and 42 per cent of purchasers, respectively. In both cases 28 per cent of customers took sales advice on these fronts (table 5.3).

In summary, the evidence showed that salespeople almost never proffered basic aesthetic advice or certain kinds of technical advice. They left purchasers to select the basic design they wanted and did not try to advise about services. Instead, they directed their effort into offering

**Table 5.3** *Nature of advice sales people offered and its take-up by respondents*

| Advice offered by salespeople | No. offered this advice | % offered this advice | No. offered advice who also accepted it | % offered advice who also accepted it |
|---|---|---|---|---|
| On choice of design | 7 | 9 | 2 | 3 |
| On position of outlets for utilities | 7 | 9 | 7 | 9 |
| On positioning of lights and plugs | 13 | 18 | 11 | 15 |
| On quality of furniture | 18 | 24 | 11 | 15 |
| On price | 20 | 27 | 14 | 19 |
| On positioning of kitchen units | 23 | 31 | 20 | 27 |
| On uses for odd spaces | 30 | 40 | 21 | 28 |
| On choice of decorative trims | 31 | 42 | 21 | 28 |

advice about the way people could finish off a kitchen. There is, of course, both a technical and an aesthetic aspect to advice about how people can utilise awkward corners and spaces in their kitchens and how they can add finishing touches to their basic design and style. Even, however, in the areas where salespeople mainly directed their sales skills, namely, in dealing with odd spaces in kitchens and the selection of final decorative trims, almost three-quarters of customers said they did not take sales help.

There may be another factor behind salespeople's offer of advice about the sale of cornices and similar extras. A number of people commented on how expensive they were and that, though they had liked some of them, they had decided to do without them because of the cost. Some buyers were suspicious that the profit margin on these was much greater than that on the basic units and worktops and they thought that was why sales staff drew attention to them. According to Mintel, kitchen furniture is a very competitive market and companies often work on tight profit margins. Possibly these buyers were right: basic units were not priced to bring in a large profit, extras were. A conversation with one kitchen retailer confirmed this belief. No systematic information was available about this, however.

To complete the picture of sales-staff–purchaser interaction and the discussion of the influence of marketing techniques on purchasers, people were asked to assess the level of help they had received from salespeople. At this juncture almost two-thirds, 62 per cent, acknowledged they had some sales help as opposed to 36 per cent who said they had had none. When asked how this influenced them, however, just 7 per cent said sales advice had made a considerable difference to their choice of furniture. In contrast, 35 per cent said they had listened to what sales staff had to say but had then made up their own minds while 45 per cent said they had made their choice with no help from sales staff. A residue, 14 per cent, gave motley answers to this question which could not be categorised.

This question tapped somewhat different information from the earlier one about contact with sales staff. But inconsistencies between the answers would have suggested that people, consciously or unconsciously, were failing to acknowledge certain cross-pressures shaping their behaviour. If one compares the answers to these two questions, however, there is no obvious inconsistency between them which would seriously cast doubt on respondents' own claims that they made an independent choice of kitchen furniture. This offers some support for the claim many respondents were emphatic about, that they were not dependent on others for reaching a decision but made their own minds up. Though willing to acknowledge they had received advice from sales staff and had listened to what they had to say, almost all were clear, indeed insistent, in stressing that the final decision about what to buy was their own. While this might not constitute incontrovertible proof that respondents acted independently, it is hard to argue for not taking respondents' claims at face value in the absence of evidence which clearly casts doubt upon such claims.

Pursuing the issue of respondent independence in the face of marketing pressures, respondents were asked how much attention they gave to fashion when choosing their new furniture (table 5.4). The bulk of

**Table 5.4** *Attention given to fashion by purchasers of new kitchens*

| Attention given to fashion | No | % |
|---|---|---|
| None | 64 | 86 |
| Some | 5 | 7 |
| Considered it important | 1 | 1 |
| Other/no ans. | 4 | 5 |
| Total | 74 | 100 |

respondents, 86 per cent, denied that fashion had played any part in their choice of furniture, often very emphatically. Just 7 per cent said they had given it some consideration and one person said they thought it important. Those who said that they had not considered fashion when they were choosing their kitchen, not infrequently gave a reason for this, namely, that they were spending a lot of money so whatever they bought would have to last a long time. It was not uncommon for people to believe they would never buy another kitchen in their lives. One effect of this was to make some people anxious to select a style they thought would not date too quickly. Some therefore described how they actively sought to avoid selecting a style they thought might just be a short-term fashion in favour of what they referred to as 'classic' styles.[4]

The National Shoppers Survey quoted earlier stated clearly that manufacturers were eager to penetrate the world of popular taste and cater to it. The subsequent examination of the influence of sales pressures on the sample in this study did not produce evidence which challenged this. The *raison d'être* of commercial companies is to make a profit, and there was evidence that kitchen furniture retailers were keen to provide consumers with the kind of goods they wanted in the interests of realising this goal.

The consumer has power. Supporting evidence for this statement was gathered by establishing contact with one of the biggest retailers of kitchen furniture, who produced a wealth of information including the description of a slate of techniques they used to find out what customers were looking for. Not only did this firm administer large sample surveys with great regularity, they were also instituting focus-group discussions on the kind of kitchens people wanted. They invited me to one of these. It was held in the evening, requiring the firm's staff to work unsocial hours. The staff sat in a separate room, where the focus-group discussion was relayed to them on television. Their running commentary on what they saw and heard showed how seriously the collection of customer opinion was taken. The fact, for example, that their own tastes and preferences were often at considerable variance with those of their purchasers was allowed, albeit sometimes with reluctance, to carry very little weight as they considered the implications of what they were seeing and hearing for the selection of future furniture designs. The firm also maintained a detailed and regularly updated record of the furniture styles which sold best, as a guide for deciding which styles to discontinue and which to develop. It will also be remembered, from the account of the history of the fitted kitchen, that Féjer (1984) acknowledged the importance of designing things that would sell.

Undoubtedly, of course, such companies are also proactive and assertive in their attempts to make sales and to this end employ a variety of promotional materials and devices with the aim of extending consumers' desires and encouraging them to buy. All the major kitchen furniture retailers produce full-colour catalogues and many manufacturers and retailers advertise, in addition, in the glossy house and garden magazines. As buyers of new kitchens, respondents were therefore asked to read four short examples of brochure writing. Three of the examples are reproduced here though, proper nouns have been changed.

> The graceful use of beautifully carved panels, combined with the light yet enchanting honey oak coloured finish, makes the Canterbury kitchen the pride and joy of many fine homes.

> The stylish, pewter effect centred handles and the excellent choice of accessories gives this exquisite kitchen that time honoured look of celebrated period furniture; a look that has stood the test of time and graced the very best kitchens throughout the ages.

> 'I, too, am a painter!' With Meyer kitchens everyone can become a painter as Correggio said. The Meyer palette puts fourteen colours at your disposal to meet your personal taste.

Respondents were then asked whether they found this kind of information useful or not. Table 5.5 below shows the overall distribution of their answers.

**Table 5.5** *Buyers' opinion of manufacturers' copy*

| Buyers' opinion of copy | No. | % |
| --- | --- | --- |
| Helpful | 1 | 1 |
| Occasionally useful | 12 | 16 |
| Dismissive of it, e.g. 'a bit OTT' | 50 | 68 |
| Contemptuous of it, e.g. 'hogwash' | 10 | 14 |
| No ans./other | 1 | 1 |
| Total | 74 | 100 |

Just 1 per cent said they thought copy of this kind was helpful and a further 16 per cent were prepared to consider that copy of this kind was sometimes helpful, though their responses were often lukewarm. Two examples suffice to illustrate the tone which coloured answers in this second category. One woman said she would read the manufacturers' copy:

> If you like the picture. If you didn't like the picture I wouldn't read [the text]. I know what I want exactly. No-one would be able to flannel round me and think I would change my mind . . . (c. 8, soc. cl. B)[5]

Another respondent in this category commented:

> It's quite descriptive, if you hadn't got a picture. (c. 47, soc. cl. C2)

There was a different and commoner response to this question, however. Respondents took the quotations and read the first few words. Then as they began to size up the tone of the writing, they stopped and, with a little gesture of irritation, such as a shrug of the shoulder or sweep of the hand, handed the cards back without bothering to read the rest. Where their words complemented these gestures such responses were coded as 'dismissive'. This category of answers accounted for over two-thirds of the replies to this question. The following quotations give an indication of the flavour of this category of answers:

> I lose interest. They annoy me. It's bad enough listening to the salesman's chit-chat. They put you off more than persuade you to buy them. (c. 5, soc. cl. B)
> Too flowery. You get bored before you get to the end. (c. 16, soc. cl. C2)
> I wouldn't take any notice of that at all. All vague opinion as far as I'm concerned.
> (c. 45, soc. cl. C1)
> A load of old waffle. I just gloss through things like this. (c. 55, soc. cl. B)

Some people responded more dramatically than this. They tautened visibly or began to gesture assertively, and a separate coding category, which had not initially been planned, was introduced for them. This new category finally accounted for 14 per cent of respondents. People were allocated to this category, however, not because of their body language, compelling though that often was, but because of their verbal language. This meant that a number of respondents whose physical reactions might have put them in this category were excluded from it. In verbal communication, however, words are quotable while gestures are only describable. This gives words a hard-edged quality as evidence which, at least in verbal forms of communication, gestures lack. This category of response therefore covered people who did not just angrily dismiss the publicity material they were offered but felt a need to be verbally abusive about what they read. Responses were thus allocated to this category if they included words like 'hogwash' and 'crap' or sexual expletives which were, if possible, even stronger.

Men were more inclined to use such language, often to the embarrassment of their wives, who sometimes felt driven to remonstrate or intervene with comments like 'John! You shouldn't say words like that in front of the lady' and 'Oh, I do apologise for my husband saying things like that.' A number of respondents might therefore have toned down their answers to this question from a sense of what was polite in front of a visitor. If we put these last two categories together, 81 per cent, or four-fifths, of respondents uncompromisingly rejected the idea that the advertising copy of kitchen manufacturers was of any use or value. Responses did not vary by social class.

Given the amount of money and time companies spend on market research, one question these responses raise is why manufacturers and retailers have such copy written. They all do, however. Of the three examples quoted here, two come from the economy and one from the luxury end of the market. It was not just that such sales talk failed to have a positive impact: more often it appeared to have a negative impact and to generate active hostility.

These responses also raise questions about the value of some academic analyses of the language of advertising. This study suggests that, left to their own devices, people frequently refuse to read advertising. Furthermore, when they do read it, it often provokes sneers and anger. In considering textual analyses of advertisers' copy, one needs to ask, therefore, just what is being analysed and exactly what can be deduced from such analyses. Whatever it is, it is not clear that it tells us anything about consumers' responses.

Apart from retailers and manufacturers, the glossy house magazines also regularly produce both feature articles and other pieces of writing giving advice to people who are considering or in the throes of choosing a new kitchen, about design, layout and other aspects of setting up a kitchen. Among the sample 16 per cent bought one of these magazines regularly and a further 20 per cent bought them occasionally or when they were actually working on their homes. Almost two-thirds, 61 per cent, never bought one. People who never bought a magazine might, of course, still see one from time to time, if only at the dentist's or hairdresser's. So, though 61 per cent never bought a magazine, a much smaller proportion of the sample, 31 per cent, said they never looked at such magazines. In one way or another a substantial proportion of the sample, 67 per cent, thus looked at glossy house magazines, at least occasionally. It is therefore worth briefly considering what kind of coverage such magazines give to kitchens.

One common feature article in the glossies is the photo survey of 'interesting' houses. These cover a wide range of houses, including modern architecturally innovative houses for individual clients, the redeployment of other kinds of building such as old schools, chapels or windmills as houses, and houses from different historical periods. The text tells the reader, in the case of an old building, what the place was like before refurbishment and then recounts the changes the present owners have made. In the case of the specially commissioned modern house we are told what the owners wanted and how they aimed to get this. Such articles are a form of socially respectable voyeurism in which the present house owners, though more particularly the women, act almost as host-esses to the magazine reader. The houses in such features are often beyond the means of many of the readers. Large country cottages in idyllic rural settings have, certainly in the past, appeared far more often in the pages of these glossies than Edwardian terraced houses in modest urban streets. Some magazines, however, are now giving more attention to how one can do up relatively cheap little houses. Some run series on this subject. And most recently television has caught on to the idea that viewers are interested in refurbished modest domestic interiors. When the research began, such programmes were virtually unknown. Now they are increas-ing rapidly, with several being shown every week.[6] Clearly audience figures are encouraging.

Both looking through the houses of the well-off and following the way a first-time buy can be made into a bright, fresh home can start up ideas in people's minds as to what they might do in their own houses. And they do so without making people feel they are being put under pressure in any way. Thus, while 35 per cent of the sample said they had consulted magazines prior to buying in comparison with 64 per cent who said they had not bothered with magazines, it remains hard to know how many people might have gleaned ideas about possible kitchen layouts and designs in a desultory, casual way from magazines, given that two-thirds of the sample looked at magazines occasionally. What was clear was that magazine copy did not cause the offence brochure blurb caused. But this does not tell us anything about the breadth or depth of its impact on people in terms of their design preferences and interests.

What we can be more precise about is that when people first embarked on looking for a kitchen just over a third, 34 per cent, said they had already developed definite ideas about what they wanted, and just under a quarter, 24 per cent, had a vague or general idea. Over half therefore had picked up or developed some ideas about design before they went to a retailer and started on the course of information collection and viewing which has been described earlier in this chapter. Another third, however, had no preconceived ideas at that juncture as to what they wanted and were uncommitted to any style. This did not mean that the selection of a style was not important to these buyers, simply that they followed a different route in choosing one.

Style, as opposed to fashion, was a matter of considerable concern to almost everyone. In the sample as a whole only 4 per cent said they thought price more important than style. Yet style was not the only factor people took into account when choosing their furniture. Durability was also important. Asked about the importance they placed on the durability of what they bought, the largest category by far is those who were emphatic that durability and style were equally important (table 5.6). The other large category is respondents who assumed that what they bought would be hard-wearing. Two points can be made about these responses.

**Table 5.6** *Importance placed on durability by purchasers of new furniture*

| Importance of durability | No. | % |
|---|---|---|
| More important than style | 4 | 5.5 |
| Equally important as style | 37 | 50 |
| Less important than style | 6 | 8 |
| Didn't think about it | 6 | 8 |
| Assumed durability of furniture would be high | 17 | 23 |
| No ans./other | 4 | 5.5 |
| Total | 74 | 100 |

Over the last decade market researchers have charted the increased sale of British-made kitchen furniture in this country, together with a decline in the sale of middle-priced foreign-made furniture. Even the sale of top-of-the-market, foreign-made kitchen units has declined. Market researchers attribute this increased sale of British-made goods to two things: improvements in its manufacture, and the help now available to buyers for erecting flat packs and for installing kitchen furniture generally. Most retailers now provide both a pre-sales planning service and an after-sales installation service, which they have been at pains to make efficient. One very large shed will give a price discount if they make an incorrect or late delivery. But, whatever the reason, the reputation of the British for producing quality goods in this field appears to have risen markedly in the home market over the last few years. We have already seen that the sample made extensive use of the planning services retailers provided. It seems reasonable therefore to take the 23 per cent of respondents who said that they took for granted that any furniture they bought would be well made at face value.

If we do this we find that almost three-quarters of the sample valued durability equally with style. This indirectly adds support to another earlier finding. People had overwhelmingly denied that they took fashion into account when buying their new kitchens. If, despite what they said, fashion was, in fact, important to people, one wonders if they would have placed quite so much emphasis on durability. If their aim was to stay even reasonably abreast of fashion, they would surely expect to restyle their kitchens within a time span that would make the question of the durability of what they bought now, not trivial, but probably of secondary importance.

This concludes the first stage of the report on how the general public goes about buying a new kitchen. It was emphasised that this study laid no claim to assessing the general impact of advertising on people. That is a large and multi-faceted field, going well beyond the remit here. This study has confined itself to looking at how buyers respond to the selling tactics they are confronted with in one particular corner of the market. Though some guesses might be made on the basis of this study about buyer behaviour in some neighbouring parts of the market, no general-isations about the public's response to advertising and marketing as a whole can be made.

With regard to the kitchen furniture market, however, this chapter has shown buyers evincing a discriminating approach which did not vary by social class. Though they by no means eschew the marketing ploys kitchen firms employ, it seems fair, on the evidence, to say that they use them rather than being swept along by them. The tenor of these buyers' behaviour suggests a reasoned, thoughtful approach to the purchase of a new kitchen. There is little support for the concept of 'the masses' or 'mass behaviour'. In summary, these respondents appeared to exercise a significant degree of independence within the market-place. Their behaviour did not support the image of an easily manipulated, non-rational herd.

One thing this chapter has not given attention to is the visual and aesthetic tastes of these buyers. There is a long history of intellectual concern about the public's aesthetic preferences. Various intellectual coteries have seen popular preferences as banal, conservative and unimaginative and have worried accordingly. This issue will be returned to and addressed. Before that, however, the question of the role gender plays during the course of the purchase of a new kitchen will be considered.

## Notes

1. Mintel (1992) *Special Report on Kitchen Furniture*. In 1992 Mintel calculated that 66% of households had fitted kitchens, 25% a mixture of fitted and unfitted and 7% non-fitted units only. The next special report on kitchen furniture in 1996, however, reported the number of households with fitted kitchens as 60%. No explanation is offered for this decline and it is hard to know what to make of it. However, Mintel also reported that people with basically fitted kitchens were also buying pieces of free-standing furniture specifically for the kitchen such as pine tables and dressers and butcher's blocks for food preparation. But they say this buying was not taken account of in the general statistics for the purchase of fitted kitchens. At the same time the number of individual households is increasing. By 1998 Mintel reports that overall levels of fitted kitchens are now pretty static at 62%. With these kinds of market research figures one can use them to indicate general trends only.
2. This kind of exercise enjoyed a considerable intellectual vogue at one time. As cited earlier, a classic example of a book based on this approach was Williamson (1980).
3. Isenstadt (1998), as noted earlier, offers a recent example of the now generally outmoded fashion for using old adverts to deduce the buyers' state of mind.
4. Design historians, of course, might prefer to call such styles cautious or conservative but the argument here is not about value judgements.

5. The notation (c. 8 soc. cl. B ) stands for case no. 8, social class B, using the Market Research classification system. This pattern of abbreviation is used throughout. It is also worth noting that none of the quotations were selected on the basis of the social class of the respondent. They were always selected for their content. This makes any similarities between the responses of the different social classes more significant, because they were not being looked for.

6. A quick glance at the *Radio Times* for any given evening shows how very numerous programmes about the home are becoming. Ten years ago there would be just an occasional one. Now it not unusual for there to be as many as eight or ten programmes a week on channels one to five. They cover almost every aspect of the home, buying, selling, building, interior décor, maintaining, modifying and the history of domestic living. Not all these programmes deal with modest homes, though many do. Other programmes deal with a mixture of large and small homes. Alongside the programmes on homes, the number of programmes on domestic gardens has also increased hugely.

# –6–

# Gender and the acquisition of a
# new kitchen

So far the analysis of buyers' behaviour has not discriminated between that of men and women. Attention now turns to this. The domestic kitchen has long been popularly perceived as a predominantly feminine domain, as women's territory. Historically, however, rather than women's possession of a special expertise in the domestic field enhancing their status, the low status from which women have suffered has been used to devalue domestic skills by association. Thus, instead of women's domestic skills earning for them a recognised area of social authority, these skills have been taken as an indication of women's lack of ability, and even of their incompetence in other social spheres. The paucity of historical, empirical or logical support for this position has attracted little scrutiny and one suspects that the real support for the argument has been a masculine concern to protect male privilege. Certainly there seems to have been little interest in trying to make a disinterested determination of the issue.[1]

This attitude to domestic work has had a spin-off. The early suffragettes, engaged in the difficult task of challenging male privilege, including the right to enter the male professions, were driven to see the feminine world of housekeeping and other domestic skills as hampering women in their campaign for equality. Progressive women put their energies into acquiring new skills and new occupations rather than insisting that domestic skills be given proper recognition for the contribution they made to social life or demanding that within the domestic arena women were given the financial wherewithal to enable them to run it independently.

For a while in the 1920s and 1930s kitchen design, as described in chapter 2, was caught up with campaigns for social and political change. But it was a brief affair. Thus, though in technological and design terms the fitted kitchen has been a radical and challenging invention, in social terms it has had a very different history. The push for fitted kitchens during the twentieth century has never been a significant part of the campaign for women's equality.

One could go further and argue that for considerable periods the development of the fitted kitchen has been interwoven with a campaign to keep women in their place. In return for the relief from drudgery, and often dirty drudgery, which the modern high-tech fitted kitchen offers, women have frequently been expected to channel more time and effort into performing their traditional roles of wife and mother. Relief from drudgery was never, from the beginning, seriously linked to a programme designed to encourage women to enter the job market.[2]

Charlotte Beecher, whose ideas helped to initiate the idea of the fitted kitchen, was, as has been shown, a conservative. She helped, indeed, to ensure that the formulation of such recognition as women were accorded for their domestic skills was widely conceptualised, right into the twentieth century, in terms of women fulfilling their God-given respons-ibilities. And neither among the suffragettes nor among the bulk of more conventional women was there generally any will for, or interest in, describing the contribution women made to society through their domestic activity in a way which would have incorporated and acknowledged that activity as an integral part of the body politic.[3] The way the conceptual distinction between the public and private arenas in social life was drawn from the middle of the nineteenth century until very recently, when a number of feminists began to recognise it as a major theoretical problem which they needed to address, also constituted a major intellectual barrier to doing this.

Christine Frederick's attitudes were more complex politically than Charlotte Beecher's. But she too must ultimately be classed as a con-servative. With her idea of scientific management for the home Christine Frederick might have encouraged a reappraisal of the idea that the kitchen was simply a site of female oppression had she possessed a more refined social or political awareness. As it was she lacked the necessary analytical social perspective which could have led her to invest her ideas with a political content which would have drawn her into mainstream political activity in terms of the campaign for female equality. In political terms she is slightly comical with her talk of 'a great band of women investigators'[4] and her very considerable number of followers was made up of basically conventional, non-political women, respectable readers of ladies' maga-zines. What they were primarily interested in were easier and pleasanter ways of coping with domestic chores and running a house, not seriously challenging the status accorded to traditional gender roles.

Because Christine Frederick always remained politically superficial, her ideas were vulnerable to conservative appropriation. When, as was described in chapter 2, male trade unionists, fearful of female competition, sought to limit the entry of women into the workforce on equal terms, her ideas proved tailor-made for incorporation into a revisionist ideology, which posited a fundamental separation between the domestic and political spheres in social life and which argued for the importance of women concentrating on activities in the private domestic sphere so as to meet the social need for better wives and mothers. Her thinking offered no serious intellectual resistance to the abandonment by official socialism of the earlier socialist concept of a woman's right to work, in favour of reformist goals which concentrated on the, undoubtedly important but ultimately gender-biased, attempt to make women's domestic round easier. Like Charlotte Beecher before her, Christine Frederick's ideas ultimately became part of the process of ensuring that any politically radical ideas which might have informed the new innovative ideas about kitchen design would disappear.

Meanwhile, the bulk of conventional womanhood had largely continued to conduct their domestic lives as before and society continued to take for granted the huge benefits derived from the domestic comforts women created on a daily basis. The effect of this was profound. Despite the fact that the First World War saw a significant breakthrough in the suffragettes' campaign for votes for women and both world wars significantly affected patterns of domestic life and altered the nature of the domestic responsibilities men and women carried, people by and large quickly reverted to old patterns of domestic conduct once war ended.

In addition, though women were now voters and it might be thought they therefore needed civic experience and understanding if they were to use their vote wisely, the British government gave higher priority after the Second World War to getting women out of the workforce so as to create vacancies for men returning from the army. The spread of the fitted kitchen in American homes facilitated by the huge American economic boom of the 1950s similarly coincided with a post-Second World War push on the part of the American government to force women employed as part of the war effort back into domesticity so as to release work for men returning to civilian life.[5] This meant that, when the increase in fitted kitchens in England occurred a decade later, it was simply perceived as just another aspect of the general improvement in the standard of living in post-war Britain and its possible potential for freeing women to strive towards greater political and social equality was ignored. The development of the fitted kitchen forms no chapter in the history of radical feminism. As far as kitchens are concerned, innovative design and political conservatism have long operated in comfortable partnership.

The campaign to get women back into the home was further boosted by a new school of psychologists in the post-Second World War years, who preached the importance of mother–child bonding in early infancy, schematically and dogmatically.[6] The subsequent cult of modern motherhood dramatically played out, during the 1950s, in millions of American homes, but on this side of the Atlantic too, as an expression of high-minded idealism was in fact inextricably intertwined with political expediency and gave rise to a new wave of conservatism, as far as women were concerned, in both post-war Britain and America. Female reaction to this came in the mid-1960s with Betty Friedan's[7] energetic broadside against the impact of these post-Second World War psychological theories and the cult of stifling domesticity they had imposed on a whole generation of both working- and middle-class American women.

In the rebellious political activity of the 1960s, therefore, the home understandably came to be seen, once again, as a major source of women's continuing oppression. Friedan's *The Feminine Mystique* became a seminal text in the new feminist movement, which burgeoned during the 1970s and produced a spate of journalistic and academic writing as well as political polemics. The view of domestic life depicted in much of this, often angry, writing coloured the study and analysis of domestic life. In this atmosphere it was hard to laud the home as a site where women could display applaudable skills, an impressive efficiency and a valuable creativity.

On the academic front Ann Oakley's book *The Sociology of Housework*[8] appeared in England in 1974 and immediately became a key text in the new scholarly writing about women. Oakley found that 70 per cent of women were 'dissatisfied' with housework, three-quarters found it monotonous and loneliness was a frequent complaint. Her findings suggested that, in the domestic sphere, women as a whole were very little better off than they had been prior to gaining the vote and that personal autonomy continued to evade them in what might be regarded as being their own special sphere. The world of domesticity seemed to have little to offer a lively independent-minded woman. It is noteworthy, however, that Oakley found it difficult to devise a typology of marriages which coherently related participants' perception of how responsibilities were allocated with the chores participants undertook, a point to which this chapter will return.

The follow-up on Oakley was desultory until 1989 when Jan Pahl's *Money and Marriage*[9] appeared. Pahl had been struck by the continued neglect, both academically and commercially, since Oakley, of economic behaviour within households and sought to open the subject up for analysis again. She argued reasonably that to achieve any purchase on the problem of measuring the distribution of power empirically within a household one had to start with some categorisation of domestic arrangements. She also recognised, however, that changes had occurred in the management of domestic life and that the way couples now managed their household finances was hugely varied. She thus set about constructing a more refined typology of households than Oakley had used. One problem she faced, however, was that she also wanted to keep it sufficiently simple for her to highlight differences in financial management by type of household arrangement. This was further complicated when she found that how people described the way they handled money was deeply coloured by their views on marriage. In other words answers were as ideological as factual, sometimes more so.

This important breakthrough in an understanding of marital relationships came as a result of Pahl's imaginative interviewing technique. She interviewed couples first together and then separately. This threw up a group in which answers changed significantly when people were interviewed separately. Thus there were 14 couples where 12 of the 14 said money decisions were joint ones when they were interviewed together but when they were interviewed separately it emerged that the wife's decisions carried much more weight.[10] In addition to this, however, Pahl devised seven questions about specific incidences of household expenditure and family decision-making with the aim of discovering whose voice carried most weight. These produced evidence to show that control over household finances widely continued to lie ultimately with the men of the house. The male voice continued to dominate, not just about buying a car but about buying a washing-machine. Many women were also expected to make their household allowance go further than it could reasonably be expected to and it was left to them to deal with this. Findings were therefore mixed. Nevertheless, the idea of joint decision-making was growing, and Pahl's data suggested a further exploration and discussion of the allocation of financial responsibility within households and the practice of 'joint' decision-making would be worthwhile.

The next analysis of household expenditure was Heather Laurie's, completed in 1996.[11] This study found the increased incidence of women bringing a significant income into the household further changing and complicating the picture of financial decision-making within marriage. One area of domestic finance of interest to this study which Laurie explored, however, was personal spending by men and women within a partnership. Revealingly, she found the mean spending money for men in her sample was over 37 per cent more than that for women. Yet, despite this, she found that women, particularly non-working women, were still much more likely to feel embarrassed and guilty about personal spending than their menfolk, and that men, and some women, often described women's personal spending as 'waste' and 'extravagance'.

This is not to say that women felt guilty about spending generally. But Laurie had access to focus-group data which indicated that people justified spending from household funds by reference to what the money was spent on. This showed that women were inclined to enjoy spending most easily and frankly when it was for the house and the children. Laurie saw this not only as reflecting the continued gendering of different areas of responsibility within adult partnerships but as a continuing denial in material terms of the social autonomy of women.

These studies paint a picture of shifting relationships between men and women in terms of the management of domestic expenditure over the last few decades, including the gradual introduction of a new ideology about the division of domestic responsibilities. But all these authors also show that old habits die hard, women continue to have less free cash and feel more guilty about spending on themselves than do their male partners.

Furthermore the picture these studies present is that women find housekeeping tedious. In addition, many women seem to exist on the brink of anxiety, sometimes even fear, with regard to the handling of household money, and, very importantly, women always appear to be the ultimate losers with regard to spending the money which comes into the home from one source or another. One feature of these studies is their success in revealing numerous little ways by which, despite various changes in domestic norms and values, current domestic decision-making conventions insidiously continue to disempower women.

These findings are consistent with the account of the history of the reform of kitchen design presented in chapter 2 and one must applaud these studies and acknowledge the insights they provide. Conducted over a period of time and highly professional in their collection of data, they make an important contribution to our understanding of the persistence of gender inequalities today within the domestic realm. I want to insert a proviso nevertheless. Despite their undoubted professionalism, I want to argue that there is something missing from these accounts.

To achieve a proper understanding of women's achievements and skills historically, women's history must embrace more than the history of the public fight for formal equality for women. A hugely important, much under-reported and still very under-written chapter of women's history, it nevertheless remains only one strand of that history. Other equally important strands of feminine history exist, strands furthermore which, in terms of recording the history of women, almost certainly reflect the lives of far larger numbers of women than the radical feminist strand.

To develop our appreciation of the role women have played in our society we need to find a way of marrying the sociological findings on household budgeting with the work on women and consumption, touched on in chapter 1. It is a commonly taken-for-granted assumption of both research and theory in the field of consumption that women have long controlled and shaped the domestic interior.[12] The household budget studies cited here make clear, however, that any unqualified assumption that women command or have commanded historically the financial means necessary to exercise such control is unwarranted. That studies in consumption characteristically neither address nor problematise the adage and commonly made assumption, 'Consumption thy name is Woman', must be considered a weakness.[13] The question is whether a more nuanced conceptualisation of women's history would enable us to make these different bodies of research complementary rather than contradictory.

The concept of feminine opportunism might help. While avoiding any overt challenge to their conventional role and concomitantly laying themselves open to possible public opprobrium, women as a social group have long been extremely adept at maximising the degree of comfort, convenience and freedom they enjoy.[14] The female population has historically developed within itself a mass of finely tuned skills for capitalising on any opportunity which occurs for improving the material and social conditions of their lives, together with a nice sensitivity about when and how to exploit these skills within the framework of marriage.

Some women are past mistresses of such activity. Rosamund in *Middlemarch* is a superb fictional example, a major triumph of literary invention. In Rosamund George Eliot combines a winsome manner and delicate beauty with an indomitable determination to maximise every opportunity for bettering her material and social position that becomes available. This is portrayed as a hugely powerful admixture which Rosamund exploits with great natural but also growing skill. There is never any doubt about who overwhelmingly dominates in her marriage. At the end of the novel we hear that 'Rosamund . . . continued to be mild in her temper, inflexible in her judgement, disposed to admonish her husband, and able to frustrate him by stratagem.'[15] It is a spare but highly convincing closing description, and one reason it convinces is that, although Rosamund is an extreme example, she displays a recognisable feminine way of dealing with the world which, in a franker, gentler and less selfish form, remains widespread. And Rosamund is far from being the only literary example one could cite. Novels alone are a rich archive of information about the way

women historically have quietly found ways of challenging their traditional second-class status.[16] Some women fail to learn these opportunistic
skills, of course, and some women live out their lives as drudges. Yet even
female drudges are often less compliant and take advantage of such
opportunities as offer to assert themselves more frequently than their
menfolk imagine.[17]

Another aspect of the sociological research cited above which we need
to examine further is the idea that women experience housekeeping as
overwhelmingly about the endless performance of tedious, repetitive
chores and putting others first. Undoubtedly housework may often seem
dominated by dreary and boring routines and undoubtedly most women
periodically groan about it, and few but the most privileged women can
have escaped the feeling from time to time of being at the beck and call
of every other member of the family. One's general experience, however,
suggests strongly that this is not the whole story of housework, that, for
many women, there are also strong positive aspects to housekeeping. It is
true Oakley acknowledged that for some women the sense of autonomy
they got from being a housewife was a positive feature of housework. To
suggest, however, as Laurie does, that when a woman enjoys buying for
the home we need to understand this as satisfaction by default, that is, a
satisfaction derived from a sense of serving others rather than a satisfaction based primarily on the realisation of an independent sense of self,
is ideologically tidy but too simplistic. The contention here is that buying
something for one's home can be just as satisfying for many women as
buying a dress: indeed, it can be deeply fulfilling. And this remains true
even if conventional mores continue to make buying for the home less
socially problematic for women than buying for oneself.

D.H. Lawrence offers a compelling and convincing account of how
significant buying for the home could be. In *Sons and Lovers* he captures
its importance for a woman's construction of a sense of self with heart-
churning nicety in his description of Mrs Morel's overwhelming desire for
a little fruit dish she sees in the market. Try as she might to drag herself
away from the dish Mrs Morel cannot leave the market until she has
bought it, which she manages with a splendid cold, calculating skill, to
ensure she gets it at a good price. And few women can have experienced
a more piercing delight as they smoothed or fondled the fabric of a new
dress than Lawrence attributes to Mrs Morel when, back in her kitchen,
she takes the fruit dish from its newspaper wrapping and gorges her eyes
on its pattern. Though both her daughter and her son chide her about her
shabby bonnet, she dismisses out of hand their pleas to do something
about it. For her, acquiring the little fruit dish is much more important than

smartening up her hat.[18] It is also quite clear that Mrs Morel buys the fruit dish for herself, no-one else. Though a fictional account the buying of the fruit dish is convincing and the emotions Lawrence describes Mrs Morel experiencing must surely have sparked off for many women feelings of complicity with her.

In addition, women have increasingly established themselves during the course of the twentieth century as the experts on home-making. Literature again alerts us to this change. In *A Room with a View,* first published in 1908, there is a moment when Mrs Honeychurch, the unassuming widow of a respectable local solicitor, exasperated by the intellectual superciliousness of her future son-in-law, turns to her daughter and says with asperity: 'No doubt I am neither artistic nor literary nor intellectual nor musical, but I cannot help the drawing room furniture: your father bought it and we must put up with it, will Cecil kindly re-member.'[19] Taking into account the proliferation of magazine articles on decorating the home directed at women at the turn of the twentieth century, one suspects that many women were taking a more active role in setting up a home than Mrs Honeychurch. The point, however, is that Mrs Honeychurches still existed at that time while it is impossible to imagine a novel, film or television play today containing lines like these. Men no longer choose the furniture. Popular opinion, indeed, now judges it proper that a woman should have the best kitchen to which the household budget can rise and kitchen advertisers today direct much of their publicity at women. One thing this study aims to consider, therefore, is the role and influence of women during the purchase of a new kitchen, including the social implications of the part they play and the effect of this on kitchen design.

In terms of both the management of money and the recognition of areas of authority between men and women, the data presented in this chapter shows that it is now a distortion to characterise the management of domestic expenditure in any simple way as a male remit. With regard to formal parity of power and control between partners in our society, a great deal still remains to be done, and we need to acknowledge and be alert to this. Studies of the management of household expenditure of the kind described earlier have had, and will continue to have, an important role on this front. However, patterns of power and control in adult domestic partnerships are commonly the outcome of a series of apparently minor negotiations regarding relatively small issues and have become highly complicated. The result is that there is more to celebrate in terms of women's achievement of certain kinds of reciprocity in the allocation of monetary resources within the household, as also in the extent of tacit or even open male acknowledgement of women's skills, than is always conceded by the kind of feminist analysis which is concerned primarily with the attainment of gender equality in terms of formal arrangements.

Against this background this chapter turns to explore the allocation of responsibility and control between men and women over monetary expenditure and the selection of goods as they embark on choosing the style of their new kitchen furniture. Such a bias has not had priority in the current anthropological and historical work being done on the construction of domestic interiors.[20] So, in tracing this, this study will help to fill a gap in the research.

Three simple questions were put to all main respondents who lived with a partner as part of establishing just how decisions about the choice and spending of money on kitchen furniture were made within households. The first question asked whether both partners were equally interested in what was bought or whether one was more interested than the other and, if so, whether the more interested person was the man or the woman (table 6.1). The second question asked whether collecting

**Table 6.1** *Who was most interested in what kitchen furniture was selected**

| Person most interested | No. | % |
|---|---|---|
| Both equally interested | 41 | 55 |
| Woman more interested | 24 | 33 |
| NA/other/no ans. | 9 | 12 |
| Total | 74 | 100 |

* If one removes the 6 people living on their own from the residual category of 9 in this table, the equally interested group accounts for 60% of the sample for whom the question was relevant.

information about kitchen furniture currently on the market was done predominantly by the man or the woman, or whether the work was shared (table 6.2). The last question asked whether the final decision about what

**Table 6.2** *Who took responsibility for collecting information about kitchen furniture*

| Responsibility for collection | No. | % |
|---|---|---|
| Predominantly the man | 12 | 16 |
| Predominantly the woman | 19 | 26 |
| Work shared | 33 | 45 |
| NA/other/no ans. | 10 | 13 |
| Total | 74 | 100 |

was bought was the man's, the woman's or whether the decision was a joint one (table 6.3).

**Table 6.3** *Who finally decided what would be bought*

| Who made final decision | No. | % |
|---|---|---|
| Joint decision | 45 | 61 |
| Man | 7 | 9 |
| Woman | 12 | 16 |
| NA/other/no ans. | 10 | 13 |
| Total | 74 | 100 |

The answers suggest that interest was overwhelmingly shared, though, where it was not shared, women were more interested and active on these fronts than men. In answering these questions, however, many respondents did not just nominate a code. They frequently made additional comments which expanded and elaborated on the code. These comments were re-corded and subsequently analysed separately.

This subsequent analysis rendered any simple reading of the three preceding tables impossible and supported Jan Pahl's suggestion that the answers people give to questions about domestic partnerships can be suffused with strong ideological colouring. The analysis of these comments also revealed that the word 'joint' is understood in significantly differently ways by different people. This was so striking that I decided to produce a formal definition of the term 'joint' and, using this definition, do a second coding of this question.

The new definition of 'joint' no longer covered respondents who thought (or perhaps wished, or found it convenient, to think) of the process of buying new kitchen furniture as being something they did in a general, but not clearly formulated, way with their partners. The term was now made to refer specifically to who made the aesthetic decisions. To put it another way, the question was now about who selected the design or style of the furniture bought. As the main determining factor of the final appearance and ambience of the kitchen, this is, in most cases, probably the most important decision purchasers make when buying a new kitchen. The effect of this new definition was to produce a much more nuanced picture of how men and women sharing a home today conduct themselves towards each other in terms of one form of high domestic expenditure. Running through the description of the new coding categories is an account both of the persistence of certain traditional gender roles and of changing and developing patterns of behaviour among men and women. The picture of couple behaviour thrown up is complex, not a simple account of the persistence of male control and domination over household finances.

Traditional male and female roles had not disappeared within the sample. What the data derived from the new coding threw into relief, however, were numerous variants of what was earlier termed feminine opportunism. The feminine ability to utilise to the full, and often with minimum fuss, any opportunity which presented for them to take on major decision-making roles in the material construction of domestic space was widespread and well-established. Other women consciously contrived situations to give them this decision-making power. The data repeatedly confirmed the considerable ability of conventional, non-political women to exploit a range of skills and devices which ensured they got the kitchens they wanted, with or without their menfolks' compliance. What also emerged from the accounts respondents gave of choosing furniture were numerous descriptions of women overseeing household expenditure, directly and openly or indirectly and circuitously. This happened regardless of social class. Class was not a significant variable.

Respondents who, on recoding, continued to be allocated to the category of 'joint' decision-makers now had to have proffered answers to this question which included some concrete backing for their claim that the choice of design or style was a matter of equal and active interest to both parties. It did, however, also include five respondents who claimed their decisions were joint but then volunteered no further information so there was no evidence to counter their claim. This produced a new picture of the role women played in the selection of a new kitchen (table 6.4).

**Table 6.4** *Recoding of question asking who finally decided what would be bought*

| Responsibility for final decision | No. | % |
| --- | --- | --- |
| Joint decision plus 5 for whom no evidence to the contrary | 16 | 22 |
| Man | 7 | 9 |
| Woman | 43 | 58 |
| NA/other/no ans. | 8 | 11 |
| Total | 74 | 100 |

Answers which continued to be classified as 'joint' decisions under this new definition still displayed a range of responses. In one case the wife wanted a new kitchen and the husband suggested that, as he had an insurance policy close to maturity, they wait until the end of the year when the money became available and then spend it on a kitchen, which they did. His wife then laughed and said, 'After that the arguments began' (c. 40, soc. cl. D). The decision-making here seemed a matter of genuine interest to both parties and the final choice the product of energetic negotiation. There was also a couple where the wife had wanted a clothes airer strung up in the kitchen on which to hang her dried flowers, and the husband, though not keen on this, had agreed to have one installed 'as a way of keeping the other half happy' (c. 46, soc. cl. C1). Also allocated to this category was the couple where the woman said,

> If you put it in and he don't like it he'll be on for evermore, so he has to like it. But we usually agree anyway. I said, 'I still like the Sandringham' and he say, 'Well, why not?' (c. 48, soc. cl. C1)

This kind of unambiguous 'joint' decision-making accounted, however, for relatively few respondents.

A good deal of decision-making which the respondents themselves had initially classified as 'joint' was now reclassified. Various new groupings emerged. A cross-section of examples drawn from these new groupings highlights the varied ways in which couple relationships could be played out while simultaneously justifying grouping them together within one coding category. They also show how the same data contributes both quantitative and qualitative information.

In one group 'joint' decisions were purely symbolic. This produced some amusingly wry responses from the inactive partner as in the following response. The wife answered the question first saying that she and her husband had made a joint decision about the choice of kitchen furniture. The husband then added,

> The wife brought these samples home and said to me, 'Which do you like?' So I said, '*That*.' So she said, 'Right, we'll have *this*.' She went through the motions so I would feel involved. (c. 7, soc. cl. B)

In another instance, as the woman was telling me that she and her husband chose the new furniture jointly, the man, wordlessly, simply jerked his finger in his wife's direction. This made her concede that 'I suppose I chose.' She immediately tacked an addendum to this, however: 'But you did come and we placed the order together' (c. 66, soc. cl. B). If one assumes an ideological commitment here to an equal partnership in which both members were active participants in domestic decision-making, this woman's responses make sense. The fact that her husband had essentially been a passive participant in the choosing process ceased to matter once she found a way of interpreting his behaviour as symbolising their shared life. This woman was not making a bad job of having her cake and eating it too. Another example of the importance some women placed on symbolic sharing was the woman who said the choice of kitchen was a shared one because 'We went together.' She then added, 'He's very good but I usually do the choosing' (c. 65, soc. cl. A).

One woman, describing her husband's role in choosing their new kitchen, had a rather different motive for categorising their decision about the new kitchen furniture as joint:

> I dragged him along everywhere because I really like to have someone with me, because I'm dreadful about making decisions. (c. 36, soc. cl. B)

This husband's job seemed confined to supporting his wife in situations when her strong propensity for indecision threatened to get the better of her. The idea that he might have an independent opinion of his own did not appear to be part of the scenario.

A final striking variation on this was the woman who asserted, 'We always get things together.' She then described how this worked. She and her sister-in-law arranged to meet and look for kitchen furniture. Together they toured the shops and decided what they liked. After this the wife went home and told her husband what she wanted him to go and look at. He did not therefore tour the showrooms independently but just looked at what she, with her sister-in-law's help, had decided she wanted. Once he had rubber-stamped her decision they went out and bought what she had selected. The reclassification of this particular response was vouchsafed additional justification when the same woman later in the interview described talking to a salesman about the purchase of another piece of kitchen equipment. In a tone of discernible irritation, she said,

> He kept going on about my husband, and I said, 'Forget about him, this is for me' (c. 59, soc. cl. D)

Recoding categorised all these answers as indicating the woman as chief decision-maker. As a group they reflect a cross-section of the quirky, informal ways in which many women effectively took over a major household decision completely while still claiming their partners played a significant role in it. Their behaviour was often transparently disingenuous. But the pretence suited them. They knew their husbands knew what was going on but they liked the idea of doing things together and the fiction they constructed could conveniently help both to avoid the need for an overt acknowledgement that they were in command and to maintain an easy-going, comfortable relationship with their partners.[21]

One effect of making the question on decision-making refer only to aesthetic decision-making was that the different gender roles adopted within some partnerships became clearer. There were a number of cases where men continued to bear formal responsibility for money matters. What was striking, however, was how rarely the formal retention of financial responsibility seemed actively oppressive of women. The narrowed reference the question now carried threw into relief how little formal financial arrangements affected women's control of decision-making in the field of taste. A cross-section of responses again provides a description of how this operated.

One man stood out as exceptional in the sample because of his extremely domineering manner. He started by stating emphatically that he was not interested in design at all. He then added brusquely:

> The wife saw what she liked and I saw what I could afford. (c. 5, soc. cl. B)

During the interview he also, as well as expressing his own, frequently tried to express his wife's ideas for her. As the interview progressed she intermittently protested, her cheeks grew steadily pinker and she found it increasingly difficult to hide her annoyance. Her behaviour conveyed the impression that she regarded her husband as usurping her territory and thought he should allow her to answer for herself. This man's assumption of the right to decide what the couple could afford was, potentially, a huge constraint on his wife. Yet, even in as unequal a relationship as this, the woman turned out to enjoy considerable aesthetic freedom. Though his manner when announcing his role with regard to the control of domestic expenditure was bruisingly aggressive, he did not interfere with her selection of the style of furniture they bought, nor was he ungenerous about meeting the cost to which her taste put him.

Though this man was particularly bullish among the male partners interviewed, judging from respondents' comments, there were probably one or two other men of similar inclination who were not interviewed. Far less extreme and much more frequently, however, both by report and from direct observation, in households where men were still seen as retaining overall financial control, the men did not conduct themselves in a simple authoritarian manner. One woman in a household of this kind recalled the process of buying.

> I nearly bought a pine one but then I thought, 'No, I like this one.' He kept saying 'I'm not buying any more units.' Because I cost him a fortune. But we went. (c. 9, soc. cl. D)

The pronouns here are revealing. Her husband meanwhile propped himself against the wall, smiled and said nothing, while installed around him in their kitchen was every unit his wife had said she wanted. Another woman in this kind of household reported her husband as saying, 'Have exactly what you want' (c. 8, soc. cl. B). And while she added 'Though obviously I knew what we could afford and what we couldn't', she proceeded to tour the showrooms, occasionally taking her daughter with her for a second opinion, and selected £10,000 worth of kitchen units. Only at this stage did her husband become involved and they returned together to the relevant showroom, where he undertook the actual purchase of the goods she had chosen. In this household, though the gendering of domestic responsibility remained very traditional, the woman was clearly the dominant actor in the domestic arena, as various anecdotes she told made clear. The man was a farmer and following his father's death he and his wife had moved into the family farmhouse. Despite the fact that it was his family home, his wife described how he found it impossible to be in the house if she wasn't there. Even on winter evenings, as long as she was out, he continued to wander round the barns and yard despite the growing dark and cold. Only when the lights went on in the house and he knew she was back was he able to make his way indoors.

This particular form of the division of domestic labour where the man continued formally to maintain financial control could also be played out, however, in a strikingly different way. There was one couple where the woman adamantly refused to take any financial responsibility during the purchasing of their new kitchen. She imposed financial control on the man. It was a deliberate and knowingly engineered tactic, motivated by self-interest, to help her cope with an ingrained inhibition she had about spending. Thus, having described how she actively refused to gather any information about the cost of the kitchen fittings she wanted and had diligently avoided taking any part in the actual purchase of them, she added:

> And I'll tell you why. Those doors are very expensive and if I went I'd always be trying to save a shilling. But I know that if he goes he'll know we can afford them. So I'll get them. (c. 74, soc. cl. C2)

That final pronoun, 'I' not 'we', is revealing. There were further variations in the sample on this pattern of behaviour.

Reviewing another group of respondents who initially saw their decision-making as a joint act, it became apparent that one factor which led to this perception derived from the way people saw themselves as carrying different kinds of responsibility within the household. Decisions in these cases were not so much joint as that each party had their own areas of activity and the process of buying a kitchen involved an orchestration of these. Thus, for example, there was the question of bargaining.

Vigorous bargaining between purchasers and retailers over price took place, after the kitchen units had been selected, in a number of cases. About 15 per cent of respondents gratuitously talked about bargaining and it seems likely that it was more widespread than this. Some buyers succeeded in driving down the final price substantially. Unaware of this aspect of modern retailing, I had included no questions about this and when it began to come up in interviews it was too late to handle it systematically. What emerged unsystematically is, however, worthy of note.

Only one woman, a young widow, mentioned bargaining, and then for a cooker rather than for kitchen units. She explained how:

> I went in and sighed. And then you've got to suck the air over your teeth. *[She illustrated this.]* Then I said, 'I could get that cheaper at . . .' (c. 28, soc. cl. C2)

She laughed as she told her story, however, and her description of her bargaining lacked the kind of aggressive edge which characterised some of the descriptions of male bargaining that were offered.

Descriptions women gave of their menfolk bargaining sometimes made it sound ferocious. Yet the same men might be perfectly happy to tell their wives to choose whatever they wanted and quite content to leave them to decide what would be within the family's means. The woman might therefore decide what she thought they could afford and make her selections without referring to the man at all. Once she had done this and was ready to buy, however, some male partners and husbands became very active. But it was an activity which had nothing to do with the selections their wife had made. Rather, respondents' descriptions suggested that certain men regarded it as a form of male duty to fight hard over the price of goods before making a substantial purchase. The women thus got what they wanted while their menfolk ensured they got it for the best possible price. Each partner fulfilled their allotted but discrete gender roles.

The womenfolk of these men, in contrast to their partners' eager engagement with fighting for a good price, often hated this part of the buying process. Some women found it so embarrassing, even painful, to be present while their menfolk haggled that they took themselves off elsewhere until it was all over. Yet to characterise these couples as still living in traditional patriarchal relationships seems too simple. Activity within these partnerships was highly gendered, but the effect of this could be to secure considerable areas of autonomy for the woman, including a de facto control over large amounts of domestic spending.

The idea that activity could be highly gendered while still leaving women with considerable control finds further support among another group of respondents who originally described their decision-making as joint but who, on further examination, were recategorised. The men in this group usually had building skills of one kind or another or were sufficiently proficient at DIY to be able to install a fitted kitchen. They represented another form of the gendering of household activity. Over half the sample installed their kitchens themselves, either alone, 16 per cent, more commonly with the help of family and friends, 35 per cent, totalling 51 per cent together. Only one woman in the sample put in the kitchen herself. Installation was men's work.

When men installed the kitchen themselves, they could play a significant role as technical requirements surfaced at this juncture and began to impose constraints on what people would have ideally liked. Such constraints did not affect the style of furniture chosen, but in some households technical considerations led men who were going to install the new kitchen to step in and make certain provisos about what could or could not be done with regard to their wives' plans for the kitchen layout. In one case the man recalled how 'my mate and me measured everything up'. He then told his wife what was possible. The selection of the design and colour of the units, however, he left entirely to her (c. 50, soc. cl. C2). So, though playing an active role in the household's acquisition of a new kitchen, these men's comments made clear that their input was limited to technical issues: the women made the big aesthetic decisions. As one man in discussing their choice of style put it,

> Oh, that's her department and I thought it was solid enough and she liked the pattern. (c. 22, soc. cl. C2)

These cases were now added to the category of women decision-makers (see table 6.4). This meant the category now covered four main groups of respondents. There were couples who lived a more or less transparent fiction about male control over household finances; couples where forms of traditional gender roles persisted with regard to money but in such a way that the woman set the ceiling on spending on a new kitchen; a smaller group of couples where the man retained significant financial control but combined this with the belief that the selection of a new kitchen was women's work and gave her free rein to get on with it; and a group where the man made a significant practical contribution to the installation of the kitchen but, unless there were technical reasons for opposing the women's aesthetic preferences, left the woman to make the aesthetic decisions.

Turning next to couples where, from the beginning, the woman was named as chief decision-maker, male disengagement from decision-making across the social classes was often total. One husband said,

> I think my words were, 'Go out and get what you want.' (c. 24, soc. cl. C2)

He even prevailed on his wife to persuade the man next door, who was going to help to fit the kitchen, to accompany her to the shops, so that he could stay at home. Another woman reported her husband as saying,

> 'It's up to you.' He left me with the brochures and said, 'You choose what you want.' (c.18, soc. cl. C1)

One woman said dismissively,

> If we'd left it to him we'd still be waiting. (c. 14, soc. cl. D)

And one man describing his role said,

> I just came along as a shadow. (c. 39, soc. cl. C1)

Whether by nature or nurture, differences in skills and sensibility between men and women were marked and widespread. So, where men could have had a considerable shaping influence over the design of the kitchen, they generally failed to exploit their opportunity. One man, for example, was a highly paid professional but did not enjoy his work. He had therefore given it up to allow his wife to pursue a career which, though less lucrative, she enjoyed, while he became a house-husband. He was thus in a position to take a dominant role in the selection of their new kitchen. Yet he did not take advantage of this. Instead, what he drew my attention to with obvious pleasure was a mass of elaborate plumbing work executed with exemplary neatness (c. 20, soc. cl. B). There was also the case of a wife who, exceptionally, broke the pattern of gender roles by having no interest in home decoration. In contrast, her husband loved working on their house and, had finances allowed, would have given up his paid employment with computers to do such work all the time. Under these circumstances the man had planned the layout, chosen the new kitchen furniture and appliances, purchased everything and then installed the kitchen, without any involvement from his wife. Yet it wasn't choosing the design that gave this man the greatest pleasure or made him feel creative, and he expressed a real anxiety about the final layout he had

**Plate 6.1** A view of the kitchen installed by the man whose wife, unusually for women, was uninterested in doing up their house. In contrast, he derived far more pleasure from installing their kitchen than from his work with computers for which he was paid. His pleasure derived primarily, however, from the physical experience of making and he was uncertain about his kitchen planning skills.

chosen (plate 6.1). What gave him a sense of well-being was the hands-on experience of measuring, cutting and hammering involved in fitting a kitchen (c. 45, soc. cl. C2).

In one exceptional case the man's life had become entirely centred on doing up the couple's house. The atypical nature of this respondent and his wife provided a critical case which allows for some generalisation. Together with the case of the house-husband, it showed how difficult many men find breaking free from conventionally prescribed gender roles with regard to the material construction of domesticity, in the absence of special training such as art schools offer.[22] The man worked in a factory in a job which provided no sense of fulfilment. So he worked his hours, starting early and finishing mid-afternoon, and refused absolutely to do any overtime. His job was simply a means of acquiring the funds to renovate the dilapidated bungalow he and his wife had bought. Each day he got home as soon as possible to work on the house, and the energy with which he tackled this work mimicked the kind of single-minded drive many men put into their paid work. His wife, in fact, in commenting on his commitment to renovating their house, described him as a workaholic.

He was certainly too busy putting a dado up in the hall to be interviewed properly. We chatted while he sawed and hammered but his wife provided the bulk of the questionnaire responses. This man was distinguished from the other men in the sample in that he made the bulk of the major design decisions in the house, including aesthetic ones, and even participated from time to time in decisions on things like wallpaper. His wife's attitude towards him mirrored that which many male respondents displayed towards their wives. She said she generally didn't interfere in his decisions as she felt he was better at this kind of thing than she was. Quite often she didn't know what she was going to get. Yet she did not show the total lack of interest in design and décor which characterised a substantial number of men in the sample. She made some significant provisos about what she wanted in their kitchen, such as some glass-fronted cupboards, and he accepted these. And she generally, though not always, chose wallpaper and curtains and decided on overall colour schemes. Even in the couple therefore where the man came closest to taking on the role normally adopted by the woman, the woman's behaviour still displayed vestiges of the classic feminine role, like the house-husband described earlier who, despite his radical role reversal, still displayed traditional male characteristics.

Yet there was a group of men who, either on their own or on their wife's account, derived a deep and touching satisfaction from the physical work of installing a kitchen and the feeling that they had done it well. It was a satisfaction clearly distinguishable from the process of choosing a design or style, however, and threw into relief a major difference in the way men and women conventionally learn to experience sensual pleasure and the effect of this on their involvement in the structuring of material domesticity.[23] This group of men was passionate about doing a really good installation job, frequently so passionate, indeed, that their enthusiasm became a burden for their wives as it threatened to make the installation process interminable. One woman pointed out a tile her husband had inadvertently put in the wrong way round. One had to look hard to see it but his wife said, with a mixture of despair and amusement, that, although he was trying his best to ignore it and get on with the rest of the installation, she knew it could only be a matter of time before her husband's need to do a perfect job drove him to take that section of tiles down and adjust his mistake.

This physical pleasure which men could experience in installing a kitchen had a strong sensual dimension to it. In describing what they had done these men would move round the kitchen pointing out various small refinements and explaining little adjustments they needed to make. As they did this they would delicately touch and stroke unit fronts, edges and corners. This tactile pleasure, however, seemed different from a pleasure in the design or style of the units in that it did not appear to derive from the overall line or form of the units. Rather it appeared to originate from memories of making, cutting and fitting. In contrast to their relaxed and unselfconscious expression of sensual delight on this front many men expressed a general sense of aesthetic insecurity not found among women respondents. Women might express frustration about not being able to find some item they wanted to complete the decoration of their kitchen but men were more likely to express bewilderment about the choices they found themselves being forced to make as they installed a new kitchen.

This was particularly true of a small group of men who were on their own, usually through divorce. They were, therefore, in the residual category of table 6.4. Few in number, no generalisations about them can be made. Nevertheless, it is noteworthy that they all confessed to feeling slightly lost domestically and uneasy about design issues, even though, by buying a new kitchen, they were clearly seeking to do something about this. They sometimes approached new women friends for advice but these women were not always keen to express an opinion when it was not their house. These men could therefore feel stranded. As one man on his own put it,

> I haven't got a clue with colours. I'm not colour co-ordinated . . . Blue and yellow go together now but they never used to, did they? (c. 54, soc. cl. C2)

Yet people could change. There was one man in this group who had begun to find himself developing new sensitivities. He was becoming conscious not only of a growing visual awareness but of the social and personal implications of this:

> I was just going to tile round the splash back. Then I just kept going. I thought it was aesthetic; it looked nicer, clean, durable and really I just liked the tiles. They had a texture plain walls wouldn't have.

Later he added,

> The experience of doing the kitchen has made me realise it's much more important to me than I'd thought. I couldn't . . . just live with the kitchen as I have in the past . . . If people come to the house and like the kitchen I realise it matters. It says something about you, your kitchen. (c. 27, soc. cl. B)

Whether by nurture or nature, though probably through a combination of these, the men and women in the sample had generally developed different forms of visual and sensual awareness. Though these were not immutable, modifying them was not easy for people. The effect of this in practice was to enhance women's control today of the material structuring of domesticity.

We have already looked at how, while men might retain formal financial control over the budget for the new kitchen, in practice women could still have great freedom in terms of choosing its style and design. If the initial budget for purchasing a new kitchen was strictly set, however, this could significantly constrain this freedom. However, while couples commonly started looking for new kitchen units with some idea of what kitchens could cost and a general feeling about what they could afford, almost none had fixed a sum they were prepared to spend. There was only one case in which the husband, in traditional, patriarchal fashion, started the process of purchasing by giving his wife a set budget (c. 31, soc. cl. B). It was quickly abandoned. The wife immediately decided that she could not buy the kitchen she had in mind with this money. So, Rosamund-style, she went out and priced up what she could buy in the quality and style she wanted, without compromising her desire for a solid wooden finish, and handed this to her husband. He doubled her budget. The wife's description of this process indicated that it was a well-rehearsed tactic on her part. While, therefore, not reflecting a formally egalitarian relationship, this wife got what she wanted, as she had on other occasions in the past, without too much fuss and without generating rancour. Indeed, as this wife recalled in another part of the interview, 'Edward was happy to spend money when the ball got rolling', to the degree that he never once demurred when she started to go hugely over budget on the lighting she wanted and she herself began to get worried about what she was spending.

Because tight budgeting was rare and most people appeared to operate with a general sense of what was an appropriate price bracket for them within the overall price framework of the market, the freedom women enjoyed in expressing their visual tastes and preferences was further consolidated. Indeed, 42 per cent of the sample had not calculated the final cost of their kitchen since it was completed. This did not mean that they had spent wildly or imprudently or that, when the request was made of them, people were unable to make this calculation. Where they were unable to come up with a total cost immediately, they usually had files of bills which they were able to check and produced the information shortly afterwards. While men and women might do this calculation together, women frequently did it alone. That women could do this further indicates that they had played a proactive role in the buying process. Altogether, financial arrangements among couples allowed considerable scope for the exercise of feminine opportunism. For all practical purposes women enjoyed considerable freedom in the selection of a new kitchen.

This still leaves the issue of equality in the overall allocation of a family's household budget to be addressed. Chapter 4 noted that when one compared what people expected a new kitchen to cost with what they expected to spend on replacing the family car half the sample expected to lay out more on the family car (see table 4.1). The point was made that if one assumes that cars are to men what kitchens are to women such a finding supports the argument that men's interests continue to be privileged in terms of family expenditure. The evidence presented in this chapter does not provide a clear refutation of this. The idea that there should be parity within the household between male and female spending was raised by various respondents, however, and a number of women with no prompting spontaneously offered accounts of how they had consciously taken action to ensure such parity was practised.

Thus, one woman began her interview with the statement, 'This kitchen is a car' (c. 32, soc. cl. B). She then proceeded to explain this. Her husband loved cars. But one day when he arrived home with the news that he had yet again indulged his enthusiasm by buying a new car her sense of grievance spilled over and she decided that it was time she too indulged herself. The result was that she and her husband agreed that she would buy herself a new kitchen to counterbalance his having a new car. In her own mind she was, furthermore, determined that her new kitchen would cost as much as it took for her to get what she wanted. And she proceeded to spend with no sense of guilt. If anything, she spent with a sense of righteousness. Nor, it might be added, was she one of the most modest spenders in the sample (plate 6.2). Another woman explained how her husband had bought a new boat with a lump sum he received on his retirement. This led his wife to decide that she wanted a new kitchen to equalise things (c. 38, soc. cl. B). And she got it. The idea that good things should be distributed fairly within a marriage came up yet again with the wife who told how her husband had purchased a 1960s E-type Jaguar, which would become a vintage car, and had it done up. She then continued:

> So my two sons said, 'Right, Dad, what are you going to do for Mum?' And
> I had a kitchen. (c. 74, soc. cl. A)

This woman had both a kitchen and enormous fun. She went out in her own words with 'an open cheque-book', and chose just what she wanted while, as she put it, 'he approved or he didn't approve'. Either way she indicated that she regarded her husband's opinion on this front as immaterial. And though she did not consciously set out to equalise their spending she cheerfully relieved their bank account of over £30,000 (plate 6.3).

**Plate 6.2** 'This kitchen is a car.' Part of the large, luxuriously appointed and thoughtfully planned kitchen negotiated by a wife whose husband bought one too many cars.

**Plate 6.3** Kitchen bought to balance off a husband's self-indulgence in buying himself a 1960s E-type Jaguar.

The interview evidence indicated that these women all acquired their new kitchens, not by default, but as the product of active choice. Earlier in the chapter, the way D.H. Lawrence in *Sons and Lovers* makes Mrs Morel experience an intense release of sensual delight over the buying of a fruit dish was cited, and the claim made that this fictional account was convincingly realistic. The women who told the stories just cited did so with a pleasure which reflected some of the same kind of feminine sensibility Lawrence described in Mrs Morel. If one accepts that the home can be a major and independent source of emotional and aesthetic pleasure for women, then stories like the ones just recounted constitute evidence that the concept of reciprocity within marriage existed among some of the sample not just as an idea but as idea translated into action. While often not expressed as directly and openly as in the stories just cited, it was widely expressed in terms of material practice.

An earlier chapter argued that the development of the design and layout of domestic kitchens over the course of the last hundred years and which now affects almost every aspect of their contemporary organisation and appearance, far from springing from the same roots as the movement for gender equality and working in tandem with that movement, worked at odds with it, both at the ideological level and for much of the time at the practical level. The modernisation of kitchen design is not an important part of the story of women's fight for their rights. What this chapter has sought to show, however, is how feminine interests and skills, emanating from, rather than challenging, women's traditional roles in our society, shape the design of the domestic kitchen today. Furthermore, not only are the feminine interests and skills which effect this shaping recognised as skills by many men but men are widely prepared to acknowledge their own lack of competence in them. Put this together with the increasing wealth of the population and the steady increase in house ownership in the country and the result is that women today now have significantly more opportunity to develop and put these skills into action. This de facto confers on women considerable control over household spending. Mrs Morel bought a fruit dish. The spending the women in the sample were engaged in was on a very different scale. They were shaping the nature of the material environment we inhabit very extensively. In doing this they were also influencing the way we experience and understand the world. If, as this chapter suggested at the beginning, the home carries considerable symbolic and aesthetic importance for women, and, as such, constitutes an arena where women consciously seek to mould and shape their material environment so as to express their values, hopes and goals, this form of feminine activity becomes highly significant in any analysis of the impact of feminine thinking on social life.

Within adult partnerships today, conventional gender roles are being played out in a way which allows women huge control over the structure and ambience of the home. In so far as the material construction of the home is a significant factor in the process of socialisation in our society, conventional women are arguably playing an increasingly significant social role, given the huge increase in house ownership and general wealth. Traditionally, of course, women have long been cast as the medium through which many familial and conservative social values have been passed on. But even where women's influence remains predominantly centred on familial values this chapter suggests that it may be unwise to assume that women mediate these values in a simple, passive and unquestioning way.

## Notes

1. Slater (1996), p. 56.
2. Adrian Forty (1989) has pointed out that the new technologies do not run themselves but have to be worked, so they do not do away with chores though they might ease them. In addition there has been the phenomenon that Betty Friedan (1964) *The Feminine Mystique*, Dell Publishing Company, discussed: the pressure women felt to constantly raise standards of domestic comfort. Friedan, for example, found women in the late 1950s who, having acquired new automatic washing-machines, were starting to change all the family's bedlinen twice a week. Ruth Cowen (1989) has also, of course, explored this phenomenon.
3. For a brief period in the 1970s, during the heyday of combative feminism, there was a call for women to be given a wage for doing housework. It was short-lived, partly because the chances of it being taken up by any political party were negligible but also because the Women's movement was more interested in getting women into jobs with better pay and proper career opportunities.
4. See chapter 2.
5. See the documentary film *The Life and Times of Rosie the Riveter* (1980), directed by Connie Field, for a vivid account of this.
6. John Bowlby was the most famous, or notorious, of the English psychologists in this school.

7. Friedan (1964).
8. Oakley, Ann (1985) *The Sociology of Housework*, Basil Blackwell.
9. Pahl (1989).
10. Ibid., p. 79.
11. Laurie (1996).
12. See de Grazia and Furlough (1996), Miller (1995) and Slater (1996).
13. Forster, E.M. (1961) *Room with a View*, Penguin Books, p. 117 and 144. In this novel, first published in 1908, Forster has one of his characters, a middle-class wife, make clear that she had no part in the choice of the sitting-room furniture. Buying furniture in that family at that time was man's work.
14. The history of women and department stores is one example of this.
15. Eliot, George (1947) *Middlemarch*, The World's Classics, Oxford University Press, p. 892, first published 1871–2. Rosamund's tenacity is made all the more steely by an intensely worldly and materialistic outlook, and a lack of that quality of moral imagination on which the development of a true generosity of spirit depends. Before the end of the novel the idealistic young doctor, Lydgate, whom she married (after crying at precisely the right moment), has become a comfortably off middle-aged doctor safely ensconced in a fashionable practice and surrounded by his pretty wife and daughters. To the outside world all looks fine. But we know that it is his wife's values that have determined the course of Lydgate's career, and that, despite surface appearances, he nurses a huge sense of disappointment. Though he may never have made a significant medical discovery, Lydgate has found that the price he had to pay for his charming wife was the abandonment of any attempt to even try to reach towards such an achievement.
16. It can be argued that Charlotte Bronte's heroine, Jane Eyre, offers an interesting variant of the dominant woman. She spends the early part of the book sparring with Mr Rochester but by the end, in the classic womanly role of nurse, she has him dependent on her.

    An example of a gentler and kindlier version of Rosamund's tactics is described openly in Stewart, Elinor P. (1989) *Letters of a Woman Homesteader,* University of Nebraska Press, p. 23. The book was first published in 1914 and comprises a collection of letters to a former employer in Denver written by a woman homesteading in Wyoming. A naturally talented and amusing writer Elinor Stewart describes in this particular letter how:

    > It is the custom here for as many women as care to to go in a party over into Utah . . . after fruit . . . They came over to invite me to join them . . . I wanted to go but it seemed a little risky and a big chance for discomfort,

since we would have to cross the Uinta Mountains , and a snowstorm likely any time. But I didn't like to refuse outright, so we left it to Mr Stewart. His 'Ye're nae gang' sounded powerful final, so the ladies departed in awed silence and I assumed a martyr-like air and acted like a very much abused woman, although he did only what I wanted him to do. At last, in sheer desperation he told me the 'bairn canna stand the treep', and that was why he was so determined. I knew why of course but I continued to look abused lest he gets it into his head that he can boss me. After he had been reduced to the proper plane of humility and explained and begged my pardon and had told me to consult only my own pleasure about going and coming and using his horses, only not to 'expoose' the bairn, why, I forgave him and we were friends once more.

17. Conversations with groups of women horrendously abused, physically and mentally, by their male partners provides ample evidence of this. It is harder to put women down even under the most inauspicious circumstances than one might imagine.
18. Lawrence, D.H. (1960) *Sons and Lovers,* Penguin Books, pp. 96–7.
19. Forster (1961), p. 117 and 144.
20. Miller (1998, 2001) and Parr (1999) provide three examples.
21. Zwick, Joel, director, *My Big, Fat Greek Wedding* (2001), offers some comic examples of women pretending to defer to masculine authority to get what they want.
22. In other areas the same must also be true of women, of course. Also, when in status or monetary terms it becomes advantageous for men to take over women's roles men regularly do so. Most top chefs are men. Given sufficient incentive, men learn to master skills normally classified as feminine.
23. The men and women in the sample were not art-school-trained. Men can and do learn to experience sensual pleasure in aesthetic terms.

# Not only but also: instrumental and expressive considerations

The last chapter showed the dominant role women played in selecting the design, the style and the size and shape of units during the purchase of a new kitchen. It also showed that the way couples handled budgeting allowed many women considerable personal freedom, including some self-indulgence, when making these choices. This does not mean that the examination of male involvement in the installation of a new kitchen will now be ignored. The sample as a whole will obviously continue to include the male component described in chapter 3 and much of the analysis will continue to draw on that sample. In addition, contributions from partners and husbands during the interviews will be used where appropriate. However, as, over the course of the next chapters, the discussion explores in increasing detail the factors and criteria which determined buyers' selection of particular layouts and design styles, the impact of the motivations and concerns of women respondents on the arrangement and appearance of the sample kitchens will carry considerable weight, given the preponderance of women in the sample and the role we have now seen that so many of them played in the purchasing process.

From the outset this study has been concerned to refine our perception of what is commonly termed the general public. It accepts that large numbers of the public share many of their values and attitudes with others, but it sees this as being true of everyone and regards it as an integral part of our human sociality. It does not see evidence of commonly shared patterns of behaviour, therefore, as justifying a view of the public as an undifferentiated mass of easily malleable people. Earlier chapters have, furthermore, presented empirical evidence which supports the view of the public as a body of people who, while sharing values with others in their society, also display independence. In examining the relationship between salespeople and the sample purchasers evidence emerged which showed that, though a minority of purchasers refused to have anything to do with salespeople, many purchasers were prepared to listen to what they had to say. Yet purchasers were still proactive about just what advice they would accept from salespeople. Similarly, the history of the public's reception of the idea of the fitted kitchen outlined in chapter 2 showed that, while people grew increasingly enthusiastic over time both about design ideas which sought to maximise the effective use of the space available and about ways of performing kitchen chores efficiently, there was less evidence of a similar enthusiasm for the styles with which professional designers dressed the basic modularised carcasses on which the fitted kitchen is based.

While the study will continues to address these issues it turns now to explore buyers' concern, first, with the efficiency of the kitchen or the kitchen as meal machine, before turning in the next chapter, to look at the kitchen as a symbol of domesticity or the heart of the home. To analyse just how these concerns shape the material appearance of people's kitchens, however, we will need to look at the visual language and aesthetic systems people command, these being the means we possess for giving material expression to such concerns. In addition, a prerequisite of our being able to make our material environment communicate these ideas is that we share our visual language with others in our society in the same way that we share a verbal language with them. We will therefore need to look at how people decipher and interpret the visual properties of different kitchen layouts and designs.

Most people would accept that we possess a visual vocabulary which we hold in common with others. It is not hard, for example, to produce examples of the highly refined and elaborate iconographies we possess for interpreting the human face or the British landscape. Nor would people need much convincing that these iconographies are both widely understood and constantly drawn on and play a central role in our daily communication with others.[1] What we need to establish here is how far we possess a similarly well-developed iconography which we use when constructing domestic interiors and which we share with others, regardless of social class. Once this has been done we can embark on looking at how people use non-verbal, visual means to communicate their values and ideals to others through their choice of kitchen layout, furniture design and general décor.

This does not involve us in making judgements of taste. Concern is simply with the extent to which people employ a shared visual language when looking at a domestic kitchen. It is important to recognise that people can do this without necessarily sharing the same visual tastes or, indeed, approving of other people's tastes, in the same way that it would be absurd to suggest that sharing the same verbal language with others involved one in sharing the same political opinions or pursuing identical moral codes. Sharing the same verbal language enables people to understand each other: it does not impose identical patterns of belief on them. Visual languages operate in the same way. This outlines the general coverage of this chapter and the concerns which run through it.

To start examining the importance the sample gave to efficiency in their kitchens, their opinions about the design of historical and contemporary kitchens were canvassed. Chapter 2 has already indicated that people have not generally had to be coaxed into using technologies which promise either to ease the burden of household chores or to improve the standard of hygiene and chapter 4 showed that this sample of kitchen buyers was committed to a high level of mechanisation in the kitchen. Among the cultural élite, however, there is a belief that the general public harbours an ingrained and sentimental nostalgia for the past. In the case of kitchens the public fascination with reconstructions of old kitchens in National Trust properties and museums, where they are becoming more common, is cited as evidence of this. It is important to be cautious, however, in interpreting a fascination with what kitchens were like in the past with a desire to resurrect them. Researching and writing popular history is an expanding historical field, reflecting the spread of a greater social equality in Britain and the impact of this in generating, among those less privileged historically, a lively interest in their past. The empirical data collected for this study, however, shows that, particularly from a utilitarian point of view, the sample for this study harboured very little nostalgia for the kitchens of the past. A strong interest in historical kitchens is not, of course, necessarily inconsistent with this.

Asked whether they thought the standard of kitchen design today was better, or not, than that of the past, 83 per cent, or over four-fifths, of the sample were convinced that modern kitchens were better than those of the past (table 7.1). The answers coded 'other' to this question also included

**Table 7.1** *Whether people considered the standard of kitchen design had improved over the course of this century or not*

| Category name | No. | % of all |
|---|---|---|
| Today's kitchen design is better than in the past | 19 | 26 |
| Today's kitchen design emphatically better than in the past | 42 | 57 |
| Quality of kitchen design now is no different from the past | 3 | 4 |
| Kitchen design today is worse than it used to be | 1 | 1 |
| No opinion | 1 | 1 |
| Other/no ans. | 8 | 11 |
| Total | 74 | 100 |

some answers expressing this view. They were classified as 'other', however, because they expressed additional opinions as well.

In expressing the opinion that kitchens of the past were inferior to contemporary ones people often couched their replies in very emphatic terms. A few examples from a long list of similar responses, convey the tone of the answers as a whole.

> Oh, definitely. (c. 13, soc. cl. C2)[2]
> A hundred times better. (c. 40, soc. cl. C1)
> A hundred per cent. Absolutely. Give me mine any day. (c. 65, soc. cl. A)
> Better? No doubt about it. (c. 44, soc. cl. B)
> Oh, God, yeah, about a hundred per cent better. (c. 53, soc. cl. C2)

When people were asked to say why they held these opinions, answers commonly mentioned advances in technology, improvements in hygiene and the reduction of backbreaking work. Many of the sample could still vividly recall the technological impoverishment of their parents' or grandparents' homes. And, while such memories were occasionally tinged with humour, nostalgia was not a feature of them. The lack of tapped water, hot water and plumbing to dispose of dirty water was repeatedly mentioned with distaste, sometimes with a visible shudder (plate 7.1):

**Plate 7.1** Many respondents remembered with distaste the kitchens of their childhoods. Here, from what has now become a series of celebrated photographs by Humphrey Spender, is a scene of washing in Stepney in 1934. *Courtesy, Humphrey Spender.*

We hadn't even got an indoor tap. The sink hadn't even a pipe out of it.
(c. 47, soc. cl. C2)
We never had running water. We had a well. (c. 13, soc. cl. C2)
My gran had a pipe from the sink into a bucket. (c. 24, soc. cl. C2)

Cooking facilities were also recalled with dismay and the kitchen range, which required blacking each week, was remembered with particular aversion. Memories of coppers and mangles were not affectionate ones either, while for some respondents, the lack of hygiene, by today's standards, was still a vivid and unpleasant memory:

a chipped white stone sink. . . and horrid wooden draining-boards, horribly unhygienic. (c. 38, soc. cl. B)
She had a coke boiler with all sorts of dirt round it and a kitchen table which had to be scrubbed – the meat juices went into it. She used soda . . . hygienically it was a disaster area. (c. 27, soc. cl. B)

At a more general level the act of recalling these old kitchens led people to reflect with pity on the hardness of women's lives in the past:

If you didn't have servants a woman's life was very hard. No-one would live like that today. (c. 39, soc. cl. C1)
When you compare what our grandmothers' lives were like, they did work hard. (c. 4 C2)
I don't know how they managed. (c. 58, soc. cl. B)
[To-day it's] better. Infinitely, from the point of view of making life better for women. (c. 60, soc. cl. B)

One man, a natural raconteur, dotted his interview with anecdotes. At one point he described his mother tackling the family wash:

When my mother used the mangle you never went near her because of the shirt buttons. They used to go flying. They'd have killed you. We used to have half buttons all down our shirts. 'I don't have time to put them flat,' she'd say.

Although the recollection made a lively story, he had no doubt about the superiority of today's kitchens, as his closing remark made clear:

Oh, it's definitely better now. (c. 22, soc. cl. C2)

Other people were led to comment on the easy assumption of comfort today:

Children of today don't know the half of it. (c. 59, soc. cl. D)
You never had hot water. We take everything for granted today. (c. 4, soc. cl. C2)

As far as the design of kitchens in the past was concerned people were not complimentary:

> I don't think they were designed. (c. 6, soc. cl. B)
> They didn't have a design. (c. 14, soc. cl. D)
> I don't think in those days it was meant to be aesthetic. (c. 68, soc. cl. A)
> . . . no conformity . . . there wasn't the colour co-ordination. I don't think there was so much pride in a house. (c. 56, soc. cl. C2)

Finally, several women imagined their mothers or grandmothers in their own spotless, fully fitted and mechanised kitchens. Thus one, recalling her nana who lived in a Nissen hut with a kitchenette tucked behind a curtain at one end, said:

> I bet she'd loved to have a kitchen like this. (c. 49, soc. cl. D)

Another mused:

> In a kitchen like this I bet she'd have worked wonders given what she cooked in what she'd got. (c. 50, soc. cl. C2)

Yet another, in a vivid and evocative analogy, thought that her kitchen

> would be like going on holiday for my grandma. (c. 70, soc. cl. A)

Altogether respondents did not harbour soft-centred, sentimental memories of the past. One woman summarised succinctly the feelings of many respondents with the comment:

> Today's kitchens look better and are more efficient. (c. 45, soc. cl. C1)

Another, as she turned the issue of memory over in her mind, said:

> I wouldn't want to go back . . . you remember the sunshiny days and they couldn't all have been like that . . . A tin bath hanging in the corner! A mangle! (c. 52, soc. cl. C2)

Overall most respondents gave unqualified approval to the technological advances modern kitchens now boast and the greater efficiency to which they give rise. Mrs Frederick seemed to hover like a ghost behind some people's recollections of the past. One woman recalling their old family kitchen described how food used to be:

> prepared in the pantry, taken to the washhouse to cook and then brought into the kitchen to eat. I wouldn't like that . . . I'll take two steps here and two steps there but not all that walking about. (c. 9, soc. cl. D)

The next step in analysing people's attitude to efficiency in the kitchen was to consider how aware they were of the demands a concern with efficiency made on the overall layout of a kitchen. It has already been noted how vigorously some buyers had struggled with the layout of their own kitchens in attempts to get the seating and eating arrangements or the positioning of services and machines as they wanted. Other buyers had been concerned to ensure easy accessibility to cupboard space or a maximising of work space. Such concerns had led them to give close attention, for example, to the height at which cupboards were hung, not only from the ceiling but above the worktop. Now respondents were asked to undertake a more general exercise. They were offered two pictures from a kitchen retailer's catalogue and asked whether or not they thought the kitchens illustrated were well laid out from a practical point of view. Plate 7.2 shows one of the pictures. The question was open and there was deliberately no prompting (plate 7.2). Only one person had difficulty with the question and felt unable to offer an opinion. Most people found the question easy. A number tackled it with visible enjoyment. And not only

**Plate 7.2** Picture of a kitchen which was offered to respondents for their views on its layout. The units were in a warm, mid-brown wooden finish, the tiles on the floor were in terra cotta and white and various bowls and pans in a celadon green. Respondents were handed a colour version of this picture. *Courtesy, Texas Homecare.*

were people happy to comment on this aspect of the picture, many displayed a keen critical acumen in doing so.

The 'work triangle' of sink, cooker and work area, a central theme in scientific household management thinking, was the most frequently and carefully scrutinised feature of these kitchens. The following extracts from the many similar responses to this question illustrate the confidence with which people from all social classes assessed a kitchen layout from the point of view of its practicality:

> A lot of walking about to do. Especially walking across a stairwell with pans is bad. (c. 58, soc. cl. B)
>
> You'd be carrying something hot across and you'd slip on the rug. (c. 51, soc. cl. C2)
>
> Impractical arrangement of sink. You'd have to walk half a mile and fall over the carpet when you strained the potatoes. (c. 61, soc. cl. C2)
>
> You'd be walking around too much and you'd be tripping over that rug all the time. (c. 40, soc. cl. D)
>
> Only a man could have designed it. To go across a doorway with a pan of water is ridiculous. (c. 39, soc. cl. C1)
>
> The sink is too far away and taking pans across an opening is hazardous. (c. 70, soc. cl. A)

Respondents therefore were both keenly aware of the overall shortcomings of kitchens historically and thoroughly versed in the rules of scientific management as they applied to kitchen layout. It does not follow, of course, that possessing a clear-sighted perception of the paucity of work-easing equipment and a strong distaste for the pervasive dirt and gunge which used to characterise so many kitchens must rule out all fond memories of kitchens in the past. As one woman said:

> It was a friendly old kitchen but . . . (c. 27, soc. cl. B)

And a comment from another respondent shows how closely entwined clear-sightedness and fond memories can be.

> . . . The scullery had a shallow stone sink in the corner, a cupboard and a copper. The kitchen had a table with a chenille cover and a range at the side of the fire and an armchair each side . . . I used to go to visit each Sunday and the meat would be roasting and it smelt wonderful . . . And she had a pulley and a dresser! What she had to do! Oh, it has to be better. People can buy those [pulleys] again and they hang their pans on them. I can't bear it. Think how greasy they must get. (c. 26, soc. cl. C1)

The past, of course, is not just about material conditions. It is also about people and relationships. Memories of the two can be separate or, as in the foregoing passage, locked together in a highly inflected relationship. While integral to the general conditions of cooking which are remembered without fondness, the recollection of the smell of roasting meat remains nevertheless richly satisfying sensually for the respondent and acts to evoke positive memories of a grandmother and a grandmother–grandchild relationship. The material environment of the kitchen has become integral to the respondent's sense of their identity, of who and what they are.

This respondent did not want her grandmother's kitchen back. Yet it held fond memories for her. This brings us back again to the kitchen as idea. People wanted efficient kitchens and high-tech machinery. But, when they were asked what importance they attached to functional as opposed to style considerations in their new kitchens, the largest group, 59 per cent, or three-fifths, said they regarded these two aspects of the kitchen as equally important (table 7.2). Unlike Mrs Frederick, these

**Table 7.2** *The relative weight respondents put on functional/practical considerations as opposed to style in their new kitchens*

| Category name | No. | % of all |
|---|---|---|
| Efficiency more important than style | 13 | 18 |
| Efficiency as important as style | 44 | 59 |
| Efficiency less important than style | 6 | 8 |
| Didn't think about it | 8 | 11 |
| Other/no ans. | 3 | 4 |
| Total | 74 | 100 |

contemporary buyers were alert to and concerned about the appearance of their kitchens. As table 7.2 shows, only 18 per cent, or under a fifth, regarded functional considerations as more important than style, while 67 per cent, or over two-thirds, of respondents had considerations other than, or in addition to, questions of efficiency in mind, when choosing a new kitchen. The appearance of their new kitchen was an important issue, in its own right, for a majority of buyers.

This leads us to the question of how interested in and alert to the various social and symbolic references borne by different design styles respondents were and how far they shared a common reading of such references with others. We already know that buyers were interested in doing more than simply maximising the efficiency of their kitchen and that they were interested in style. To establish that respondents shared an extended and highly inflected visual language with each other would establish that people possessed the means of consciously giving their kitchens material form in ways that not only expressed a range of social and aesthetic values but that other people could read.

Respondents were given pictures of two kitchens of sharply contrasting design and asked to say what kind of atmosphere they thought the people who had constructed these kitchens were aiming at. It was stressed that the question was not about whether respondents liked or disliked these kitchens. That did not matter. It was also decided to provide no prompting, even initially, for this question to ensure that people were left entirely free to develop their answers in an open-ended way. Only three people, or 4 per cent, hesitated over this question. The great majority offered full and detailed answers readily and easily. Equally significantly, people read these pictures' visual messages in such similar ways and there was such an extensive overlap in the vocabulary they employed to describe them that very few categories were needed for coding the answers. This in itself was compelling evidence of a shared visual language.

One of the pictures used for this question was also the one used for reporting people's assessment of the efficiency of a given kitchen layout (plate 7.2). Two main categories of response were identified from the answers to this question. One related primarily to the social ambience people saw the kitchen's physical attributes as creating; the other related to the emotional resonances people saw as imbued in these physical attributes. The first category was designated '*farmhouse/country*'. This rubric also embraced '*cottage, rural, olde worlde, traditional*'. The second category, termed '*warm/homely*', also covered '*comfortable, cosy, family*'. The distribution of answers this categorisation produced is presented in table 7.3. Between them the first three categories account for 84 per cent of responses, indicating a high level of shared visual understanding.

**Table 7.3** *Respondents' interpretation of ambience of kitchen shown in plate 7.2*

| Categories | No. | % of all |
|---|---|---|
| Farmhouse/country | 16 | 22 |
| Warm/homely | 32 | 43 |
| Both the above | 14 | 19 |
| Other | 6 | 8 |
| Don't know | 3 | 4 |
| No ans. | 3 | 4 |
| Total | 74 | 100 |

**Plate 7.3** Picture of a top of the market, prize-winning kitchen, in a high-gloss aubergine and black lacquer with satin-finished stainless-steel cooker and hood. Respondents were handed a colour version of this picture and asked for their views on its design. *Courtesy, Poggenpohl Ltd.*

Respondents were further asked to undertake a variant of this exercise. They were given a picture of a top-of-the-market, design-award-winning kitchen (plate 7.3),[3] though the information that it was an expensive kitchen and had won a design award was withheld. They were just handed the picture and a list of eight adjectives, *'friendly, comfortable, streamlined, warm, cool, elegant, clean, practical'*. They were then asked to select the two adjectives they considered most appropriate for describing this kitchen followed by the two they regarded as least appropriate.

Two of the adjectives were not widely chosen. Over three-quarters of respondents, however, chose *'friendly'* as one of the two least appropriate adjectives to describe this kitchen, while over half selected *'streamlined'* and a third of respondents thought *'elegant'* one of the two most appropriate words for describing the design. The distribution of the choice of adjectives is given in table 7.4. Again, it offers evidence of a shared visual interpretation and understanding of material conditions.

Having established that respondents shared a visual language, it became possible to ask how conscious they were of the opportunities this gave them for expressing themselves creatively, that is, for using design

**Table 7.4** *Respondents' choice of appropriate and inappropriate adjectives for describing the top-of-the-market, design-award-winning kitchen*

| Least or next least appropriate adjective | % of 100% | Most or next most appropriate adjective | % of 100% |
|---|---|---|---|
| Friendly | 78 | Clean | 56 |
| Comfortable | 59 | Streamlined | 52 |
| Warm | 43 | Elegant | 32 |

N.B. Because respondents were each selecting two adjectives the columns do not add up to 100.

to communicate their ideas and feelings. The idea that planning a kitchen was a creative exercise was suggested in two of the advertising blurbs. One example is the following.

> Planned in another way in another room, this beautiful design could create an entirely different feel . . . here it is spectacularly modern. It . . . illustrates the design quality inherent in all our furniture . . . Your imagination and ideas are the other essentials.

Following the discussion of the advertising blurbs respondents were therefore asked whether they themselves saw the planning of a new kitchen as an artistic/creative process (table 7.5).

**Table 7.5** *Respondents' response to the idea that kitchen planning could be a creative project*

| Category | No. | % |
|---|---|---|
| 1 Yes, it is creative | 10 | 13 |
| 2 Yes, it's creative but the blurb is silly | 26 | 35 |
| 3 It's a silly idea | 19 | 26 |
| 4 Blank response | 6 | 8 |
| 5 Other | 11 | 15 |
| 6 No ans. | 2 | 3 |
| Total | 74 | 100 |

The largest group of responses, categories 1 and 2 in table 7.5, accounting for 48 per cent, or almost half, were open to the suggestion that installing a new kitchen was a creative process and some respondents took the idea for granted:

Definitely a creative process. (c. 19, soc. cl. A)
Of course it's a creative process. (c. 63, soc. cl. C1)
Making a home is a creative project. (c. 64, soc. cl. D)

But other answers in this category, while concurring with this, expressed other feelings too:

It's nice to make something nice, though I'm not very creative. (c. 58, soc. cl. B)
I don't think it's silly. It's quite a creative effort. But I find it difficult. I'm a struggler. (c. 21, soc. cl. C2)

And among other respondents the answers shaded into a more defensive kind of reply:

Yes, though I'm more practical than artistic. (c. 15, soc. cl. C1)
Yes, though I didn't go out to choose something artistic. I wasn't planning to do it that way. I'm practical. (c. 70, soc. cl. A)

These respondents, while accepting the idea that there is artistry in designing a new kitchen, were insistent about emphasising the importance of a practical approach. There was little difference, in fact, between these last two replies and one offered by someone who, having said they disagreed with the idea that designing a kitchen involved an artistic element, then added:

I don't see myself as a creative, arty person though some people see me as that. I wanted a practical kitchen. (c. 60, soc. cl. B)

This group felt the need to dissociate themselves from a charge of being artistic.

There was one group, however, who thought the idea of planning a kitchen as being a creative or artistic venture was just plain silly, and another of people who seemed unable to take in or comprehend the idea that planning a kitchen could be a creative project. Together these groups accounted for 34 per cent, or a third, of respondents. The 'other' answers also included a number of people whose responses included similar sentiments. As part of his answer to this question one respondent in the 'other' group said:

I'd have to scratch my head and say 'What *are* they on about?' (c. 61, soc. cl. C1)

Another respondent allocated to the 'other' category because of his rather complicated overall response also concluded his answer with the words:

. . . [It] makes me think 'What are they talking about?' (c. 10, soc. cl. B)

It was also a feature of this question that, once people had allocated themselves to a category, they not infrequently proceeded to elaborate on their initial answer in ways which then problematised the initial categorisation. The following answer, for example, began on one note and ended on another and finished up in the 'other' category:

> It is creative. But I wouldn't call it creative. It's a bit of an arty word. I just want to make it home. (c. 28, soc. cl. C2)

One reason for the mixed-category answers to this question was again the strong discomfort some people felt about being seen as artistic. Quite a number of people expressed their sense of unease or nervousness about this both verbally and in terms of body language. One respondent provided a clue as to what sometimes lay behind this discomfort.

> I think it's pandering to one's ego really. (c. 49, soc. cl. D)

In summary, this question revealed a substantial number of respondents who were uneasy about being thought to be creative because they did not want to be associated with styles which might be labelled arty. These respondents seemed to see the art world as consisting of people with whom they had nothing in common, artistically, socially or morally, and they wanted to establish their distance from them.

It does not follow, of course, that this group of respondents therefore had no strong opinions about different kinds of kitchen design, or that they lacked a developed visual aesthetic or were uncreative in the way they refurbished their own kitchens. Indeed, there is already evidence that the contrary was true.

We know from their responses to plates 7.2 and 7.3 that people shared a visual vocabulary. The next question was how far they drew on this facility in interpreting the material environment other people constructed around themselves as part of locating those people socially and morally. To explore this the picture of the award-winning kitchen was once more utilised and respondents were invited to say what they thought of it as a design and then what kind of person they thought might buy it. They were still given no indication of either the make or cost of these kitchen units.

The responses were assured, voluble, forceful and vivid. In addition, though the question was open-ended, the themes of many of the answers were strikingly similar. Regardless of social class the design was not one to which most people responded warmly. Only a few liked it or were positive about it. Many people expressed their dislike of it with considerable feeling. Answers at the less passionate end of the negative response spectrum included things like:

Not something I would choose. (c. 16, soc. cl. C2)
I don't like it, full stop. (c. 25, soc. cl. C2)

One step up from this came answers like:

Horrid. (c. 5, soc. cl. B) (c. 55, soc. cl. B)
Awful. (c. 22, soc. cl. C2) (c. 35, soc. cl. C1)
Dreadful. (c. 41, soc. cl. C1)[4]

At the top of the scale responses included:

Horrendous. I'd rather die than be in something like that. It looks like hell on earth. (c. 27, soc. cl. B)
Awful. I wouldn't even like to go into one. (c. 34, soc. cl. B)
Anyone who bought a kitchen like that I can't think would be a friend of mine. (c. 38, soc. cl. B)

At the positive end of the spectrum answers included:

You'd expect to see it somewhere like Lloyds of London. In the right place it could be OK. (c. 45, soc. cl. C1)
OK if you had a very modern house. (c. 20, soc. cl. A)

And a small number of people responded to it enthusiastically:

Very interesting, exciting. Very elegant, very sophisticated. (c. 37, soc. cl. C2)
I like it very much. Unfortunately I wouldn't be able to afford something like that. (c. 73, soc. cl. B)

As interesting, however, as whether people liked this design or not was how they described it and how they positioned it socially in terms of taste. While many people described it simply as 'very modern' or 'ultra-modern', twenty-nine respondents, or 39 per cent, described it as 'space-age, space-shuttle, futuristic, sci-fi'. And, when asked who they thought might buy such a kitchen, 66 per cent, or two-thirds, of the answers slotted into three categories: twenty-eight, or 38 per cent, opted for some variant of the young, trendy, rich yuppie bachelor; eleven, or 15 per cent, for some kind of celebrity, such as an actor or pop star; and ten, or 14 per cent, for an architect, designer or other member of the art world. So, for example:

City-oriented, a stockbroker with a bachelor pad. (c. 35, soc. cl. C1)
Young – in show business-cum-celebrity. (c. 46, soc. cl. C1)
An architect because they have some funny ways. (c. 41, soc. cl. C1)

Fifteen, or 20 per cent, gave what seemed for these respondents to be a variant on this first group of answers. They saw this kitchen design as catering to a desire for self-display or showing off. Buyers would therefore be:

Some one out to impress . . . a sort of 'look at me' kitchen. (c. 37, soc. cl. C2)

A successful business man or someone into design who thinks it's the kind of thing to have, the latest fashion in kitchens . . . It's a bit like Vivienne Westwood clothes. People just buy them to say, 'Oh, it's a Vivienne Westwood.' (c. 66, soc. cl. B)

or someone who wanted:

A talking-point kitchen, a 'look at me' kitchen (c. 72, soc. cl. B)

or simply:

. . . a showpiece. (c. 58, soc. cl. B)

People did not see the potential owners of such kitchens, however, in traditional class terms but rather in terms of smaller occupational groups.

Opinions about who would own such a kitchen were sometimes combined with another commonly expressed opinion, that this kitchen was never intended for eating or, even, for cooking in. One respondent struggling to capture their feeling about this came up with the inventive expression, 'the unfood-like look of it'. Variants of this feeling about the kitchen occurred in nineteen, or 26 per cent, of the replies to this question:

A professional single man would buy a kitchen like that, someone who's never going to cook. He brings his take-away in and eats it in the other room. (c. 13, soc. cl. C2)
It's the sort of kitchen they don't cook in – just bring home a Chinese. (c. 51, soc. cl. C2)

People often felt strongly about what they saw as the acute limitations of this kitchen's design as a family kitchen One way they sought to convey this was to say where they thought the kitchen would be appropriate. Twenty-three, or 31 per cent, of respondents did this. While suggestions ranged widely, there was, nevertheless, a kind of generic link between them. The list included a hotel, a restaurant, a school, a commercial kitchen, a hospital, an operating theatre, a bathroom and a lavatory. Nearly all these suggestions were offered more than once. Some, such as the lavatory comparison, were offered several times. Many of the suggestions seemed to be as much poetic, expressive responses as analytical ones. A number of people suggested the design would suit an operating theatre. The interchange this generated between one husband and his wife makes clear the expressive as opposed to literal intent behind such comparisons:

*Wife:* It looks like an operating theatre.
*Husband:* It doesn't look at all like that. But I know what you mean. (c. 3, soc. cl. B)

One man saw the design as appropriate to:

> a posh hotel's ladies' loo. (c. 49, soc. cl. D)

In view of the respondent's gender, it seems unlikely that he had an extensive experience of such places and more likely that the respondent's aim was less to be precise about what would be a suitable location for such a design as to communicate his feeling about the design's aesthetic ambience.

Despite being given no indication of its cost, the feeling that this was an expensive kitchen was widespread. Together with their sense of the kind of people they imagined might buy such a kitchen, this pushed a small number of people into loosely relating design preference to social class.

> It's not a working-class kitchen. (c. 17, soc. cl. C1)
>
> It's not for an ordinary person. (c. 47, soc. cl. C2)
>
> It would be like aspiring to a BMW or a Merc but that is outside my lifestyle. I'd feel awkward in it if I was living like I am now . . . It gives the impression of exclusivity. You'd be a long way from going round MFI. (c. 21, soc. cl. C2)
>
> It wouldn't even suit my sister-in-law and she's got much higher taste than what I've got, and more money. (c. 59, soc. cl. D)

Class, however, was not a strong referent for most people in thinking about this kitchen. For the bulk of respondents there were stronger and more cogent reasons for rejecting this kitchen. People repeatedly complained that they would not be able to 'live' in this kitchen. Such a complaint was hardly intended to be taken literally, but rather seemed a shorthand by which people expressed their feeling that this was not a friendly, comfortable kitchen, and that it lacked the aura of domesticity they felt they wanted in a kitchen. One man, stolidly silent for almost the entire interview, was impelled by this picture into saying to his wife:

> When I come in in my muddy boots from clay shooting you'd be shouting at me all the time. and my boss wouldn't be able to throw his wellie boots down. (c. 9, soc. cl. D)

Another couple had a similar discussion.

> *Wife:* If you left anything out it would look untidy. You'd have to keep it just like that.
>
> *Husband:* No good my putting my boots and grub box in the corner. It would look right out of place. (c. 13, soc. cl. C2)

So far the quotations illustrating people's responses to the award-winning kitchen have all been snippets from answers given. But to conclude the discussion of this question and to illustrate something of the quality and subtlety of many of the answers a small number of longer quotations are offered. Whatever sense of unease respondents harboured about the art world in general, their answers to this question left no doubt about their capacity for sophisticated visual interpretation. As unrehearsed spoken answers, they often wander, but they place the kitchen socially with great nicety; convey, often vividly, the different reservations people had about this kitchen; and are articulate about their desires for their own kitchen. None of these answers has been quoted so far in the discussion of this question.

> I couldn't possibly live in it. It's not relaxed or comfortable. It wouldn't fit in with my character or lifestyle. Too cleaned up. I like clutter. I've deliberately introduced clutter in my kitchen. You wouldn't want to stay in that kitchen even to cook. It's for a very smart, high-powered young bachelor Not a family kitchen. It's a singles kitchen . . . male and unmarried. You couldn't have toddlers in. (c. 44, soc. cl. B)

> Nobody cooks in this kitchen . . . It looks expensive. It looks as if you've got a kitchen for a kitchen's sake. It seems like something a megastar from Hollywood or a rock star like Mick Jagger would have. They certainly don't eat in this kitchen. I can't imagine anyone actually doing anything in that kitchen. Someone might walk in and have a glass of wine but that would be about it . . . Very posh. (c. 2, soc. cl. C2)

> I don't hate it but it's a bit like a toilet. It's very functional but it's a bit too not-of-this-world. I don't dislike it. It's going on my lines, but it's a bit too cool. I'd like to think mine was friendly as well. I can see a master chef in there. Nobody I know would buy a kitchen a bit like that. It would be a professional person, a yuppie. I can imagine it in Canary Wharf where someone comes home and shoves something in the microwave. As my mother would say, 'Can't they have a mat on the floor?' (c. 26, soc. cl. C1)

> Horrible absolutely. I thought it was a bathroom to begin with. It's too ultra-modern. Nothing warm, cosy, just practical. A bachelor might buy it, a yuppie in his thirties making lots of money on the stock exchange – in a penthouse flat. (c. 30, soc. cl. C2)

Most people, then, did not like this kitchen. And even those who did might add a proviso, that it wouldn't 'go' in their house:

> [It] could look stunning in the right place. Try putting it into our house and it would look absolutely gross. (c. 20, soc. cl. A)
> In the right place it could be OK. In here the building just doesn't allow it. (c. 45, soc. cl. C1)

While confirming the existence of a shared visual language among respondents, the picture of the expensive award-winning kitchen elicited a wide a range of colourful opinions about design tastes from respondents. It showed both that people had strong aesthetic preferences and were adept at relating visual tastes to socio-economic groups, not in traditional social-class terms but in terms of smaller occupational groups. At this level their reading was both shared and highly inflected.[5]

This raises the question of the extent to which people took advantage of their visual prowess, actively using it, as they installed their own kitchens, to tell others what kind of people they were and what kind of values they cherished. Before looking at how people related their design preferences to the decoration of their own houses, however, it was necessary to establish what those design preferences were. To begin on this, respondents were offered pictures of five kitchens depicting as widely varied and contrasting styles currently on the market as could be found. As the choice of design was huge, some arbitrariness in selection was unavoidable. In addition, all the pictures were packed with detail and a short verbal description can only convey their appearance and ambience in very general terms. To give readers a broad idea of their variety some of the main features of these kitchens are listed. There was a kitchen with pine units bearing simple knob handles, and a solid, rectangular table, all in light yellow wood; a farmhouse-style kitchen with rich brown wooden fittings adorned with scrolled bronze handles and an ample table for eating; an expensive, top-of-the-market kitchen sporting a good deal of stainless steel, unit doors laminated in bright, shiny turquoise and black metal stools tucked under a high eating bar; a kitchen with dark, gun-metal-grey cabinets which reflected the light sharply, dark olive-green floor and wall tiles, a considerable number of chrome fittings and high bar stools: and, finally, a kitchen equipped with completely white units, down to the handles, red lino flooring, a large stainless-steel cooker hood, small white folding table and slatted folding chairs, which could be opened up when eating and stacked away at other times.

While all the kitchens were supplied with an abundance of modern kitchen technology, their designs were geared to creating very different kinds of ambience. At one end there were the kitchens in pine or brown wood which sought to emanate a simple or warm domesticity and, by implication, familial values. At the other end there were the shiny laminate, chrome and stainless-steel kitchens, celebrations of high tech.

People were asked to rank-order these pictures in terms of their preference (table 7.6). The farmhouse-style kitchen with its rich brown wooden unit doors emerged as most popular. Almost three-quarters, or

**Table 7.6** *The sample's stylistic preferences*

| Category | Choice | No. (total = 74) | % | Combined % |
|---|---|---|---|---|
| Farmhouse kitchen | 1st | 30 | 41 | 72 |
| | 2nd | 23 | 31 | |
| Pine kitchen | 1st | 19 | 26 | 61 |
| | 2nd | 26 | 35 | |
| White kitchen | 1st | 14 | 19 | 38 |
| | 2nd | 14 | 19 | |
| Shiny turquoise laminate kitchen | 1st | 8 | 11 | 15 |
| | 2nd | 3 | 4 | |
| Dark gun-metal kitchen | 1st | 4 | 5 | 15 |
| | 2nd | 7 | 9 | |

72 per cent, of respondents ranked this kitchen as their first or second choice. In terms of popularity, the pine kitchen followed the farmhouse kitchen, the white kitchen fell in the middle and the two high-tech kitchens, the dark gun-metal kitchen and the shiny turquoise laminate top-of-the-market kitchen, shared being least popular. In both cases, just 15 per cent of respondents made them their first or second choice. The dark gun-metal kitchen might be regarded as marginally less popular than the shiny laminate kitchen in that fewer people made it their first choice.

Despite the pattern of preferences expressed, some caution in interpreting these findings should be exercised. On the one hand, the findings show that there was a preference for what would be read in the visual language of our culture as homely kitchens over those kitchens which visually read as lauding technological innovation and masculinity. That is clear. On the other hand, although the farmhouse kitchen was overall the most popular design, almost 60 per cent of the sample made another design their first choice. Any interpretation of these results needs to take this into account.

What was increasingly apparent, in fact, was that when people embarked on selecting a new kitchen design they soon found themselves juggling with a number of competing factors because in designing a new kitchen they had a variety of considerations in mind which they were keen to accommodate. Thus, what people said they liked when presented with an array of pictures of different kitchen designs but no specific context and what kind of kitchen they actually chose to install in their homes did not necessarily correspond. This does not mean that respondent reactions to the pictures of different kitchen designs were irrelevant to an understanding of how people chose a new kitchen. But it does point to the importance of considering the range of factors people took into account when choosing a kitchen and the interplay between these factors. For it was this interplay that ultimately determined both the final choice of design and the final appearance of people's kitchens.

As they selected their new kitchen furniture a strong sense of what might be termed architectural propriety, that is, a strong concern to establish what they saw as an appropriate harmony between the architectural style of their house and their interior décor, was a key issue for people, cross-cutting other important considerations. One woman, who lived in a 1900s house, expressed this sense of propriety through her exasperated comments on her builders. She wanted an extra window in her new kitchen but had great difficulty in getting the builder to do this in what she considered the correct way:

> They gave no importance to the window being a proper sash window that would fit in with the house. Any old window would have done for them. (c. 31, soc. cl. B)

In similar vein a woman living in a 1930s house with Sunspan windows said:

> I haven't put everything in the house that is in 30s style but I have avoided a cottagey look as inappropriate. (c. 33, soc. cl. B) (see plate 9.1, p. 186)

Another couple who built their own wood-framed house went up to the Midlands to look at one already constructed. What concerned the wife when she saw the prototype was that the house was:

> traditional except the kitchen, which was entirely white. It was very nice but seemed out of keeping. I wouldn't have felt comfortable in that room. (c. 32, soc. cl. B)

When they came to construct their own house, therefore, she saw to it that this was changed.

This sense of propriety had been apparent in some of the responses to the award- winning kitchen when a number of people remarked that in the right place and the right kind of house they would not object to such a kitchen. Other people, basically pursuing the same line of reasoning, said that, while they would have liked a farmhouse-style kitchen, they felt it would be inappropriate in their house. Thus one woman described how:

> I went to a friend's who's got a converted barn and I was dribbling all over her kitchen. She had a red Aga and clothes above and dried flowers. She

had the clothes there even though she had visitors coming. That really impressed me, that she hadn't put the clothes away. But my house isn't suitable.

And she specifically made the point that, conscious that she had a modern house, she had:

kept to a modern style in a general way. (c. 28, soc. cl. C2) (see plate 9.1, p. 186)

This is not to say people wanted their kitchen to mirror the style of the house but they did want it to complement that style, in the rather formal sense in which they understood that word. This could significantly change their initial uncontextualised design preferences. What people might ideally, in an unconstrained world, have selected and the style they actually chose for their kitchen could be markedly different.

A concern with trying to make a kitchen emanate an overall visual coherence while realising several goals was apparent in the seriousness with which people approached the selection of the furnishing accessories for their kitchens. It became clear that the choice of floor covering, curtains, lampshades and tiling could absorb a huge amount of time, involve a lot of legwork and generate considerable frustration when people couldn't find what they wanted. Even then, a number of people were still prepared to wait rather than compromise over these items, an indication of their importance to them (table 7.7).

**Table 7.7** *Respondents' opinion of the importance of accessories in a kitchen*

| Importance of accessories | No. | % |
| --- | --- | --- |
| Superficial/cosmetic | 3 | 4 |
| Fairly important | 12 | 16 |
| Essential to the kitchens' success | 56 | 76 |
| Other/no ans. | 3 | 4 |
| Total | 74 | 100 |

Having often accepted with equanimity a range of structural and financial constraints, the desire to make their kitchen perfect within the framework of these impositions could be very strong.[6] And when people felt driven to make do with second best this could be a source of continuing disappointment and an ongoing visual irritant. A year after the units were installed, some kitchens still lacked curtains, light shades or other accessories as people were still looking for the right thing. Several recalled that their budgets went awry at this stage when they found that what they wanted was going to cost more than they had planned to spend. While some felt obliged to retrench, others decided there was:

> No point in spending all that money if you aren't going to finish it off properly. (c. 5, soc. cl. B)

or:

> It's not worth spoiling the ship for a ha'p'orth of tar. (c. 70, soc. cl. A)

It took six months and innumerable shop visits, during which her husband recalled she had bored him stiff, before one woman found a lampshade in the colour she wanted (c. 22, soc. cl. C2). Another woman describing the choice of wallpaper recalled that:

> It took me months and months and months and months to decide. (c. 38, soc. cl. B)

And a couple remembered how:

> We had tiles standing about all over the show. (c. 4, soc. cl. C2)

Final selections were, indeed, recalled by a number of respondents as hard work, sometimes bordering on the painful:

> Each choice was agonised over . . . But I have a worrying type of nature. (c. 21, soc. cl. C2)
> I spent ages working out all the colours . . . [and] it took a long time to match all the colours up. There's still a table which is all wrong – the wrong green, and I've spent a long time trying to get the right table for there. And when I do then that awful little stool will have to go. (c. 34, soc. cl. B)

The phrase which occurred most commonly in respondents' explanations of why these things were so important was that they 'finish it off'. The second most frequently used phrase was 'they make it or break it'. In themselves neither phrase is very informative. But as people became more expansive they imbued these vague little phrases with substantive content. As one woman put it:

> If you don't spend time on them you can ruin the whole . . . accessories can change your whole kitchen. If you had a geometric pattern, for example, it could change the whole feel of the kitchen. (c. 66, soc. cl. A)

Another said they were important because:

> Otherwise you've only got units. You want the thing to be a whole, a room – not just units. (c. 39, soc. cl. C1)

There was also a group of answers which dealt with the role of accessories in creating a specific effect people wanted in their particular kitchen. To take just one example from this group, one woman explained that accessories were very important to her:

> because the kitchen was white with blue tiles and I wanted to pick up a bit of colour to add softness and warmth so it didn't look too clinical. (c. 65, soc. cl. A)

This last comment begins to highlight another concern, namely that people could want their kitchen to be read in two ways which were not obviously compatible. On the one hand, they might seek to ensure an efficient working kitchen but, on the other, be equally concerned that their kitchen was 'friendly', 'warm', 'cosy', that is to say, inviting to people. This made a number of respondents express a concern that their kitchen shouldn't have too spare a look which, while it might be part of creating a practical kitchen, would be read as clinical.

What the discussion over accessories threw into relief, indeed, was how many respondents consciously and actively sought ways of softening the appearance of their kitchen despite their concern with creating a practical and efficient workplace. Clearly the former concern could work against maximising a reading of the kitchen as practical and clean. A consideration of the effect of this on the overall design of many of the sample kitchens also leads us from looking at respondents' attitudes to efficiency in the kitchen to considering the kitchen as a symbol of domesticity or the heart of the home. This also raises the question of the role this latter concern played in the construction of a personal aesthetic. The impact of this on people's handling of the design and furnishing of a new kitchen takes us into the next chapter.

# Notes

1. There is a long-standing and deeply engrained Western tradition which links facial attributes to moral traits. At its simplest it is found in the fairy story. We know that the princess is good because she is beautiful, but also that she is beautiful because she is good. Similarly the witch's ugliness tells us that she is wicked. And the convention remains very much alive. It is a mainstay of contemporary film and television, where

some actors are constantly offered parts as heroes while others, simply because of their looks and body build, are repeatedly cast as baddies. And this is only the start. Close-set eyes are shifty, a high forehead indicates intelligence, a receding chin denotes a weak determination. As we get older we recognise and respond to clues in novels, plays and films which posit a far more refined relationship between the inner and outer person but the basic iconography of the fairy story is rarely discarded entirely.

2. Case categories here make clear that a wide array of cases have been drawn on and therefore the widely held nature of these opinions and their accompanying experiences.

3. This exercise was not concerned with whether people liked or disliked this kitchen but only with how they read it. However, it was a kitchen which had been designed with a great deal of self-consciousness and came from a design series which had won a number of awards in different countries.

4. Single words may scarcely seem to warrant being identified by case and all were used more than once, some several times. For the sake of completeness, however, usage by individual cases is identified.

5. The urge to express their visual responses accurately more than once edged people into constructing a new vocabulary to meet their needs, as in the case of the respondent who, groping for precision, described the top-of-the-market kitchen as 'a bit too not-of-this-world'.

6. It could belie earlier protestations that installing a kitchen was not a creative project.

# –8–

# Finishing off and adding the clutter

In tracing the history of twentieth-century kitchen design, chapter 2 outlined two major developments: the adoption of ideas drawn from theories of scientific management by a number of women writers in the United States whose aim was to ease the domestic burden women laboured under, and the translation of these ideas into a design style by the modernist European avant-garde. The influence of these developments on the appearance of today's domestic kitchens has been profound. At the same time a very different image of the kitchen has persisted within English social consciousness and the indigenous imagination. Vernacular memory has continued to cherish a concept of the English kitchen as the heart of the home. This kitchen is a multi-purpose eating–living–working room. It is open to all age groups and both sexes without discrimination; it severely limits privacy, lauds shared activity and celebrates informality. Its origins lie in a time when social and economic exigencies forced a large segment of the population into shared and confined living conditions.[1] Today, new economic developments in conjunction with changing social mores are effecting huge modifications both to the patterns of occupational life and the structure of personal relationships, and, as usual under such conditions, this leaves many people feeling socially and mentally uncertain and somewhat insecure. Meanwhile the passage of time has softened people's memories of the harshness of life and dimmed their recollections of the less attractive aspects of many family relationships in the past. As a result the idea of the living-kitchen has acquired an appeal as a potential means of creating material conditions conducive to and supportive of domestic solidarity.

A central concern of this chapter is to look at how the idea of the living-kitchen informed the way contemporary buyers planned and decorated their new kitchens. The account provided in chapter 2 made clear that the idea of the living-kitchen was never part of the professional design concerns which developed the concept of a fitted kitchen. In so far, therefore, as purchasers today are concerned to intermesh technological efficiency with a kitchen décor which reads as the heart of the home, such an endeavour cannot be characterised as the public deferring to the interests and values of the world of professional design. Rather, such concerns show contemporary buyers acting as independent agents. By a process of selection, in which they take what they want from the world of professional design and reject what they are uneasy with or dislike, they construct a material environment for themselves which suits their needs as they define them. An examination of the process by which buyers do this raises a number of aesthetic issues and, by the end of the chapter, leads to an explication and analysis of popular taste in contemporary kitchens as revealed in the finished kitchens of the sample.

It will help to start by looking at a quintessential written account of a living-kitchen from the past, namely, the kitchen Laurie Lee describes in his autobiographical work, *Cider with Rosie*:

> our waking life and our growing years were for the most part spent in the kitchen, and until we married, or ran away, it was the common room we shared. Here we lived and fed in a family fug, not minding the little space, trod on each other like birds in a hole, elbowed our ways without spite, all talking at once or all silent at once, or crying against each other, but never I think feeling overcrowded, being as separate as notes in a scale.
>
> That kitchen, worn by our boots and lives, was scruffy, warm, and low, whose fuss of furniture seemed never the same but was shuffled around each day. A black grate crackled with coal and beech-twigs; towels toasted on the guard; the mantel was littered with fine old china, horse brasses, and freak potatoes. On the floor were strips of muddy matting, the windows were choked with plants, the walls supported stopped clocks and calendars, and smokey fungus ran over the ceilings. There were also six tables of different sizes, some armchairs gapingly stuffed, boxes, stools, and unravelling baskets, books and papers on every chair, a sofa for cats, a harmonium for coats, and a piano for dust and photographs. These were the shapes of our kitchen landscape, the rocks of our submarine life, each object worn smooth by our constant nuzzling, or encrusted by lively barnacles, relics of birthdays and dead relations, wrecks of furniture long since foundered, all silted deep by Mother's newspapers which the years piled round on the floor.

Lee does not gloss over the physical shabbiness of this kitchen, nor, more importantly, its dirtiness. And his description of the matriarch whose kingdom this was combines affection and admiration with critical distance.

> Our mother was a buffoon, extravagant and romantic, and was never taken seriously. Yet within her she nourished a delicacy of taste, a sensibility, a brightness of spirit, which though continuously bludgeoned by the cruelties

of her luck remained uncrushed and unembittered to the end. Wherever she got it from, God knows – or how she managed to preserve it. But she loved this world and saw it fresh with hopes that never faded.[2]

The physical features of the domesticity with which this mother surrounded herself and in which she raised her fledgling children reflect both her irredeemably chaotic, yet indomitably vital, approach to life and the world. Her kitchen becomes the materialisation of maternity, a life-force in its own right, and thereby a concrete expression of the power of family life to provide both a sense of belonging and a sense of self in a turbulent world. For if Lee's description of this kitchen eschews sentimentality it is deeply suffused with sentiment, offering a powerful evocation of a mode of family living which gives its members a sense of being wrapped in a warm embrace from which they derive a sense of physical and emotional security. It is in polar contrast to the Schutte-Lihotsky kitchen described in chapter 2 which sought to valorise very different concerns.

We have seen that many respondents welcomed equally the decline in poverty and the growth of domestic technology and onset of mechanisation. Their attitudes to these issues suggest that they would have reacted with fastidious distaste at the shabbiness and dirt of the Lee kitchen. At the same time a strong attachment to the *idea* of the kitchen as the heart of the home emerged repeatedly during the interviews. It was apparent, for example, in the considerable number of respondents who, offered pictures of different styles of kitchens, placed a farmhouse-style kitchen, which represented a cleaned-up and modernised version of the Lee kitchen, high on their list of preferences. And when asked to describe a similar kitchen popular adjectives were 'traditional', 'family', 'warm'. The discussion of respondents' attitudes to selecting floor covering, curtains and tiles with which the last chapter closed also indicated that, while people wanted practical kitchens, they did not want ones which looked clinical. The desire for efficiency had to compete with other considerations.

To explore this, respondents were directly asked, towards the end of the interview, whether they saw their own kitchen as 'the heart of the home' or 'a meal machine'. Bearing in mind that architectural factors precluded one group of respondents from using their kitchens for much more than cooking, a very high proportion of those who could make their kitchens operate, in some sense, as 'the heart of the home' did so. Almost two-thirds, or 62 per cent, said they saw their kitchen, either primarily or importantly, as 'the heart of the home'.[3] Demonstrably, the desire to own a clean, efficiently organised, technologically advanced kitchen was widely combined with a desire that it should also be read as and feel family-oriented and family-sustaining. This raises two issues. First, there is the question of whether this view of the role of the kitchen should be regarded as the product of an essentially sentimental or mawkish view of family life. Secondly, there is the issue of how purchasers expressed this view of the role of the kitchen through design and decorating decisions.

An interdisciplinary approach, drawing on the tools of traditional literary critical analysis[4] of Laurie Lee's description of the kitchen of his childhood, helps in thinking about the first of these questions by raising the issue of whether, despite the apparent realism, Lee nevertheless offers a glamorised description of family life. It might well be argued, of course, that all this will tell us is whether or not Lee glamorises his account of the kitchen he grew up in and people might want to ask what this has to do with the sentimentality or realism of the respondents in this study. Certainly a literary analysis of the Lee description is not, in itself, germane to this study. But a full analysis of the entire passage is neither necessary nor proposed. Only as much commentary will be offered as is needed to assess the general value of such descriptions, over and above the immediate narrative in which they occur, for what they can tell us about the broader society in which they were written. The contention is that the Lee description offers an entrée into considering the nature of and relationship between idealist and idealistic concepts.

Lee uses the first paragraph to establish the general ambience of the kitchen and the way it shaped the experience of family relationships and a sense of self. An account of the material conditions of the kitchen, such as details of the furniture and its dispersal, comes in the second paragraph. So in the first paragraph we hear how the family tumbled over each other 'like birds in a hole'. It is a charming simile conjuring up a sense of harmony with nature. And this suggestion then colours the claim which immediately follows that they 'elbowed each other without spite'. It would be an exceptional family, however, where bad temper and an impulse to hurt and damage others didn't sometimes surface, where people always 'talked', never shrieked or swore at each other even though the space they occupied was highly confined. Being able to move away from others, to separate oneself physically, is a well-tried method of defusing tension and, where this is not possible and feelings start to run high, they become difficult to contain and manage. The description also implicitly assumes an uncomplicated impulse to gregariousness among family members. Yet, while the living conditions described by Lee were likely to encourage gregariousness, in a society where the need for privacy has become deep-rooted it seems likely that there were times when different members of the family yearned profoundly for solitude.

Textual analysis of the whole passage would support the argument that Lee's description of the family kitchen, while in many respects offering a realistic and honest account of the material conditions a large and poor family shared as they grew up, is also an account of social relations heavily gilded by fond memories. However, to demonstrate this is not necessarily to denigrate the quality and significance of Laurie Lee's writing. The description comes from Lee's account of his early childhood and is part of an account of childhood itself. The literary stance Lee adopts is thus a precarious and delicate balance between seeing the world through a child's eyes and seeing it through adult eyes, additionally complicated by the fact that it also includes the adult's meditative return to the lost world of childhood. So, while Lee is revisiting some of the fantasies of his childhood, he is simultaneously reconstructing that childhood as an adult looking fondly back on it. And, though he never relinquishes a concern for accuracy and a core of clear-sighted recall informs the writing, autobiographical fact is constantly entangled with autobiographical fantasy. Indeed, much of the writing's power to attract and beguile us lies in the tension between fact and fancy. Ironically it is also where the book's most moving and honest insights about family life are ultimately located. Realistic accuracy is neither the only or necessarily always the most effective way of capturing the truth.

The relevance to the argument here of this kind of analysis of Lee's account of their family kitchen is that Lee's description has many of the attributes of a concept which the style preferences of the sample suggested many respondents were attracted by. It is essentially an idealist concept of the kitchen as the heart of the home, a concept suggesting a way of giving material form to widely held hopes for family life which continue to pervade our culture. The management of space in kitchens regarded as the heart of the home, so as to foster the mixing of various domestic activities, cooking, eating and leisure pursuits, also provides a way of giving symbolic expression in material form to the idea of the family as a close-knit group, in which members offer each other mutual support, pulling together and standing by each other, both in terms of action and in emotional terms.

It might be charged that such kitchens represent not only an idealist but an idealistic concept of family life, if not one positively shot through with sentimentality. Few of us seriously believe that most contemporary families function smoothly or consistently in this way. There is also enough historical evidence to suggest that they were equally rare in the past. But this is to take the idea of the kitchen as the heart of the home literally instead of seeing it as an ideal. And it is to forget that ideals are by definition idealistic and may thus reflect aspirations whose importance for us is not necessarily diminished because we fail to achieve them.

Against this background, discussion turns to consider the degree to which the respondents in this study looked for ways of expressing in material form the values found in the Laurie Lee passage through the layout and furnishing of their new kitchens. To put it another way, the aim is to see how people used design to express various social values and aspirations that were important to them. Whether respondents realised these aspirations personally in terms of their own familial relationships does not need to be and is not part of this study.

It was noted that, when looking at the top-of-the-market kitchen (plate 7.3), a number of respondents said emphatically that they 'couldn't *live* in it' (my emphasis) and their tone of voice indicated clearly that this was not intended as praise. The choice of word was striking and, because the statement was made on several occasions by different respondents, it attracted attention. It was clear that the word was not intended to be taken at face value: it carried a diffuse meaning. For example, though people often wanted the facility for eating in the kitchen, which might be interpreted as being one aspect of living in the kitchen, they often also had, and valued having, a separate dining-room as well. The word 'live' was used rather to denote a certain ambience people wanted to feel pervaded their kitchen. It was not simply having a table and chairs available for eating, but having a certain kind of table and chairs which people felt were stylistically appropriate to a kitchen. When people complained that they could not 'live' in the top-of-the-market kitchen, it seemed another way of saying that it was not a warm or friendly kitchen, not that it lacked facilities for eating, which, in fact, it did not.

Responding in a literary, as opposed to literal, way to what people said can help in analysing attitudes to design. Distinguishing between what people said and what they meant, indeed, was not infrequently integral to an understanding of respondents' comments on issues of style and design. Insisting on sticking to a literal interpretation of answers could, for example, leave a respondent appearing silly when they clearly were not. One woman, for example, commenting on the top-of-the-market kitchen said:

My cat wouldn't like to sit in it. (c. 36, soc. cl. B)

Cats, of course, do not make judgements about design when deciding where they will sit. Rather, this response seems to represent a heavily abridged line of thinking about cats and kitchens in which the presence of a cat in a kitchen is seen as lending an aura of domestic comfort to the room. What this respondent thus seems to be expressing is a feeling that it would be inappropriate to have a cat in a kitchen where the design motives behind the styling of the furniture were clearly not aimed at creating an atmosphere of informality and intimacy. She also, by her reference to having a cat herself, implies that an atmosphere of informality and intimacy was one she herself valued in a kitchen. To cut through this complicated line of thought, however, the woman simply anthropomorphised the cat so as to distil her essential meaning.

Chapter 2 discussed the role of the kitchen in terms of the way people distinguished between different kinds of relaxation and the way different kinds of furniture denoted different kinds of relaxation for people. One product of this was the sample's sense of what was an appropriate use of the kitchen. The lounge with its plushly upholstered and padded easy chairs was for clean relaxation. It was where you congregated after you had washed off the grime of work and changed into clean clothes. But you could sit on an upright chair, even if it was prettily cushioned, and you could sprawl across the kitchen table all evening in your work clothes, despite the fact that the kitchen was normally as clean as the lounge. The proper use of domestic space was determined by historical considerations and by the style of the furniture. Issues of cleanliness and hygiene were not necessarily relevant.

As noted in chapter 2 most people were keen to have a table in the kitchen for informal eating and entertaining. In modest households in the past, the distinction between formal and informal living frequently did not exist,[5] and the popular image of the living-kitchen which has come down to us commonly has the table as a prominent central feature of the room, the axis around which family life rotated. The only other feature which might vie with it would be the hearth. In the modern kitchens of the sample, hearths rarely existed; the table was left to bear the full burden of this role.

However, in only one case had a table been placed squarely in the middle of the room. Significantly this was in the kitchen of a farm worker who still lived in a tied house.[6] Not only this arrangement but the kitchen as a whole, replete with aged Aga, had a feeling of the past about it (plate 8.1). And the table in the middle of the room was a key aspect of this. No-one else had placed their table like that. This was not only true of the 23 per cent of the sample who had kitchen-diners of one kind or another, where the hand of the original architect rather than the current house owner's might still be regarded as wielding a significant control over the organisation of domestic space. It was equally true of the 32 per cent, or third, of the sample who, when they possessed the space, deliberately introduced a table.

**Plate 8.1** This kitchen, with its large table placed squarely in the middle of the room and its refurbished Aga was the most traditional kitchen in the sample.

The lessons of scientific management in the home had been well learnt and people wanted practical functional kitchens incorporating an efficiently constructed work triangle of cooker, sink and worktop. But they also wanted tables in their kitchens. In order not to flout the rules of functionality, tables were thus, with the one exception, placed at the side or at one end of the room, thereby ensuring a clear passage between the sink, cooker and worktop. Such an arrangement simultaneously made various kinds of socialisation in the kitchen comfortable and possible.

However, it was apparent that for a substantial number of the sample the desire for a functional, efficient kitchen was a dependent, rather than independent, variable in many people's design and aesthetic decisions, in that people did not feel a need to ensure that their concern with efficiency was mirrored in their design decisions generally. Some people went so far as to try to hide the functional aspects of their kitchen. A striking example of this was the way some of the sample had hidden their kitchen machines, such as the dishwasher and fridge, in cupboards. They thus retained all the benefits of modern technology and yet anyone entering the kitchen would face an unbroken row of cupboards which, depending on their design, might speak of very different values. As one woman said:

> I wanted a fitted kitchen for the convenience, but I didn't want it to look like a fitted kitchen. (c. 44, soc. cl. B)

By hiding their machines the owner could more easily give expression to the social messages they wanted to convey without sacrificing efficiency.

Another tactic some people adopted for handling the dual role of their kitchen, that it is in part an efficient meal machine and in part represents the warm heart of the home, was to divide the kitchen spatially. In such kitchens one end was given over to being functional while the other became a locus for the expression of the familial values which were so important a feature of the Lee kitchen. By making a 180 degree turn in one of these kitchens you might almost feel you were in another room. One end of the kitchen might parade a sleek, spare arrangement of fitted cupboards and kitchen machinery, the window above the sink might carry a neat Venetian blind and anything not in use be meticulously tidied away. This end of the kitchen could look as though it had been lifted straight from the floor of the retailer's showroom. On turning round, however, one could find oneself facing a table, chairs with chintzy seat cushions and a scatter of loosely folded newspapers, and behind this a shelf or other display facility bearing an array of bric-a-brac, the odd greeting card and a litter of holiday postcards (plates 8.2 and 8.3).

There was one particularly striking example of this Janus-faced kitchen. Because the kitchen entrance was at one end the owner had had to insert the alternative face of the kitchen down a side of the room, so it had a somewhat different format from the one just described, but the organisational principle was the same. The functional part of the kitchen was textbook modernism, stark, black and white units, innocent of all ornamentation. The owner's opinions also displayed a strong modernist spirit:

> I can't bear doors over machines. They're pretending to be what they're not. And I go to these people's houses and they are so proud of them [machines in cupboards] and I think, *why*? Sometimes I say that.

She displayed her own kitchen machinery consciously and assertively. Facing this and constituting an equally emphatic visual presence, however, the owner had placed a dark oak Welsh dresser, typical in its design and ornamentation of the flourishing East London furniture trade of the thirties, catering to popular taste and priced for those on modest incomes. Arranged on this was a 1930s coffee service with demitasse cups and black and gold ornamentation made in pre-war Japan for the Western market, together with a collection of other small black and gold ornaments of various kinds and origins and some general odds and ends. Despite the fact that the colour of the ornaments matched the colour of the kitchen units, the entire feel of this display was at variance with the aesthetic of the units.

**Plates 8.2 and 8.3** One of the Janus-faced kitchens, showing two markedly different styles at the opposite ends of the kitchen. Note, for example, the window with patterned curtains at one end in contrast to the severe blinds at the window at the other end.

The owner, furthermore, had relocated the kitchen from its original position at the back of the house. It now no longer looked out over the garden but onto the street. This meant she not only got a good view of what was going on in the street but was well placed to invite passers-by in. This was no accident. The new arrangement represented a carefully thought out rationale:

> When you put kitchens at the back of the house mothers in them get cut off from the family. I've put it [the kitchen] at the front of the house. You can see what's going on in the street.

She also added that when people entered the house:

> I've designed it so that people have to pass through it [the kitchen]. (c. 10, soc. cl. B)

This kitchen was designed to serve the owner's very personal mixture of expressive and instrumental requirements involving the kitchen both as a meal machine and the heart of the home.

The concern to make the kitchen expressive as opposed to functional made many respondents keen to incorporate display facilities into their kitchens for showing off non-functional items in terms of the work done in kitchens (table 8.1). If one adds the first three categories in table 8.1

**Table 8.1** *The incidence of display facilities in the sample kitchens*

| Display facility | No. | % |
|---|---|---|
| Had special display rack or glass case | 39 | 53 |
| Had a dresser | 3 | 4 |
| Had both of these | 1 | 1 |
| Had none of these | 23 | 31 |
| No ans. | 8 | 11 |
| Total | 74 | 100 |

together, 58 per cent of the sample had organised display facilities for themselves in their new kitchens. In their construction and design these frequently combined features from the traditional dresser and the display cabinet, and were equally frequently deliberately planned as an integral part of the overall kitchen design, sometimes at considerable expense.

In another variant of the double-faced kitchen, for example, one wife decided she wanted to demarcate the eating area from the cooking area. To this end she arranged to have a display cabinet raised above the end of the worktop and at right angles to it to create a partial room divider. It turned out to be a far from simple construction job and her husband toiled over it. When he finally got it up safely and realised just how his wife proposed to use it she recalled how he turned and looked at her:

> He said, 'I'm not being funny but did we pay all that money to have you go round car boot sales to buy bits of green glass to put in this?' And I said, 'Well, yes.' (c. 56, soc. cl. C2)

In terms of their symbolic messages a display cabinet full of green glass sits uneasily with the proselytising of Mrs Frederick and the celebration of efficiency early modernist kitchen design sought to convey. It derives from a differently grounded aesthetic altogether (plate 8.4).

Buyers across all the social classes were prepared both to sacrifice a degree of efficiency and to expend sizeable sums of money in the interests of this differently grounded aesthetic. The husband of another woman[7] owned a glass collection which he had lovingly put together over a period of years. In their spacious house they could have displayed the collection in a number of places. The wife, however, decided she wanted to show off the collection in the kitchen despite the fact that it meant she had to sacrifice kitchen cupboard space. And not only was she prepared to do that. In order that her display case should arouse memories of the traditional dresser, she had the cabinet doors built to meet the worktop,

**Plate 8.4** Kitchen with a specially built glass-fronted cabinet for displaying the wife's collection of green glass bought at car boot sales.

**Plate 8.5** Large, carefully appointed display cabinets installed to show off a husband's much loved collection of quality glass.

thereby sacrificing a significant amount of worktop space as well. What made these decisions particularly interesting was that this respondent had been one of that minority, 18 per cent of the total sample, who earlier reported that they regarded practical considerations as *more* important in planning a kitchen than the choice of design style. It afforded a classic example of the way actions are often more revealing than words (plate 8.5).

This case raises questions about the kinds of things people displayed in their kitchens and the importance of these items for them. These items belonged to quite a different category of objects from the 'accessories' discussed in the previous chapter. Clusters of pictures, wall plaques, flowers, fresh, dried or artificial, family photographs and collections of china or pottery animals abounded. There were also plates on specially made racks which were clearly never used for eating, bowls of plastic or wooden fruit, lush but inedible, and teapots from which a cup of tea had never been poured and, in all probability, never would be. Despite their apparently disparate nature, however, many of the objects shared a generic similarity, and it seemed appropriate to categorise most of them under the general heading of bric-a-brac. Under this heading respondents were asked how important these items were for them as part of their new kitchen décor (table 8.2). By summing the first two categories in table 8.2

**Table 8.2** *The importance of kitchen bric-a-brac for respondents*

| Attitude to bric-a-brac | No. | % |
|---|---|---|
| Had 1 or 2 items of bric-a-brac and considered them important | 38 | 52 |
| Had 3+ items of bric-a-brac and considered them important | 14 | 19 |
| Had 1+ items of bric-a-brac but did not regard them as important | 12 | 16 |
| Other ans. | 9 | 12 |
| No ans. | 1 | 1 |
| Total | 74 | 100 |

we see that 71 per cent of respondents not only had bric-a-brac in their kitchens but regarded it as important. Women regarded it as more important than men, however. Of 59 women, 46, or 78 per cent, regarded bric-a-brac as important. In contrast, of the 15 male respondents, 6, or 40 per cent, regarded bric-a-brac as important. Another 6, or 40 per cent, of men gave answers which fell outside the main categories, in contrast to 3, or 5 per cent, of the women. While some of these numbers are small, the differentials are considerable.

The ubiquitous presence of bric-a-brac in so many of the sample kitchens brings us back to *Cider with Rosie*. The bric-a-brac which featured so prominently in many of the new kitchens visited seemed to be the equivalent, in contemporary terms, of the accumulation of debris which was such a marked feature of that kitchen. The Laurie Lee kitchen, however, belonged to a poorer age and the accumulation of debris there just happened. In contemporary kitchens the presence of bric-a-brac was rarely just fortuitous.

People did still acquire items by chance and other items arrived as unsolicited presents. Such objects might finish up in the kitchen because people could not find another place for them, though they could be there because, having come into possession of them, people felt that the kitchen was an appropriate place to locate them. But with more money to spend the gathering of debris had become, at least in part, a planned and self-conscious process. And, though people might choose the style of their new kitchen, select the actual units of furniture with great care and put a huge amount of effort into the acquisition of accompanying accessories, a majority of buyers did not regard their kitchens as completed or, as it was frequently put, 'finished' until they had their 'knick-knacks' or 'bits and pieces' in place. The reasons people gave for the importance of apparently trivial 'knick-knacks' fell into three main categories.

One reason for regarding bric-a-brac as important was a dislike of bare walls. What might be called an anti-modernist aesthetic was widespread.

Respondents frequently saw simplicity and minimalism as 'stark', 'wooden' or, vaguely but feelingly, as 'horrible'. The kind of modernist aesthetic which celebrates a spare, undecorated style did not communicate the kind of visual messages people wanted to convey with their kitchen décor. One virtue of bric-a-brac, indeed, for some people was precisely its ability to 'kill' or 'break up' bareness, to 'fill plain areas' and thereby, as they put it, to 'soften' a room. A second reason for favouring bric-a-brac arose from the desire to 'personalise' and 'individualise' the kitchen, so as to 'give it character'. Ornaments, souvenirs and family mementos were often felt to perform such a role. Respondents' concern that their kitchen should feel 'homely' and emanate a sense of family, however, was the most frequently voiced reason for favouring the inclusion of bric-a-brac in the kitchen. For a sizeable group of respondents the display of bric-a-brac was central to the creation of such an ambience.

This is not to say people thought there was just one way of making a kitchen resonate with familial values. The array of objects people employed to this end, while falling under the general rubric of bric-a-brac, was wide-ranging. People, for example, were often as happy to use new, shop-bought ornaments as old sepia photos of granny or other faded bits of family flotsam and jetsam which had drifted down from the past. One wife had a collection of pottery chickens. This had grown over the years as she came across suitable new additions. It also tended to increase, as she laughingly noted, each time she had a birthday. For her these chickens were as important in generating a sense of family as the old holiday photos she had on display. Both were, as she put it, part of 'the home thing'.

In discussing the importance of bric-a-brac for them, many respondents often offered more than one of the above reasons as well as including others. The following extracts illustrate some of the kinds of responses given.

> I don't like bare walls. It cheers the place up. (c. 25, soc. cl. C2)
> I like knick-knacks all over the place. They make the place look lived in and homely. For me it's what makes a home rather than a house. (c. 42, soc. cl. C1)
> I like to arrange things . . . my little bit of artistic talent! I can express myself. It includes a lot of rubbish I've had bought. I couldn't hide them because they don't fit in. I try to find a place for them. They make my home what it is. They have memories. It's welcoming. (c. 29, soc. cl. C1)
> [They're] important because they're personal to you. I can tell you a story about each of them. We've got to a stage when we look at those things and they're our life. (c. 39, soc. cl. C1)

It was these kinds of reasons and concerns that underlay the thinking of the woman who explained that, although she had undertaken an initial foray to the 'knick-knack' shops and knew what the market had to offer, she had still not decided on all the bits and pieces she felt the kitchen needed. In her eyes, therefore, her kitchen remained unfinished.

Similar concerns also informed another respondent's attitude as she discussed her response to different presents she had received from members of her family. As she put it:

> I'd never not put it up just because I didn't like it. (c. 29, soc. cl. C1)

The way this woman stacks her negatives lends the statement an emphasis a simpler syntax would have lacked. The statement also, however, articulates a conscious aesthetic position on the speaker's part. The significance of this position derives from the way in which it defines aesthetic values by criteria quite unrelated to traditional definitions of what constitutes either aesthetic beauty, aesthetic innovation or good design. It implicitly assumes that aesthetic pleasure can be grounded in non-aesthetic concerns. Though historically this was a common position, the last century witnessed its widespread demise in professional art circles.[8]

If, in these new kitchens, consciously acquired bric-a-brac had widely replaced the casual accumulation of debris found in the Laurie Lee kitchen, there remained a group of people for whom clutter was important in itself. In seeking to understand people's feelings about their kitchens, this group is worth a mention. At one end of the spectrum there were the people whose bits and pieces, despite their often disparate nature, were largely selected and certainly carefully displayed. The air of informality or the casual quality they frequently imparted to the kitchen was managed, to a significant degree. At the other end of the spectrum were the people who felt acutely uncomfortable in such a managed environment. As one woman succinctly put it, 'I like clutter.' For such people genuine comfort involved a degree of real untidiness, such as the wellies thrown into a corner mentioned earlier during the description of attitudes to the top-of-the-market kitchen. Such people found kitchens in which everything was put away in its proper place not merely unrelaxing; they found it unattractive and the sense of displeasure[9] it gave them had an aesthetic dimension.

This chapter has sought not simply to detail the ubiquity of knick-knacks in the sample kitchens but to look at the importance respondents attached to them, more particularly in the case of women, though also in some men. In doing this, the chapter has begun to look at the interplay between people's social and aesthetic values and the way social concerns mark and shape aesthetic decisions and preferences for many people. The final chapter will now take this up.

# Notes

1. Simple poverty was a major factor in shaping such kitchens and the absence of central heating for a long time accounted for their persistence. Many houses had only one warm room, invariably the kitchen; during the winter, people steeled themselves to go to the lavatory because it was so miserably cold and climbing out of bed each morning into a freezing bedroom required gargantuan resolution. Such houses are now largely a thing of the past. But what the advent of central heating has not dislodged is the concept of the kitchen, within general social consciousness, as the warm centre of the home.

2. Laurie Lee (1962) *Cider With Rosie*, Penguin Books. Permission for quotation on p. 156 granted by Peters, Fraser and Dunlop on behalf of the Laurie Lee Estate.

3. It has also been noted how hard some respondents had worked at organising the means of eating with other family members in kitchens which had not been designed for this purpose, seeking to add a social role to a kitchen architecturally planned simply as a workplace.

4. There are now a number of post-modernist-inspired approaches to textual analysis within literary circles, which derive from Heidegger. The analysis offered here, however, is based simply on the traditional literary belief in the value of close and careful reading.

5. By the late nineteenth century the parlour had become an important room in many modest homes, though one which was virtually never lived in. Everyone crammed into the poky kitchens provided, leaving the parlour for funeral breakfasts and other solemn or very special occasions.

6. The arrangement might have been traditional but interestingly the table was not scattered with the debris of daily living as it might well have been in the past. When visited it was covered with a clean tablecloth on the middle of which stood a bowl of perfect yellow roses.

7. C. 31, soc. cl. B.

8. For centuries it was taken for granted that the highest form of painting had a classical or religious subject-matter and that the aesthetic properties of painting were dependent on and derived from this.

9. A historical example of such feelings is provided by the American writer Emerson when he visited a Shaker community. He is said to have found the spare neatness of their décor so acutely uncomfortable that he could not wait to get away.

# –9–

# Reviewing the endeavour and endeavouring to conclude

The aim of this study has been to deepen our understanding of the concerns which underlie and shape one example of popular visual taste, namely that expressed in the style and design of the new domestic kitchens people are purchasing today. While this required a review of the development of professional thinking in the field of kitchen design, not least for the relationship between this and commercial manufacture, it also demanded a review of the kinds of kitchens people actually install in their own homes. The study therefore drew a sample of purchasers of new kitchens and a major part of the research consisted of conducting an empirical examination of the process by which people finished up with a particular kitchen layout, style and décor. This fieldwork made it possible to explore the interplay between professional design concerns and popular tastes. It also moved the study into still cursorily charted territory. Design history, with its background in art history, still contains relatively little analysis of the considerations and values which lie behind and underpin the visual preferences embodied in popular tastes,[1] even though such preferences are expressed everywhere in the material construction of our domestic environment.

Among the reasons for choosing to look at popular visual tastes in kitchens, as opposed to other domestic spaces, two predominated. First, not only is it widely believed that, in terms of patterns of household expenditure in this country, the amount of money spent on refurbishing domestic kitchens is very considerable, it was also possible to establish early on that nationally the retail market for kitchen furniture enjoyed an annual turnover of more than a billion pounds and during the research turnover continued to rise steadily. The market for kitchen furniture today is thus very substantial. And the study subsequently provided corroboration for popular beliefs about the high level of popular spending on kitchen refurbishment. The fieldwork showed that there was a strong tendency among the sample to spend more on refurbishing their kitchens than on refurbishing any other room in the home.

Secondly, the kitchen has historically played a notable role within popular mythology and the literary imagery of our society as a vehicle for expressing ideas and aspirations about domesticity and family while simultaneously functioning as a major workroom in terms of daily household practice. On this latter front the kitchen has undergone huge changes in recent years. For, as the second half of the twentieth century has witnessed an explosion of inventions for mechanising many of the household tasks commonly undertaken in the kitchen, there has been a steady growth within the English population in the number of people with sufficient money to buy these inventions.

The kitchen was therefore interesting, not only because people spent a considerable amount of money on it but also because it promised to be a domestic site where both powerful symbolic and major functional concerns simultaneously jostled for attention. The ways in which people sought to manage these two different and potentially conflicting aspects of the kitchen through their handling of its layout and design promised to be fruitful in terms of enhancing our understanding of one aspect of popular visual taste.

An enquiry into these issues, however, required a sample in which popular tastes in kitchen design and style were properly represented. To obtain this a sample was drawn which reflected the proportion of the market the main kinds of retail outlet for kitchen furniture commanded. So, the more heavily patronised the form of outlet, the larger the proportion of the sample who had bought from that kind of retailer.

Another aim from the beginning was that the book should attempt to conduct an interdisciplinary study in which sociology rubbed shoulders with design history and aesthetics in the belief that the intermingling of different disciplinary perspectives would produce insights into popular tastes not otherwise achievable. This raised a number of problems regarding the presentation of the themes of the book and the data collected. Chapter 1 touched on some of the presentational problems posed here by the interdisciplinary nature of the exercise. In a conventional sociological study the theoretical issues, imitating the practice of the natural sciences, are laid out in the opening chapters. This provides the researcher with a means of collecting the data in an orderly manner and then of analysing its significance systematically. The adoption of an interdisciplinary approach forced the layout of the book to follow a rather different pattern. Rather than having a formal theoretical chapter, different chapters have introduced and explored particular theoretical issues. In a similar way, this final chapter will not perform a general summarising role. Instead, using the data and ideas of the earlier chapters, it will seek to construct a description of the overall aesthetic approach which was found among the sample.

In attempting to understand popular taste the study made no attempt, however, to erect criteria for making aesthetic judgements about the quality of different popular visual tastes and, by association, evaluations of their owners' visual sensibilities. A major concern driving the study was, rather, that there have been too many diatribes against the evils of so-called massification, which have largely rested on untested assumptions about the nature of popular visual preferences. One recent response to this has been to celebrate the popular, sometimes solely on the basis of its popularity. The contention here, however, was that, before arguments either about the socially stultifying effects of massification or the socially energising impact of popular taste could start to carry intellectual weight, they required solid evidential support. As with earlier arguments about the evils of massification, to date too many judgements about the aesthetic value of popular taste have been characterised by an absence of intel-lectual rigour and a paucity of empirical evidence in equal parts.

This argument carried no accompanying logical imperative, however, that the study should ignore people's aesthetic preferences. In addition, the fact that the aesthetic criteria underpinning popular taste might be deeply at odds with the criteria underlying what is commonly termed high culture was not and cannot, I believe, constitute a cogent defence for relegating popular aesthetic preferences to a marginal role in design history today. While at one time design history, as an offshoot of traditional art history, was biased towards being object- and creator-centred, it has now signific-antly shifted its perspective. Today design history is far more user- and consumer-centred.[2] This is to be welcomed but, as the introduction to the book noted, it raises the issue of the consumer as actor or acted upon, a long-standing sociological issue. This has coloured much of the discussion in this book. The growing interest in popular taste has also opened up the question of the status and significance of different sets of aesthetic criteria to fresh debate.

Design history is increasingly taking on board the fact that the general populace's desire to express aesthetic partiality is both strong and widespread. Indeed, it seems plausible that the desire to express aesthetic partiality in strong terms is an inherent feature of human nature. And, even if that is unprovable, many people indubitably put a great deal of time and energy into expressing their taste preferences within their homes. Cer-tainly, during the course of the study members of the sample repeatedly expressed both positive and hostile opinions about different styles of kitchen planning and furniture with considerable passion.[3]

In so far, then, as the expression of aesthetic preference appears to be a powerful and virtually universal impulse, it had to be a concern of the study.[4] Similarly, the experience so many people have of responding positively or negatively to certain forms of visual expression, often apparently spontaneously, just as we do to the taste or texture of certain foods, was an important issue for the study. These impulses and experiences constituted important data in the search to understand popular aesthetic experiences and values and their role during the refurbishment of a kitchen.

Interest in people's aesthetic partialities was further heightened, however, by the fact that, on top of the inherent aesthetic propensities people display, people's aesthetic partialities historically have frequently been intimately intertwined with and shaped by an array of intellectual, religious, moral and social values. In many periods these have been powerful, taste-forming considerations. Indeed, non-aesthetic factors have frequently operated as intervening variables in the process by which people have come to regard decisions about aesthetic preferences as a matter of importance. Such factors have also helped to imbue people's aesthetic preferences not only with strong passion but sometimes with considerable dogmatism.

Certainly, many of the sample for this study had decided and emphatic opinions about the appropriate criteria to employ when making judgements of taste. Some held these opinions both dogmatically and inflexibly. Nor does it seem likely that this will change in the near future. It is too deeply entrenched and widespread within our culture. Yet neither does the empirical evidence in the study suggest the world would be an obviously better place if people abandoned expressing strong aesthetic opinions *per se,* even if the adoption of a more moderate tone might be thought beneficial at times. The discussion undertaken in chapters 7 and 8, for example, suggested that the expression of strong aesthetic preference is frequently triggered because people are busy engaging with important social issues and, even if we do not share their aesthetic tastes, we would not wish people to take the issues they bear upon lightly.

Two major assumptions have, in fact, underpinned much of this study. One is that one important role judgements of taste play is as a means of helping people construct a form of meaningful social order around them.[5] Another assumption underlying the study, and part of what made it seem worth doing, is that the process of actively and positively making judgements of taste adds to the quality of our lives as such judgements represent the expression of various material, sensual, emotional and intellectual responses to the world we find ourselves in. From this perspective, judgements of taste also become part of the analysis of people as actors and people as acted upon, which has informed this study.

One thing the study found which supported the assumption that aesthetic judgements reflect a common human impulse was that the urge to make such judgements was not confined to particular social groups within the sample. Although numbers were small, at no point did the empirical evidence suggest that the impulse to make judgements of taste varied significantly by social class. The data quoted during the course of the analysis has continually shown people from all social classes expressing aesthetic opinions with equal vigour. Where there was a nervousness about making aesthetic judgements, the discriminating variable was gender, not class.

Some design historians might charge, of course, that, even if this is so, we still need to address two questions: first, whether different social groups display different patterns of visual ability and skill; and, secondly, if they do, that any analysis of the way popular taste develops or of the social import of different expressions of popular taste needs to address this, particularly in view of the long-standing debate about massification.

Though the term 'massification' is relatively new, the concern it refers to, as chapter 1 indicated, has long been a central issue in discussions of popular taste. It was argued, however, that this debate has been led overwhelmingly by a group of self-appointed guardians of so-called high culture, mostly intellectuals, comprising a heavy complement of art and design historians as well as more general social commentators.[6] This group is not, however, generally regarded in conventional social class analysis as constituting a class in its own right. Rather, it constitutes a subgroup of a larger social class.

This brings us to Bourdieu and a sociological perspective again. Among discussions which have sought to systematically relate people's socio-economic standing to their aesthetic tastes and cultural styles, Bourdieu's analysis, though dating from the late 1970s, still stands out as the most detailed and wide-reaching review of the relationship between class and taste. It is helpful, therefore, in approaching the question of the frequently presumed differential ability of different social classes to make aesthetic judgements which are intellectually defensible.

Bourdieu's interest in the relationship between class and taste arises from his interest in the struggle for social power, which is for him the pivotal force in social life. In Bourdieu's analysis of this struggle, taste is theorised as a major mechanism of social exclusion. By dint of their particular taste preferences certain groups in our society are able to claim status for themselves at the expense of other groups who do not share their tastes. Certain sets of aesthetic preferences are thus a key factor in the legitimisation of patterns of social power. This line of argument pulls questions of aesthetic preference in from the margins of social analysis and makes them part of the mainstream debate. Though the remit Bourdieu sets himself has a far wider embrace than this study, his theory of taste is clearly relevant to the search here for a better understanding of popular visual preferences.

In analysing the distribution of social power, Bourdieu sees the power and status of the bulk of the dominant social class as primarily founded on and sustained by a solid body of economic wealth, including money. In contrast, the bulk of the cultural élite lack significant economic wealth. This excludes this group from the mainstream of the dominant class. With little but their asserted possession of good taste to rely on to maintain their high social standing, the cultural élite ranks as a subgroup, or fraction, of the dominant class. Thus, for Bourdieu, an analysis of the way aesthetic taste is formed becomes part of the process of identifying the mechanisms by which the cultural élite, despite generally possessing only modest economic power, are able to exploit their aesthetic preferences as a means of legitimising a privileged social status and concomitantly a significant degree of social power. The fact that the cultural values of this subgroup are not only different from but often in marked contrast to those of the bulk of the dominating members of the dominating class is for Bourdieu no accident. His scheme theorises such differences as structural prerequisites on which the cultural élite depends for maintaining its social standing. A detailed account of Bourdieu's argument is not necessary. But it is worth noting that one effect for Bourdieu of the success with which the cultural élite have exploited their aesthetic preferences in pursuit of social status is to throw into relief:

> the difference between the legitimate culture of class societies . . . and the culture of little differentiated or undifferentiated societies, in which . . . culture is fairly equally mastered by all members of the group and cannot function as . . . an instrument of domination.[7]

Bourdieu is not, of course, a disinterested observer of all this. Despite a style which combines an overt commitment to intellectual dispassion and a labyrinthine syntax to accommodate the endless qualification of every statement, *Distinction* is not a piece of value-free cultural analysis. Bourdieu's partisanship seeps through every page of the text.[8] For Bourdieu, indeed, high culture in our society is a class weapon used to support and legitimise a deeply inegalitarian system. And, though he would be in the forefront of those enumerating the difficulties confronting anyone attempting to create a more equal society, he clearly continues to be committed to greater social equality. It is also clear that he sees a more equal society as characterised by a more exploratory approach to different cultural styles and by less supercilious evaluations of them by the dominant cultural groups. He would reject, for example, the almost automatic categorisation of immediately accessible pleasure or direct, unmediated sensual responses to art as 'facile', 'superficial', 'meretricious' or 'syrupy', all descriptions favoured by the cultural élite.[9] Bourdieu nowhere expresses these feelings about the use of taste preferences to divide and stratify more directly or clearly than in the postscript to *Distinction* entitled 'Towards a "Vulgar" Critique of "Pure" Critiques'. The chapter opens with a robust and sweeping rejection of the whole paraphernalia of philosophical and literary aesthetics. As Bourdieu puts it 'this project has required . . . a readiness to renounce the whole corpus of cultivated discourse on culture.'[10]

This study shares Bourdieu's position in a number of respects. Integral to the basic conception of the study is the belief that, in the face of cultural élitism, we need to seek to understand popular visual tastes on their own terms before embarking on attacking their standards and values. Yet Bourdieu's concerns and the concerns of this study also diverge. One reason for this is that a major issue in the 'cultivated discourse' to which Bourdieu refers has been around the question of the utility of art objects and the elevation of the concept of art as an end in itself.[11] This drives much of Bourdieu's analysis of the role of art in the legitimisation of ongoing patterns of social stratification. For this study to have engaged with Bourdieu's argument about the cultural élite would have called for a sample which included a substantial group of people who saw themselves as the guardians of high culture. And to ensure this it would have been necessary to draw the sample quite differently. One would expect, for example, to find this group significantly less likely than the bulk of the population to use the main retail outlets for kitchen furniture if they decided to refurbish their kitchens.

In the event, the study did not seek to nor did it produce a group of respondents whom one could identify as committed members of the world of high culture. Despite a considerable socio-economic spread, the sample for this study turned out to be largely homogeneous in terms of their general aesthetic approach. Had sample membership been weighted to ensure a larger complement of social classes A and B, differences might have started to show up; it is impossible to know. For one would still have needed to distinguish between members of the dominant and the dominated fractions of that social group. As it was, the study showed that the aesthetic concerns of those members of the sample whose occupation put them into social class A or B were not clearly distinguishable from those in social class C or D. While exploiting certain aspects of Bourdieu's theory of taste, it is not, therefore, a purpose of this study to address Bourdieu's theme about the role of élite culture as a form of social power.

Since the publication of Bourdieu's mammoth work, post-modernism in its various forms has decisively entered the intellectual arena, bringing with it a fresh interest in and a new, even defiant, celebration of various forms of popular culture, as well as a fresh acknowledgement of the agency of the actor. Reservations about the value of post-modernist theories for this study were touched on in the introduction. The numerous variants of post-modernist theory now enjoy such wide circulation, are so endlessly and energetically debated and attract so many adherents, however, that the decision not to exploit them or the analytical concepts they have introduced for the analysis of popular taste and behaviour in a study which deals four-square with trying to expand our understanding of the motives and considerations underlying an expression of popular taste is briefly returned to here.

One problem with trying to use a post-modernist perspective for understanding the dynamics which drove behaviour in this study, and the role of culture and cultural artefacts in this, is that the interview data suggested that much of the analytical theorising which characterises post-modernist thinking was tangential to the personal perceptions of the sample in this study. Post-modernist theories of culture and consumption have not addressed the kind of issues which occupied and engaged these people's thoughts and attention as they were installing their new kitchens. It is acknowledged that one cannot assume that the actors' own perception of the impulses which drive their actions are accurate, and that it is notoriously difficult for anyone located within a situation and actively engaged with it to make a clear and balanced appraisal of their behaviour.[12] The way they see their actions and the way an outsider reads their behaviour can vary widely. But this does not mean that the researcher can just ignore their sample's interpretation of their own behaviour. A researcher wishing to challenge their respondents' own accounts of their behaviour must be able to offer cogent reasons for doing so.[13]

The way people discussed the purchase of a new kitchen, however, did little to encourage an analysis of the process in terms favoured by these post-modernist analyses of consumption, which depict people as going out to select a lifestyle calculated to reflect an image of the self characterised by playfulness, an image which might be equally easily donned or dropped. Nor did the data suggest that people's perceptions of themselves were dependent upon and the product of an effort to construct a sense of self under the invasive influence of global images in conjunction with the insidious pressures of the media. The search for a plausible and meaningful account of the process of installing a kitchen on the basis of the empirical data collected neither required recourse to such explanations nor gained from it. The data lent itself to a simpler interpretation. It suggested that the amount of money people were laying out in their kitchens made them regard the project as a business to be approached carefully. Both people's demeanour and actions indicated their keen desire to feel they had spent their money well. The evidence also suggested that spending one's money well meant carefully thinking through both one's objectives and the means of implementing them in material form. Until clearly discredited, simple explanations like this must be preferred.

The study traced the way in which people's practical concerns became intermeshed with their socio-moral ones in the process of their setting up a new kitchen, giving rise to a concept of the English kitchen which was widely shared across the social classes, though rarely articulated systematically as a generalised, abstract idea. Instead, its articulation was indirect, taking the form of physical or material description offered by purchasers, or even just a general expression of feeling about what people wanted for their kitchens. But the absence of a detailed articulation of the kitchen as idea did not deny the role the concept played for purchasers at a practical level. The kitchen as idea was both strong enough and powerful enough to colour and shape purchasers' imaginations and visual tastes demonstrably and significantly. Planning the refurbishment of a kitchen is a practical, concrete exercise, and the finished kitchens essentially communicated their meaning by visual and material means, not through philosophical homilies on the part of the purchasers. This takes us to the considerations which underpinned the design of the sample kitchens.

The concept of the English kitchen was characterised not only by having efficiency as a goal, but also by seeking to parade its efficiency. It did this through an enthusiastic embrace not just of the mechanisation of kitchen work and related technological developments, but, along with and as part of this, of some of the basic tenets of early twentieth-century avant-garde modernism and the aesthetic principles which drove that movement. Thus people were highly receptive of the idea of modularisation in the design of kitchen units as a means of maximising the effective use of space. Similarly they welcomed the introduction of long, sweeping worktops. Many also seemed to feel that such features possessed inherent aesthetic properties. They liked the look of a fitted kitchen. It pleased them. But at the same time many people wanted their kitchen to reflect their concern over and ideas about domesticity and the kind of family relationships they desired and wanted to encourage. For many this concern was equally strong and an equally significant factor in shaping the design and appearance of their kitchen. The aesthetic values which this concern drew into play in the design of the sample kitchens, however, derived from very different sets of criteria from those which informed mainstream modernist design.

The study has traced the way people actively managed their two sets of concerns for their kitchens. One device some people adopted was to arrange the kitchen so as to separate food preparation and its accompanying technology from the familial aspects of kitchen activity such as eating and informal socialising, in a way which ensured that these latter activities were not marginalised but remained a clearly integral part of kitchen life without affecting the efficiency of the kitchen as workplace. Chapter 8 explored this feature of the kitchens visited, looking, for example, at the way kitchens were divided so that people made different ends of the room speak to different concerns and emanate a different ambience. The way kitchen tables were positioned was often a crucial factor in reconciling these two concerns within the layout of their kitchens.

Another way in which people married design features which spoke of efficiency to those which spoke of familial values was through the choice of design veneers, of which, as was noted, there is now a huge selection available. These veneers left the basic construction of the kitchen carcasses intact but radically weakened the visual impact of their straight, clean, structural lines so favoured by the modernists. So, while the modernist structural skeleton remained a pervasive presence, the application of panelled doors, cornices and other decorative touches acted to ensure that its power to project itself visually as the dominant feature of the design was significantly impaired. People, as chapter 7 described, also used pattern and texture to help create the kind of ambience and social message they wanted their kitchen to communicate. And it did not stop here. Chapter 8 described the importance of decorative and ornamental objects and even ephemera for generating atmosphere and feeling and expressing values, communicating sets of socio-moral ideals which were important to people and establishing complementary sets of aesthetic values and standards.

The diversity of décor and appearance which this produced might again appear to raise issues about the effect of globalisation. One argument currently put in some theories of globalisation is that the new globalised world we now inhabit is encouraging a major questioning of the old bastions of social structure, leading them to crumble fast. Arising from this and currently enjoying some support is the further argument that global changes are bringing the development of new freedoms in their wake. These are stimulating the growth of an interest in individuality, which is encouraging a fresh emphasis on the pleasure to be derived from the ongoing construction and reconstruction of the self. This argument perceives the emergence of a new self-conscious construction of personal identity as filling the void left by the collapse of the old social system and as heralding a new form of social order.[14] In summary, this variant of globalisation theory sees people today as attracted to selecting and adopting individual lifestyles for the promise such lifestyles offer of achieving release from the social constraints which historical group attachments, through their shared norms and values, have traditionally imposed on people. Again, however, the evidence gathered here about the way people exploited texture, colour, design variations and other decorative and ornamental possibilities in their kitchens offered little empirical support for this account of to-day's lifestyles and their roles. There was little evidence that the sample were rejecting established social values. Instead, this study strongly suggests that, though the families to whom these kitchens belonged might be very different in a number of respects from the English family of fifty years ago, the concept of the family generally continued to be of central importance to people and their manner of refurbishing their kitchens reflected this.[15] Rather than seeking to set up their kitchen so as to escape from established systems of norms and values, many people appeared to be actively engaged in devising arrangements which would help to reconfirm a commitment to some long-standing tenets of family life.

This kind of concern also distanced people socially and imaginatively from the kind of post-modernist world which is fascinated by the stance of the *flâneur*, celebrates irony and enjoys playing with the concept of a world turned upside-down. The interest in visual and verbal quotation in the dressing of the basic kitchen carcasses in some of the sample kitchens, which might, at first sight, seem to constitute a link between the world of these popular kitchens and a post-modernist perspective, was, in fact, handled in such a way that it served rather to highlight their distance from than to reflect that perspective. Irony was not a striking feature of these purchasers' refurbishment of their kitchens. In place of the knowing, tongue-in-cheek, self-distancing positions which characterise various branches of post-modernist cultural analysis, this sample of contemporary buyers were engaged in a straightforward tussle to make their surroundings reflect some long-standing, deep-seated concerns to which they continued to be strongly committed.[16] The sample kitchens showed both individualisation and individuality. But these were located in, emerged from and reflected long-standing, conservative values.

Though there was little evidence that people buying new kitchens subscribed to either a post-modernist outlook or aesthetic and only partially subscribed to a modernist one, the refurbishment of their kitchens was, nevertheless, a conscious aesthetic exercise for most people which they saw as involving aesthetic decisions based on aesthetic criteria. And, though they did not talk at a high level of abstraction, people had ways of enunciating their criteria of judgement. These purchasers did not lack a design aesthetic and the data collected allows for a description of the aesthetic principles which underpinned and shaped the tastes of the sample.

One aspect of popular taste of particular interest to design historians is the relation between popular taste and the idea of art as an abstract concept. The concept of art as 'an abstract capitalised Art, with its own internal but general principles'[17] is, in terms of the history of ideas, very recent. Painting, sculpture, textiles, pottery, together with an array of other arts, crafts and different forms of design, all have long and impressive histories of service to social and moral goals beyond and outside themselves. Across the world and the centuries artwork of all kinds has derived both its most important meaning and its social value from this. In such work it is always difficult, and sometimes impossible, to separate the aesthetic impact of the work from its social role.[18] Today, though the concept of art as an end in itself currently dominates thinking about art within professional art circles in the Western world, such an idea still has a weak hold in many parts of the world. In many societies art in the modern Western art world sense would be a bewildering and confusing, even incomprehensible idea.[19] Though the functions art performs are numerous and vary according to place and time,[20] art, throughout the world, continues to be widely made because it performs a function external to itself. Much anthropological work, for example, operates on the assumption that what we would call art is, by definition, innately functional. Even in the Western world the idea of works of art and design as ends in themselves is largely limited to members of a small self-defined professional art world. The sample, in contrast, continued, for the most part, to embrace an older concept of art and design.[21]

The data showed that people had both clear and detailed views about what they wanted the design of their kitchen to achieve, that, while deeply influenced by functional considerations, many also wanted to use their kitchens to give material expression to general moral and social values. The experience of sensual pleasure was thus often intimately tied up with extra-aesthetic concerns. The evidence, however, did not suggest that the sample suffered any dilution of sensory experience as a result of this.

Thus, in describing how they had reached a decision about décor, it was unusual for people to do so simply in terms of finding a missing piece in a jigsaw. Whether or not one shared the respondents' tastes was immaterial. What was significant was that so many expressed a sense of aesthetic satisfaction and pleasure, as well as describing their decisions. Thus, in talking about how she had had her kitchen decorated one woman said:

A good artexer is a joy to watch. (c. 22, soc. cl. C2)

Simple and short, this statement nevertheless communicates, economically and clearly, the visual pleasure watching the assured, rhythmic movements of a skilled decorator gave this woman.

Given the intimate relation for so many people between socio-moral considerations and aesthetic values and the widespread general perception of the enduring importance of family life, the visual conservatism which characterised so many of the sample, their attraction to the visual language of the past together with some of its accompanying aesthetic criteria, was understandable. Related to this, and a striking feature of many respondents' approach to design, was a widespread sense of aesthetic propriety.

People did not, of course, employ the term aesthetic propriety. Nevertheless, the concept captures one of their major aesthetic concerns. Thus many respondents were at pains to explain how important they felt it was to ensure that the different aspects of one's house were 'in keeping' with each other. Furthermore, the concept of propriety, related as it has been to eighteenth- and nineteenth-century social and aesthetic values, has also historically had moral undertones and we have noted the link between moral concerns and aesthetic partialities among the sample. In addition, while undoubtedly interested in technological development, there was little to suggest that respondents would have been troubled by the charge that commitment to propriety might make them aesthetically conservative. People were not particularly interested in aesthetic innovation or experimentation and few were interested in it in the way that modernism in particular and, to a lesser extent, post-modernism have been and which has given the new and the different huge aesthetic cachet in art-world circles.

In a similarly pre-twentieth-century spirit, respondents were not aesthetic purists. Accusations of supporting the ersatz would have caused most respondents scant concern. Few of the sample were therefore worried by the thought that the concept of propriety might be difficult to operationalise. They generally compromised happily over stylistic matchings. If it were possible to acquire an authentic fitting easily, then

**Plate 9.1** A new kitchen installed in a 1930s Sunspan house. The owner felt this style of kitchen, while not directly reflective of the style of the house, did not jar with it, and satisfied her sense of aesthetic propriety.

**Plate 9.2** Though the owner of this kitchen described how she had drooled over a friend's farmhouse-style kitchen she felt such a kitchen would be inappropriate in her own 1970s home. Instead she had this white kitchen installed.

people might insist on correctness, as in the case of the woman noted earlier who insisted the builder did not replace a sash window with a modern window just because it saved him trouble. Mostly, however, if the stylistic spirit of an item was right, people were prepared to overlook any historical inaccuracy in its detail.[22]

Within this framework certain perceived stylistic inconsistencies could worry people, however, and a number described how they actively sought to avoid such inconsistencies in the pursuit of propriety. Thus in chapter 7 the point was made that what people liked and what they installed were not necessarily the same. A respondent who lived on a 1970s estate and another who lived in a 1930s Sunspan home both said they felt that to install a farmhouse-style kitchen within those kinds of architectural shells would be inappropriate. Both were careful to select furniture styles and a general décor which they considered more in keeping with their homes' architecture (plates 9.1 and 9.2). Other examples of the way people expressed their sense of propriety were found in some of the stylistic and decorative detail they adopted. People spoke, for example, of how they had tried to select cupboard handles so that, in their judgement, they 'matched' the style of the cupboard doors. Again, people were guided in making these decisions by reference to past styles and, again, they were not generally worried about an ersatz element creeping into the design of the furniture. It was not an aesthetic criterion they considered relevant.

Along with the idea of propriety, and sometimes it seemed to be an extension of it, many of the sample were strongly committed to the idea of harmony in the design of their kitchens. In this context harmony nearly always involved careful matching and colour co-ordination. Floor coverings, light shades, wall paint, splash tiles, curtains, blinds and seat cushions, right through to bread bins, knick-knacks, decorative plates and pictures, all had to 'go' with each other. Some respondents expended a considerable amount of time and attention on this and were prepared to wait a long time to get what they wanted. So there were respondents who had waited months to get the right lampshade or splash tiles. Others, forced to make do with something they felt was less than ideal, continued to keep a lookout in case something which 'went' better and which they could substitute for the offending item turned up. One woman was still looking for the right side-table, another for the right bread bin. Other people told of how they had almost given up their search for the right thing and then, unexpectedly, found just what they were looking for. Thus one woman recounted how, on a visit to Australia some time after the installation of her kitchen, she came across some wonderful artificial grapes. She immediately realised that these would add just the right finishing touch to the Mediterranean ambience she had tried to create in her kitchen back home. She promptly bought them and wryly described how she had carried them all the way back to East Anglia.

The concern to ensure the design of their new kitchen was in keeping with the overall architecture of their house could clash with people's desire to use the design of their kitchen to express their sense of the cultural importance of the continuity of family life. This did not mean that people abandoned their desire to make their kitchens speak of what they regarded as enduring familial values. Instead they devised stylistic compromises. An earlier chapter looked at the importance of the kitchen table for people and this offered one source of compromise. A simple modern table with upright but cushioned chairs in an appropriately patterned fabric, that is, a table, chairs and furnishing fabric which avoided a strong farmhouse reference but which created a 'feeling' of conviviality, might perform this role satisfactorily. The use of various display facilities offered another way of introducing references to family without directly employing a farm-house style.

One common complaint voiced by art and design professionals about the kinds of kitchens which have been examined in this study is that they are all the same. The foundation of this accusation tends to be twofold, first, that the use of modularised units tends to impose a design similarity on all fitted kitchens and, secondly, that most fitted kitchens are bought from one of the big retail sheds, whose style ranges, despite their apparent variety, nevertheless, essentially lead to kitchens which are very similar to each other. One reply to this is that such arguments are theoretical and not based in practice. The development of greater modularisation combined with the wide choice of unit finishes now available has, in practice and demonstrably, facilitated huge variations in design and layout in even the most architecturally standardised kitchen within today's houses. An earlier chapter looked at how people actively exploited the modularisation of kitchen units so as to maximise the use of the space they had available and to make their kitchens serve their own personal idiosyncratic needs.

Far from fitted English kitchens being all the same, fitted kitchens all display an individuality. At this juncture, the critic might counter that, whatever the variations in the combinations of the base units and dressing, tying them together by running a continuous work top above them standardises the look of every fitted kitchen and that those who argue that fitted kitchens are very different from each other are concentrating on cosmetic differences and ignoring the basic structural similarities. Warming to their argument, they might also point out that much of this study has been spent showing how purchasers of domestic kitchens today share both a visual language and a number of practical and social concerns and that it has been part of the burden of the book to show how these factors have operated to produce some common patterns in kitchen layouts. They might cite the incorporation of a compact work triangle incorporating worktop, sink and cooker, the positioning of the kitchen table and the division of the kitchen into work and socialising zones as three such common design arrangements noted in the sample kitchens. Not only, they might charge, do such features support the claim that one popular kitchen is much like the next, but it has consciously been part of the aim of the study to reveal the common design features in the sample kitchens.

At one level this is true. A main driving impulse behind the sociological endeavour is to identify shared patterns in human behaviour in the belief that through the creation of typologies of human behaviour and interaction sociology achieves the formulation of generalities which enable it to impose some kind of order on the labyrinthine complexity of human affairs. It is, indeed, a major premise of sociology that identifying patterns of behaviour within the sprawling turmoil of human activity enables us to give that activity meaning, and that this is a prerequisite for realising any hopes we have of refining our understanding of society. Classification, including the classification of behaviour, is therefore a major sociological tool.

At the same time, sociologists are acutely aware that their attempts to extract behavioural patterns from the mass of constantly shifting human activity which confronts them are always problematic and can only ever offer partial truths. For, even while they are helping us discern common strains in human behaviour, sociologists are conscious of a mass of human behaviour which their analysis does not embrace. Equally importantly, they face the constant development of new behavioural patterns as people respond to changes taking place in the world around them. So there is always evidence threatening to crowd in and erode newly won sociological generalisations.

On the one hand, therefore, sociology can claim to have shown the benefits empirical work offers in identifying patterns in social behaviour and concomitantly a fuller understanding of ourselves, thereby offering us the promise of greater control over our lives. On the other hand, sociologists are constantly forced to recognise the intrinsic and irresolvable tension between the detail and the generalisation in the sociological project. In an interdisciplinary exercise like this it is important, if we are to progress interdisciplinary understanding, to acknowledge this tension. This highlights yet again a theme which has run through this study from the beginning, namely, the tension within the sociological narrative between people as actors and people as acted upon, between people asserting their independence and people accepting various constraints under which they live. Recognising this tension and the fact that it is intrinsically irresolvable, however, allows us to address some of the behavioural and other details which cannot be contained within the typologies which this study has employed. It also offers an escape from ignoring what we cannot classify. This allows us to pursue the charge that popular fitted kitchens are basically the same.

Evidence collected during the study showed that the sample kitchens shared certain design traits. Some of the similarities found emerged because their owners shared a number of socio-moral goals. It has also been acknowledged that the fitted kitchen as a design concept involves a number of features which tend to imbue all fitted kitchens with certain similarities. It was likely that design similarities within the kitchens in this study would be further compounded because the respondents were neither very rich nor very poor, generally fell into a fairly restricted spending band, had not gone through art and design training and socialisation, and a substantial number had selected their kitchens from the offerings of the large retail sheds. Even when they had bought from other kinds of retailers, such as small-town builders' merchants or up-market design studios, the goods on offer did not generally differ radically in their overall range of designs. Though chapter 3 made the point that retailers were keen to respond to their clients' preferences, it was to be expected that the sample kitchens would also reflect what the market had to offer. Many of the resulting kitchens therefore bore a generic similarity to each other. Like domestic interiors across the ages, they reflected their time and place. These kitchens could only have been found in a rich, late-twentieth-century Western country.

To accept this, however, does not mean that each of these kitchens was not also different from every other. Chapter 7 noted that a significant number of the sample were chary of the idea of creativity and some had strong reservations about being labelled artistic. However, when respondents' attention was not consciously drawn to these attributes so that they were not tarnished by their supposed association with élite culture, the study found some of these same respondents being consciously and energetically creative. People, for example, displayed a lively inventiveness as they set about making the space and facilities they had available serve their aims and desires, squeezing a machine in where it seemed impossible, hiding a fuse box, introducing eating arrangements in the face of considerable structural and spatial difficulties, and catering for personal family needs such as the accommodation of lemonade bottles. Many of the kitchens were also characterised by a rich abundance of idiosyncratic detail. These include the kitchen where a 1930s dresser from the East End furniture trade of the time was juxtaposed with kitchen equipment deliberately selected for its stark, high-modernist style; a specially built cubby-hole for the family dog; a carefully housed and much loved collection of fine glass, as well as an equally carefully housed collection of glass picked up at car boot sales. There were no end of examples.

All this acted to differentiate the kitchens in the sample from each other and give each its own character. But there was also another category of individualising items of which these kitchens sported a vast miscellany. Pottery chickens, postcards and family photographs were some examples noted. Sometimes very small details could encapsulate a striking expression of individuality, such as the carefully tended pot plant whose owner simply commented.

> every time I went in I thought, 'You *do* look nice.' (c. 17, soc. cl. C1)

There were also items lovingly displayed, not because the owner wanted, liked or had any use for them, but because they were presents from people the owner cared about. Such items were often invested with some of their owner's most important feelings and concerns. The end result of such features was kitchens which vividly conveyed their owners' personal quirky, even eccentric, individuality.

In the face of this kind of evidence, the charge that popular kitchens are all the same is overly sweeping and visually insensitive. Indeed, when one treated popular kitchens to the kind of careful examination which the work of prestigious interior designers and architects would automatically receive from the professional art and design world, the variety of individualising detail these kitchens contained began to leap out. The claim that kitchens of this kind lack significant distinguishing features or that the differences between them are at most superficial and cosmetic cannot be sustained. Depending on the viewer's judgement, the differences which characterised the sample kitchens might seem quixotic, funny, touching, awkward, ugly or beautiful. It is not the purpose of this study to ask anyone to like or dislike any of the kitchens described here. All it asks is that people approach this form of popular culture with a concern to understand it before launching into a debate about its merits and demerits.

The final word is reserved for the interdisciplinary approach the book has adopted. An interdisciplinary approach raises not only a wide range of theoretical and methodological difficulties, it even raises questions about one's writing style. This is not just about using the jargon of one discipline side by side with that of another, though that is not always without difficulty. There are decisions to be made about how one uses connotive as opposed to denotive language, even to how one uses adjectives and adverbs. This book has only just started to address these various issues. One difficulty is that there is as yet no tried and tested mode of meeting the intellectual expectations and customs of two or more different disciplines simultaneously. Trying, for example, to draw the different threads of the study together to tie them off coherently in this last chapter has not been easy. Not only has it led this chapter to deal with fresh theoretical issues it has even presented fresh material and ideas. And unfinished issues still remain.

If this study has done sufficient, however, to convince people that combining a sociological and design-history approach can yield a quality of understanding it would otherwise have been difficult to achieve, it will have been worthwhile. It will also hopefully encourage others to improve and refine on the tentative beginnings made here. Our current disciplinary specialisms with their ever-increasing progeny of sub-specialisms and their continuous struggle to make their methodologies ever more rigorous undoubtedly have huge benefits to offer in helping us gain more insight into the societies we create around us. But these same specialisms can also act as prisons, prisons in which some of us now wilfully incarcerate ourselves in ever smaller cells. The result is that we threaten to dissipate the advantages of the enlarged vision which specialisation can afford by wrapping ourselves in the intellectual myopia it can also engender. We can therefore benefit from a group of people who step outside the disciplinary cage. Certainly, in doing this they are likely to find themselves in uncharted terrain and stumble as they try to mark a path forward. But the endeavour can also sensitise them to various limitations of intellectual approach which are not even perceived but are simply taken for granted by those who operate within the security of a well-developed, intellectually sophisticated discipline. One hope of this book is that it will encourage a greater intermingling of and discussion among today's academic tribes, resulting in our greater intellectual refinement.

# Notes

1. Particularly if you exclude a small number of privileged groups such as young people in their late teens and twenties.

2. The dominant art-historical perspective has also shifted steadily over the course of the last twenty-five years and art criticism is no longer so dominated by monographs on individual artists and detailed analyses of individual paintings. It ranges widely and there is a growing body of art commentary informed by increasingly nuanced and refined socio-historical and political perspectives.

3. Attfield, Judy 'Inside Pram Town: A Case Study of Harlow House Interiors, 1951–61', in Judy Attfield and Pat Kirkham (eds) (1989) *A View from the Interior: Feminism and Design*. The Women's Press, p. 215, also noted that women making homes in post-war Harlow often had opinions about the décor of their homes which they implemented, unconcerned about whether they matched those of the town's architects. Roberts, Marion (1991) *Living in a Man-Made World: Gender Assumptions in Modern Housing Design*, Routledge, p. 156, has a sharp comment too about the tendency of the educated world to underestimate the sensitivity of other groups towards their surroundings.

4. For myself I certainly responded much more warmly to some design features than to others in the sample kitchens, and was more strongly drawn to the ambience some people had created in their kitchens than to that found in other kitchens. However, visiting so many homes and discussing their new kitchens with their creators also touched me in other ways. As I came to understand what their owners were trying to achieve, I sometimes found my aesthetic responses to some of the kitchens I saw changing. Though it seems worth noting this, these personal responses were always tangential for me to the main purpose of the study, which was not concerned with trying to erect a philosophical argument for the aesthetic superiority of some forms of visual taste over others. That was not part of the brief I had set myself. Rather, I was conducting a preliminary foray into the exploration of popular visual taste with the aim of achieving a greater understanding of what shaped it and how it operated in one domestic location.

5. The study assumes, indeed, though it does not develop this thesis, that judgements of taste play both a varied and a positive role on this front, helping us to cope with a world which can constantly appear to teeter on the edge of disaster and is essentially uncontrollable.

6. Adorno would be one example of this latter group.

7. Bourdieu (1984), p. 228.

8. One example of this will suffice, Bourdieu's discussion of the 'apocalyptic denunciations of all forms of "levelling", "trivialisation" or "massification"' (ibid., pp. 468–9).

9. Ibid., p. 486.

10. Ibid., p. 485.
11. Prior to the advent of modernism the celebration of things which could be seen as an end in themselves had already been rehearsed by Newman, John Henry (1964) *The Idea of a University*, Holt, Reinhart and Winston. The book, a collection of lectures Newman gave, was first published in 1852. The dictum that a work of art is an end in itself, however, became a central tenet for disciples of twentieth-century high culture. It thus became part of the canon of high art that functionality in art objects demeans them. One way, therefore, for artists to proclaim their membership of the world of high art is for them to ruthlessly eliminate from their work anything which suggests functionality, thereby freeing it from the coarsening and narrowing effect usage is perceived to impose.
12. A classic example of this would be the case of a husband and wife in the process of separation, when the difficulty in seeing the breakdown of the relationship from any perspective other than their own can become enormous for them.
13. At the same time, this study makes no claim that what triggered purchaser action when buying a kitchen would necessarily operate similarly in other areas of popular consumption in our society, even, indeed, where the same purchasers were involved. The question of the degree to which the findings here may be replicated on other fronts remains open.
14. Giddens, A. (1991) *Modernity and Self-Identity*, Polity Press, offers an example of this kind of thinking.
15. It is true certainly that the rising level of divorce in the West and the incidence of long-term partnerships outside marriage indicate that people are rejecting erstwhile conventional concepts of what constitutes a family. And an increasing number of people are in new kinds of family structures and clearly reject some aspects of the way family life was structured in the past. But this, in itself, is not evidence that they are rejecting the idea of the family *per se*.
16. The ironic post-modernist perspective, indeed, seems to lend support to Bourdieu's contention, *Distinction*, p. 257, that the iconoclastic counter-cultures of the young frequently act, despite immediate appearances, to sustain rather than challenge élitism. They simply give it a new face. Certainly, the features of post-modernist thinking as described above, which now widely inform the new post-modernist art and shape the appreciation of it, encourage the establishment of a body of post-modernist art as cerebral and esoteric as the old modernist art canon and equally at odds with the aesthetic partialities of the non-professional art world.

17. Williams, Raymond (1985) *Keywords: A Vocabulary of Culture and Society,* Flamingo, p. 41.

18. Meiss, Millard (1964) *Painting in Florence and Siena after the Black Death: The Arts, Religion and Society in the Mid-Fourteenth Century*, Harper Torchbooks, points out that all European painting was at one time religious. And Kristeller, Paul Oskar (1952) 'The Modern System of the Arts', in *Rennaissance Thought and the Arts*, Princeton University Press, 1980, traces the modern concept of aesthetics from the German philosopher Baumgarten in the mid-eighteenth century and notes that the concept of aesthetics as a modern idea and word only appears in English in the nineteenth century.

19. Even in the Western world, as Williams (1985) points out: '*art* and *artist* acquire ever more general (and more vague) associations, even while, ironically, most *works of art* are effectively treated as commodities and most *artists*, even when they justly claim quite other intentions, are effectively treated as a category of independent *craftsmen* or *skilled workers* producing a certain kind of marginal commodity' (p. 42.).

20. It is not difficult to find examples to support this contention. Two contrasting ones are offered here.
    i.  Baxandall, Michael (1974) *Painting and Experience in Fifteenth Century Italy,* Oxford University Press, discusses the role of church frescoes in Renaissance Italy. However they are perceived today, Baxandall argues that a central purpose was originally educational, to teach the stories of the Bible and the doctrine of the church and to help to generate the right kind of religious experience in the viewers.
    ii. Both the style and much of the hugely decorative detail in the clothing of non-urban peoples often still today denotes kinship and life stages. See, for example, Lewis, Paul and Lewis, Elaine (1984) *Peoples of the Golden Triangle*, Thames and Hudson, where, despite the impact of the modern Thai state and Thai nationalism and the spread of tourism, clothing is both readable and continuously read by members of the hill tribe groups in these terms. And this remains true even when people in these tribes also find ways of expressing aspects of their individuality through their dress. Whether this will still be true in another twenty-five years is hard to know, however.

21. Raphael Samuel (1994) argues that modernism might well turn out to be a kind of aesthetic 'blip' in that the fetishisation of the new that characterises modernism is unusual while revivalism has historically been common (p. 110).

22. Eighteenth- and nineteenth-century classical borrowings architecturally operated in this way, of course, right across Europe.

# Bibliography

Attfield, Judy 'Inside Pram Town: A Case Study of Harlow House Interiors, 1951–61', in Judy Attfield and Pat Kirkham (eds) (1989) *A View from the Interior: Feminism and Design*, The Women's Press.

Barthes, Roland (1977) 'The Death of the Author', in *Image Music Text, Essays selected and translated by Stephen Heath*, Fontana Paperbacks.

Baxandall, Michael (1974) *Painting and Experience in Fifteenth Century Italy*, Oxford University Press.

Beecher, Catherine E. and Stowe, Harriet Beecher (1869) *The American Woman's Home, on Principles of Domestic Science, Being a Guide to the Formation and Maintenance of Economical, Healthful, Beautiful and Christian Homes.* University Microfilms Inc., Ann Arbor, Michigan.

Bernstein, Basil 'On the Classification and Framing of Educational Knowledge', in M.F.D. Young (ed.) (1971) *Knowledge and Control*, Collier-Macmillan.

Bourdieu, P. (1984) *Distinction: A Social Critique of the Judgement of Taste*, Routledge and Kegan Paul.

Bratlinger, P. (1983) *Bread and Circuses: Theories of Mass Culture as Social Decay*, Cornell University Press.

Bullock, Nicholas (1988) 'First the Kitchen – then the Façade', *Journal of Design History*, vol. 1, numbers 3 and 4.

Burnett, J. (1979) *Plenty and Want: A Social History of Diet in England from 1815 to the Present Day*, Scholar.

Cook, Guy (1992) *The Discourse of Advertising*, Routledge.

Cowen, Ruth Schwartz (1989) *More Work for Mother*, Free Association Books.

Davidson, Caroline (1982) *A Woman's Work is Never Done*, Chatto and Windus.

De Grazia, V. and Furlough, E. (eds) (1996) *The Sex of Things: Gender and Consumption in Historical Perspective*, University of California Press.

Dobash, Emerson and Dobash, Russell (1998) *Rethinking Violence Against Women*, Sage.

Docker, John (1994) *Postmodernism and Popular Culture: A Cultural History*, Cambridge University Press.

Eliot, George (1947) *Middlemarch*, The World's Classics, Oxford University Press.

Féjer, George (1984) *Design Process: Inside Story of Familiar Products*, Exhibition catalogue, Manchester Polytechnic.

Field, Connie (director) (1980) *The Life and Times of Rosie the Riveter* [film].

Forster, E.M. (1961) *Room with a View*, Penguin Books.

Forty, Adrian (1989) *Objects of Desire*, Thames and Hudson.

Frederick, Christine (1912) 'The New Housekeeping', *Ladies Home Journal*, vol. 26.

Frederick, Christine (1919) *Household Engineering: Scientific Management in the Home*, American School of Home Economics.

Freeman, June (1989) 'The Discovery of the Commonplace or Establishment of an Elect: Intellectuals in the Contemporary Craft World', *Journal of Design History*, vol. 2, nos. 2 and 3.

Freeman, June (1990) 'The Crafts as Poor Relations', *Oral History*, vol. 18, no. 9.

Friedan, Betty (1964) *The Feminine Mystique*, Dell Publishing Company.

Giddens, Anthony (1984) *The Constitution of Society: Outline of the Theory of Structuration*, Polity Press.

Giddens, Anthony (1991) *Modernity and Self-Identity*, Polity Press.

Giedion, Siegfried (1948) *Mechanisation Takes Command*, Oxford University Press.

Gilbreth, L. (1930) 'Efficiency Methods Applied to Kitchen Design', *Architectural Record*, March, pp. 291–2.

Hardyment, Christina (1988) *From Mangle to Microwave: The Mechanisation of Household Goods*, Polity Press in association with Basil Blackwell.

Harrison, Molly (1972) *The Kitchen in History*, Osprey.

Isenstadt, Sandy (1998) 'Visions of Plenty: Refrigerators in America around 1950', *Journal of Design History*, vol. 11, no. 4, p. 311.

Keynote Market Survey (1990) (2000).

Kristeller, Paul Oskar (1952) 'The Modern System of the Arts', in *Rennaissance Thought and the Arts*, Princeton University Press, 1980.

Laurie, Heather (1996) 'Household Financial Resource Distribution and Women's Labour Market Participation', Ph.D. thesis, University of Essex.

Lawrence, D.H. (1960) *Sons and Lovers*, Penguin Books.

Lee, Laurie (1962) *Cider With Rosie*, Penguin Books.

# Bibliography

Leiss, W., Kline, S., and Jhally, S. (1990) *Social Communication in Advertising*, 2nd edition, Routledge.

Lewis, Paul and Lewis, Elaine (1984) *Peoples of the Golden Triangle*, Thames and Hudson.

McCulloch, Andrew (1983) 'Owner Occupation and Class Struggle: the Mortgage Strikes of 1938–40', Ph.D. thesis, University of Essex.

McRobbie, Angela (1999) *In the Culture Society: Art, Fashion and Popular Music*, Routledge.

Market Research Society (1991) *Occupational Groupings: A Job Dictionary*, 3rd edn, Market Research Society.

Meiss, Millard (1964) *Painting in Florence and Siena after the Black Death: The Arts, Religion and Society in the Mid-Fourteenth Century*, Harper Torchbooks.

Meyer, Erna (1926) *Der neue Haushalt, ein Wegweiser zur Wissenschaftlichen Hausfuehrung*, Franklische Verlagshandlung.

Miller, Daniel (1987) *Material Culture and Mass Communication*, Basil Blackwell.

Miller, Daniel 'Appropriating the State on the Council Estate', in T. Putnam and C. Newton (eds) (1990) *Household Choices*, Futures Publications.

Miller, Daniel (ed.) (1995) *Acknowledging Consumption: A Review of New Studies*, Routledge.

Miller, Daniel (ed.) (1998) *Material Cultures: Why Some Things Matter*, University of Chicago Press.

Miller, Daniel (ed.) (2001) *Home Possessions: Material Culture Behind Closed Doors*, Berg.

Mintel, Marketing Intelligence (1989) (1996) (1997) (1998) (2000)

Mintel, Marketing Intelligence (1992) *Special Report on Kitchen Furniture*.

National Shoppers Survey (2000) Summer.

*New Earnings Survey*, Office of National Statistics, 1997.

Newman, John Henry (1964) *The Idea of a University*, Holt, Reinhart and Winston.

Oakley, Ann (1985) *The Sociology of Housework*, Basil Blackwell.

Oedekoven-Gerisher and Frank, P. (1989) *Frauen im Design*, Haus der Wirtschaft, Exhibition catalogue, Design Centre, Stuttgart, vol 1 & 2.

Pahl, Jan (1989) *Money and Marriage*, Macmillan.

Parr, Joy (1999) *Domestic Goods: The Material, the Moral and the Economic in the Post-war Years*, University of Toronto Press.

Poggenpohl Möbelwerke GmbH & Co. (1992) *100 Years of Poggenpohl: Tradition Orientated Towards the Future*, Poggenpohl.

Roberts, Marion (1991) *Living in a Man-Made World: Gender Assumptions in Modern Housing Design*, Routledge.

Samuel, Raphael (1994) *Theatres of Memory*, Verso.

Saunders, Peter (1990) *A Nation of Homeowners*, Unwin Hyman.

Slater, D. (1996) *Consumer Culture and Modernity*, Polity.

*Social Trends* (1996) Office of National Statistics.

Stewart, Elinor P. (1989) *Letters of a Woman Homesteader*, University of Nebraska Press.

Tilly, L. and Tilly, R. (1975) *The Rebellious Century*, Harvard University Press.

Valentine, G. (1999) 'Doing Household Research: Interviewing Couples Together and Apart', *Area*, vol. 31, no. 1, pp. 67–74.

Walley, Joan E. (1960) *The Kitchen*, Constable.

Warde, Alan (1997) *Consumption, Food and Taste: Culinary Antinomies and Commodity Culture*, Sage.

Williams, Raymond (1985) *Keywords: A Vocabulary of Culture and Society*, Flamingo.

Williamson, Judith (1980) *Consuming Passions: The Dynamics of Popular Culture*, Marion Boyars.

Willis, Paul (1990) *Common Culture: Symbolic Work at Play in the Everyday Cultures of the Young*, Open University.

Woodforde, J. (1969) *The Truth about Cottages*, Routledge and Kegan Paul.

# Index

# Index

nostalgia, 131
Nunn, George, 42, 47

Oakley, Ann, 102–3, 106
oral testimony, 1
Ouds, J.J.P., 37, 39, 41

Pahl, Jan, 102–3, 109
parity between sexes, 122, 124
personal spending, 104
plans and drawings, 83
Poggenpohl, 43–4, 46, 79
popular culture, 180
popular taste, 173–5, 177
post-modernism, 14, 180–4, 194n16
power and control, 107
practical, 67, 69, 140
price, 4, 83, 95, 115, 121
process of
  buying, 77, 81–2, 111, 115, 119,
    121
  constructing a material environment,
    156
  housekeeping, 34
  problem solving, 87
  usefulness as concept, 8, 9
professional design/er, 15–16, 156, 173,
  191
propriety, 36, 149, 185–7
public and private, 100

qualitative, 2, 16, 58, 111
quantitative, 2, 16, 58, 111

radio, 76
reciprocity between couples
  *see* gender roles
refridgeration, 57, 69
refridgerators/fridges, 48–9, 162
relaxation, 75, 161
  *see also* leisure
Rfg, 38
role reversal, 119

sales advice, 88
salesmanship, 79
salespeople/staff, 81, 87–9
Samuel, Raphael, 13–14
Schutte-Lihotsky, Margarete, 38, 40–1,
  52n28, 85, 157

scientific management and
  American origins, 4
  buyers of kitchens today, 136, 162
  Christine Frederick, 29–30
  European avant garde, 35
  European middle class fastidiousness,
    37–8
  Lillian Gilbreth, 33
sentimentality, 158
servantless household, 35–6
servants, 35–6
showing off, 143
showrooms, 82, 163
Slater, D., 8, 14
snacking and grazing, 57
social class and
  aesthetic judgment, 177
  concept of the English kitchen, 181
  house ownership, 6
  intellectual condescension, 11
  its explanatory power, 8, 68, 93, 96,
    142, 144–5
  middle class concepts of decency, 36–7
  occupational change, 155
  ownership of machinery, 60–1
  sampling, 60–1
  variable imposition of design ideas, 42
  visual vocabulary, 130
  working class housing, 34
    *see also* Bourdieu
social dupes, 80
social power, 177–8
socialising, 75, 182
socialist, 33–7 passim, 101
social order, 176, 183
sociologists, 18, 57, 189
sociology and
  empirical work, 16–17, 189
  role in book, 1–2, 192
  theoretical perspectives, 10, 175, 177
socio-moral, 77, 181, 184, 190
standardisation, 35, 50
standardised, 35, 46, 50, 56, 79, 188
structural functionalist/s, 10
suffragettes, 99–101
symbolic interactionist/s, 10

television, 76, 107
trade unions, 34–5
tumble-driers, 55, 57